COMPUTER SUPPORTED
COOPERATIVE WORK

Also in this series

Mike Sharples (Ed.)

Computer Supported Collaborative Writing

Springer-Verlag
London Berlin Heidelberg New York
Paris Tokyo Hong Kong
Barcelona Budapest

Mike Sharples, BSc, PhD
School of Cognitive and Computing Sciences
University of Sussex
Falmer, Brighton BN1 9QH, UK

Series Editors

Dan Diaper, PhD
Department of Computer Science
University of Liverpool
PO Box 147, Liverpool L69 3BX, UK

Colston Sanger
GID Ltd
69 King's Road
Haslemere, Surrey GU27 2QG, UK

ISBN 3–540–19782–6 Springer-Verlag Berlin Heidelberg New York
ISBN 0–387–19782–6 Springer-Verlag New York Berlin Heidelberg

British Library Cataloguing in Publication Data
Computer Supported Collaborative Writing.
– (Computer Supported Cooperative Work
Series)
  I. Sharples, Mike II. Series
  808.00285
  ISBN 3-540-19782-6

Library of Congress
A catalogue record for this book is available from the Library of Congress

Typeset from authors' disks by Fox Design, Bramley, Guildford, Surrey
34/3830–543210 Printed on acid-free paper

Contents

Contents

6 A Survey of Experiences of Collaborative Writing
E.E. Beck 87

7 Multimedia Conferencing as a Tool for Collaborative Writing: A Case Study
S. Baydere, T. Casey, S. Chuang, M. Handley, N. Ismail and A. Sasse 113

Contributors

Sebnem Baydere

Department of Computer Science, University College London, Gower Street, London WC1E 6BT, UK

Eevi E. Beck

School of Cognitive and Computing Sciences, University of Sussex, Falmer, Brighton, Sussex BN1 9QH, UK

Tom Casey

Department of Computer Science, University College London, Gower Street, London WC1E 6BT, UK

Shaw Chuang

Department of Computer Science, University College London, Gower Street, London WC1E 6BT, UK

Ian Denley

Ergonomics Unit, University College London, 26 Bedford Way, London WC1H 0AP, UK

Andrew Dillon

HUSAT Research Institute, Elms Grove, Loughborough LE11 1RG, UK

Alan Dix

HCI Group, Departments of Computer Science and Psychology, University of York, Heslington, York YO1 5DD, UK

Steve M. Easterbrook

School of Cognitive and Computing Sciences, University of Sussex, Falmer, Brighton, Sussex BN1 9QH, UK

James S. Goodlet

School of Cognitive and Computing Sciences, University of Sussex, Falmer, Brighton, Sussex BN1 9QH, UK

Mark Handley

Department of Computer Science, University College London, Gower Street, London WC1E 6BT, UK

Michael Harrison

HCI Group, Departments of Computer Science and Psychology, University of York, Heslington, York YO1 5DD, UK

Nermeen Ismail   .

Department of Computer Science, University College London, Gower Street, London WC1E 6BT, UK

Steve Jones

Department of Mathematical and Computer Sciences, Dundee Institute of Technology, Bell Street, Dundee DD1 1HG, UK

Anthony R. Kaye

Institute of Educational Technology, The Open University, Milton Keynes MK7 6AA, UK

Jon May

Standard Elektrik Lorenz-AG, Hirsauerstrasse 210, D-7530 Pforzheim, Germany

John McCarthy

Department of Psychology, University College of Cork, Cork, Eire

Victoria Miles

GMAP Ltd, University of Leeds, Springfield House, Leeds, UK

Andrew Monk

HCI Group, Departments of Computer Science and Psychology, University of York, Heslington, York YO1 5DD, UK

Julian Newman

Department of Computing, Glasgow Polytechnic, Glasgow G4 0BA, UK

Rhona Newman

Department of Sociology, University of Ulster at Jordanstown, Newtonabbey BT37 0QB, UK

Lydia Plowman

School of Cognitive and Computing Sciences, University of Sussex, Falmer, Brighton, Sussex BN1 9QH, UK

Angela Sasse

Department of Computer Science, University College London, Gower Street, London WC1E 6BT, UK

Mike Sharples

School of Cognitive and Computing Sciences, University of Sussex, Falmer, Brighton, Sussex BN1 9QH, UK

Andy Whitefield

Ergonomics Unit, University College London, 26 Bedford Way, London WC1H 0AP, UK

Charles C. Wood

School of Cognitive and Computing Sciences, University of Sussex, Falmer, Brighton, Sussex BN1 9QH, UK

Chapter *1*

Introduction

M. Sharples

1.1 The Collaborative Tradition

Collaborative writing is nothing new. The description below is from the introduction to a book published in 1911:

> Every page, however, has been debated and passed by the three of us. Our usual method has been, first to pick up a subject that interested us, perhaps a subject we had been talking about for a long while, then to discuss it and argue over it, ashore and afloat, in company and by ourselves, till we came to our joint conclusion. Then on a rough day, in a set-to discussion, I would take down notes, which frequently amounted in length to more than half the finished article. From the notes I would make a rough draft, which, after more discussion, would be re-written, and again, after revision, typewritten. We would go through the printer's proofs together and finally, after reading the matter in print, we have once more revised it for book publication. Collaboration could not be more thorough. (Reynolds, et al. 1911, p. x)

The book, *Seems So! A Working-class View of Politics*, was written by an academic working closely with two fishermen. What makes it unusual, now as then, is its insight into the sharing of ideas and feelings as part of writing, and also its open celebration of joint authorship, as a means of recording the authentic voice of English working men:

> Thus, the three of us have done together, as well as we could, what neither of us separately could have done at all – which, surely, is the essence of collaboration. (Reynolds et al. 1911, p. xii)

To gain from such a close collaboration each writer has to offer up ideas and experiences and has to be willing to accept the identity and consensus of the group. It can bring the rewards of creating a text which transcends the identity and knowledge of any single contributor, but at the cost of hard work to overcome conflict, to coordinate the activities and to arrive at a shared understanding. Reynolds, in his own introduction to *Seems So!*, says that "every page was debated and passed by the three of us".

If the work is intended for publication then co-authorship may well not be worth the effort. Disincentives include the refusal of some universities to accept co-authored works in review for promotion, the omission of all but the first author in citations, and the difficulty for joint authors of fiction to fit into the whirl of book signings and publicity appearances. Ede and Lunsford (1990) offer as an example of co-authored fiction a novel, *The Whole Family*, published in 1908 by twelve authors including Henry James; although it is a unique exercise in collaborative literature, the novel gains no mention in the *Oxford Companion to English Literature*. We work in a culture which values individual responsibility for ideas and which promotes the ideal of the lone author struggling for self-expression. It is not surprising that (apart from scientific literature where research requires team effort) joint authorship is rare.

Far more widespread than acknowledged co-authorship is the practice of loose, informal collaboration: the sharing of ideas and opinions, supportive but critical reading of drafts, emotional support during the dark days of writer's block. Behind the imprint of a single author there lies a complex web of friends, colleagues and unacknowledged influences. Couture and Rymer (1991) differentiate between *group writing*, in which all or part of a document is jointly authored, and *interactive writing*, where the writer depends on a degree of interaction with colleagues at some point during the process of writing. This interaction may lead directly to text, as when a discussion in the pub or common room offers a writer new ideas or a new line of argument. Or it may come indirectly, from a circle of friends and the culture of the work-place. All writing is interactive in the sense that it arises out of an author's interactions with the surrounding world of talk, correspondence and activity.

Intellectuals have traditionally used written correspondence as a source of ideas and inspiration. The collected letters of Charles Darwin fill seven volumes and the foreword to the first volume notes that:

> These letters place him in his social and intellectual contexts and clarify the extensive scientific network of which he was a part. The nature of his work and his poor health left him more than usually dependent upon correspondence in carrying out his investigations. (Burkhardt and Smith 1985, p. xv)

The inspiration of correspondence may not always be benign and abstracted. In *Six Studies in Quarrelling*, Brome (1958) picks out some delicious feuds conducted by letter among George Bernard Shaw, H.G. Wells, Hilaire Belloc and others.

Authors of fiction have formed into literary groups for mutual support and as a safe haven from which to sail out and challenge the literary establishment. The most celebrated of these was the Bloomsbury Group, but

others included the friendship of Wordsworth, Coleridge, Sc(
Quincey, and the circle of Keats, Percy and Mary Shelley, Byron a
In some cases the influence of informal groups on writing can be
quite direct. In her introduction to *Frankenstein*, Mary Shelley wrote:

> But it proved a wet uncongenial summer, and incessant rain often confined us
> for days to the house ... "We will each write a ghost story", said Lord Byron, and
> his proposition was acceded to ... At first I thought but of a few pages – of a short
> tale, but Shelley urged me to develope the idea at greater length. I certainly did
> not owe the suggestion of one incident, nor scarcely one train of feeling to my
> husband, and yet but for his incitement it would never have taken the form in
> which it was presented to the world. (Shelley 1985, p. 52–56)

1.2 New Ways of Working Together

The distinction between loose, informal collaboration in private and single
authorship or formal co-authorship in public has been crumbling for some
years. The growth of interdisciplinary studies, of international research projects, of team-based news reporting, of distributed work groups within
large companies, of consortia to carry out pre-competitive product development, have all exerted political and organizational pressures on writers to
be seen to be collaborating.

These writing groups often consist of people who rarely meet face-to-
face and who come from widely differing cultures and organizations, yet
they are expected to collaborate closely, and to tight schedules. For
example, to gain funds from the ESPRIT European research initiative, a
consortium must consist of partners in three or more different countries
and be able to make revisions and write technical addenda to a proposal
within days. An ESPRIT proposal, running to around 100 pages, must be
jointly written and agreed by all the partners. There is no time for leisurely
academic discussions or the painstaking work of scientific cooperation. The
tools for this new high-speed semi-formal collaborative writing are the telephone, the fax and the computer.

At first sight, computers seem merely to extend the traditional means of
collaboration: electronic mail (email) substitutes for letter writing, computer
conferencing substitutes for meetings, shared databases stand in for filing
systems and libraries. But each of these systems offers new ways of working and blurs the boundary between informal and formal collaboration.

The speed with which computer-based messages can be formed and
transmitted means that email and bulletin boards are often used for informal discourse. They enable unstructured interest groups to form,
exchanging knowledge and opinions rapidly across national boundaries;
much of the academic debate about the possibility of "cold fusion", for
example, was conducted over email. Studies of email discussion (Siegel et

al. 1986) have also shown that contributions tend to be more antisocial and the decisions more extreme than in face-to-face conversation. "Flaming" is the term coined to describe intemperate use of email; and a lack of social cues and responses which moderate spoken dialogue, combined with the computer programmers' culture of informality and free expression, mean that many an email message is sent in anger and regretted a moment later. But the computer serves to formalize and preserve. Unlike speech, email leaves a permanent trace and so does not offer the possibility of denial – your views, however ill-judged, are set in text ready to be incorporated into documents, or transmitted onwards. On a number of occasions, bad-tempered email disputes among academics have been passed on to wider audience or have found their way into print.

The technologies of email, electronic conferencing and shared databases not only change the nature of collaboration but can undermine its very basis. The journalist Keith Waterhouse (1992) laments the move of news-paper offices away from London's Fleet Street, with its social world of pubs and wine bars, into palaces of technology:

> Fleet Street was, for better or worse, quite a delicately balanced, intricate social system ... a meeting place of minds. ... What's left? ... I think a form of journalism where you don't talk about it much but just sit in front of a screen and get on with it may suit a few computer journals and trade papers but it's not good for newspapers – that way blandness lies.

1.3 Grand Plans or Small Tools

Despite being blamed for a multitude of ills from repetitive strain injury to bland journalism, the computer has become an indispensible tool for writers. In her survey of 1279 professional authors, Jane Dorner (1992) found that 74% of authors already use a computer and a further 11% were considering buying one. She discovered a great deal of enthusiasm for word processors. The authors, in general, believe that word processing makes writing more of a pleasure, saves time and increases their output.

The survey also revealed that the authors make little use of additional facilities such as outliners, style checkers and on-line databases. The only extra tools employed by more than a third of word processor users were word counters, spelling checkers and templates. The main needs identified by the survey were for better ways of presenting work on disc to publishers, advice about what to buy, and improved contracts and licensing agreements.

Those of us who wish to design software for the support of collaborative writing must tread very warily. If we rush in proffering our shared editors, coordination tools and negotiation support systems then we are, at best, likely to be ignored or, at worst, seen as a Trojan Horse of new technology intruding into the writer's world of formal agreements and structures, and informal alliances, unacknowledged collaboration and tacit social support.

Early software designed to support collaboration and coordination has been seen as inappropriate (Neuwirth et al. 1990), poorly integrated with other writing tools, and inclined to force partners into "premature commitment", committing themselves to courses of action (such as selecting a social role or a type of message) when they may not have a rational basis for making the decision, or may prefer to leave their options open. Johnson-Lenz and Johnson-Lenz (1991) and Hewitt et al. (1990) propose that the best systems to support collaboration are not all-embracing environments, but toolkits which enable groups to build software appropriate to their needs and which can be incorporated without disruption into their working practices.

This book does not propose any grand plans for computer-supported collaborative writing: we know far too little about writing practices to do that. Rather, it offers studies of formal and informal collaboration, and preliminary designs for computer tools.

In Chapter 2, Sharples, Goodlet, Beck, Wood, Easterbrook and Plowman set the scene by suggesting some issues central to research in collaborative writing. The chapter surveys literature on single-person writing as a cognitive process, on small-group working, and the few studies on collaborative writing itself, and develops a composite picture of collaborative writing as an open-ended design task carried out in a social setting.

Chapter 3, by Newman and Newman, discusses writing in a larger social and organizational context, through two case studies in which documents were written collaboratively as part of a decision making process, using computer and communications technology. The studies highlight the influence on collaborative writing of social practices, the micro-politics of the organization, the purposes of writing and the patterning effects of time. They also bring out mismatches between the computer support and the social practices represented by the writing activity. Collaborative writing at large is not a rational cognitive act, but a complex game played between people with their own organizational interests, a repertoire of skills for manipulating the situation to their own advantage, and a burden of misunderstandings and mistaken premises.

Although Chapter 4 is ostensibly about the use of computer networking for the development of distance education courses at the UK Open University, the issues it raises are broad and relevant. Kaye contrasts the model of course development prescribed to Open University academics with experiences of course team members. Private factors, discussed only with trusted friends, such as individuals' beliefs about the course content and teaching approach, individual commitments, the chairperson's personality and experience and the quality of team interactions are all seen as being just as important to course production as the public issues such as the subject matter and audience of the document. There is little evidence that even the simple but functional tools for electronic collaboration already available are being used to any great extent in course team production – any new system will either have to fit in with the complex work patterns (of meetings, deadlines, and home or office working) or else require a (possibly revealing and upsetting) re-examination of the public and private sides of course team work.

In Chapter 5, Dillon presents an analysis of the production of two technical reports. He finds that the general sequence of activities was similar for the two groups: identification of need, pre-draft discussions, identification of a primary author, production of a draft according to an agreed plan, incorporation of responses from the other group members. A study of the document versions found little evidence of explicit collaboration beyond querying of details, objections to certain points, and requests for clarification in the early drafts. Any debate about content and issues was concluded largely before production of the first draft and handled verbally rather than through annotation of the document. He concludes that, for collaborative writing at a distance, the greatest need is not for dedicated writing environments, but for better tools to support communication and general group working.

Beck's survey in Chapter 6 of the experiences of collaborative writing is at odds with Dillon in finding that authors discussed content and structure more often during writing than they did before starting the first draft. It finds that the groups had a range of leadership styles and that fluctuations in membership and commitment to the group were common. The broad picture of writing presented by the survey is of a dynamic group process, with re-negotiation of task, leadership and responsibilities as the writing progresses.

In Chapter 7, Baydere, Casey, Chuang, Handley, Ismail and Sasse attempt the cognitive equivalent of standing on one's own shoulders, by writing about the process by which they wrote the chapter. The six authors employed as writing tools a combination of a prototype multimedia conferencing system, email and a shared filestore. They found that the synchronous communication offered by the conferencing system was effective in substituting for face-to-face meetings and that the provision of facilities for shared minute-taking and documenting improved communication between the authors. They conclude that it is quite feasible to produce a complex document by using multimedia conferencing supplemented by other computer-based tools, but that a set of protocols should be established to improve the efficiency of communication and minimize conflict.

The three remaining chapters offer designs for collaborative writing tools which, despite their differences of emphasis, have much in common. They all suggest the need for integration of writing with other tasks, for keeping track of the progression of work on a document, and for exchanging ideas and plans.

Chapter 8, by Miles, McCarthy, Dix, Harrison and Monk, reviews designs for a group editing environment. It starts from a conceptual model of cooperative work, which describes group writing in terms of direct communication between participants and interaction with and through the artefact of the document. The different types of communication and work coordination require different, but integrated, software tools: direct communication requires "conversation spaces" apart from the document, whereas interaction with and through the document suggests the need for a choice of tools that can enforce a document structure or that encourage users to structure their own interaction. The tools should provide interrelated and complementary channels of communication among the authors, with document segments acting as a channel for indirect communication *through* the document, and annotations providing a channel of direct communication *about* the document.

Denley, Whitefield and May, in Chapter 9, describe a prototype multi-author multimedia document production system whose design was informed by a task analysis of document production. The analysis suggests the need for a "shared workspace" which allows users working independently to have access to shared work objects, for a distinction to be made between *plans* and *documents*, and for a "workgroup overview" which indicates all the people working in the group, their roles, and their availability.

In Chapter 10, Jones discusses MILO, a writing tool to support distributed, asynchronous authoring of structured documents. MILO provides a hierarchy of "notes" (data elements, each of which contains text and graphics) and tools for viewing, editing, communicating and filtering the notes.

This book is itself a product of informal and formal collaboration. It coalesced around a meeting of the Department of Trade and Industry (DTI) Special Interest Group on Computer Supported Cooperative Work, on the topic of *Collaborative Writing*. The authors of each chapter sent an email copy of their draft to Sussex where it was passed to "knowledgeable locals" for comment. The comments were sent back by email and the chapters were revised. The authors exchanged copies of their drafts at the meeting and, after presenting their papers to an audience of around eighty people, made final revisions in the light of any comments they had received at the meeting and to take account of the other authors' work. The chapters were submitted both in ASCII format and in paper copy and then went in to the publishing process of review and copy editing, with the authors' own ASCII text used as the source for the typesetting and printing of the book. Behind this public display of electronic collaboration lay many hours of discussion conducted in meeting rooms, common rooms and corridors. Collaborative writing can be a long and complex business.

Chapter *2*

Research Issues in the Study of Computer Supported Collaborative Writing

M. Sharples, J.S. Goodlet, E.E. Beck, C.C. Wood, S.M. Easterbrook and L. Plowman

2.1 Introduction

In this chapter we set out issues central to the investigation of computer support for collaborative writing, extending previous work to develop cognitive support systems for single writers (Sharples and O'Malley 1988; Sharples et al. 1989). The most successful computer tools to support complex tasks such as writing are those that fit in with the user's normal patterns of work (Norman 1986). All writers have strategies of working that suit the context of the task and that have been acquired over many years, through apprenticeship and trial and error. It is difficult to uncover and analyse these strategies, and more difficult still to design computer systems that will support them. Our method for single-person writing was to develop a task model that drew on research in the writing process and to extend it through empirical studies of those aspects of writing (for example, the writer's use of external representations such as notes and plans) that could be supported by computer tools.

Collaborative writing brings in a new dimension of social interaction. Not only do collaborating writers have differing strategies for writing that need to be reconciled, but they also form a social group, with its own personality and dynamics. We suggest that computer support of collaborative writing should be informed by a broad understanding of the cognitive and the social processes of collaborating writers.

2.2 Background

There are a number of ways to approach the design of systems to support collaborative writing. It may be tempting to begin by extend existing single-user tools, such as word processors or outliners, to support multiple users. For example, facilities could be added for logging different versions of a document, or enabling two or more users to work simultaneously at a task and to merge the results. Extending systems that already exist has the advantage that users may already be familiar with the original system. However, there is no guarantee that the extensions will offer any improvement on existing means of collaboration and forms of communication. At worst, they may require unnecessary effort to use, or prescribe an unnatural way of working.

To avoid these pitfalls, we need to investigate existing practices in collaborative writing. This might involve observational studies, task analyses, and interviews of writers; from these a descriptive account of current ways of working can be developed. But without a methodological framework to guide the investigation there is no guarantee that it will capture the important aspects of collaboration and writing, or that it will cover a sufficiently wide range of situations to provide general advice for the design of writing support systems. There is also the danger that the researcher may become submerged by a deluge of irrelevant data.

In this chapter we set out a range of cognitive and social issues that should be considered before starting to build computer programs to support collaborative writing. We begin with a brief survey of research on the writing process and on small group working and then cover four areas in more detail:

1. *Task issues*   These include strategies used by writers for partitioning and coordinating the work, and the interleaving of tasks.

2. *Group issues*   These include the adoption of roles by group members, substitutability and interdependence between members, and management of conflict.

3. *Communication issues*   These include the context in which communication takes place, the effects of different media on communication, and the structuring of communication.

4. *External representation issues*   These include types of representation used by writers, the specification of constraints, the effects of media on representations, and version management.

For each of these areas we set out questions that need to be answered through studies of collaborating writers. The empirical studies should give a deeper understanding of the process of collaborative writing, which can then be consolidated with analyses by other researchers to inform the design of computer supported cooperative work (CSCW) systems for collaborative writing.

2.3 Writing and Group Working

Writing is an open-ended design task. Unlike playing chess or solving mathematical equations, there is no fixed goal, or formal transitions between states. It is under-constrained, in that there are innumerable possible texts that could fit a writer's goals and possible actions that a writer might take at any stage. Actions include deleting any part of the existing text, adding more text at any point, generating new ideas, revising plans, looking for reference material, and so on.

When writers choose to collaborate in the production of a document, the complexity of the task is magnified many-fold. Writers must be able to express their ideas and attitudes toward the document to other members of the group, they must share and discuss their thoughts if the group is to establish a shared understanding of the task, and they must negotiate about the constraints on the task and the strategies for carrying out the work.

2.3.1 Single-Author Writing

Over the last twenty years the study of writing has moved from a concern with the written product to descriptive accounts of the writing process, beginning with the work of Flower and Hayes in the mid-1970s (Flower and Hayes 1980). They studied writing as a problem solving process and, from analysis of the verbal protocols of writers in action, they developed a model of the cognitive processes involved in a writing task (Flower and Hayes 1981). The model identified three main component processes:

1. *Planning*, including the generation of information relevant to the task, organizing information, and setting goals.
2. *Translation*: the turning of plans and ideas into text to meet the goals.
3. *Reviewing*, which combines evaluating the text and editing either the text itself or the ideas and goals.

The interactions of these processes can account for a variety of writing strategies, and the model offers a plausible explanation for problems such as writer's block and for the differences between novice and expert writers.

The picture that has emerged from cognitive studies of the writing process is of a complex and demanding task involving the juggling of multiple constraints. Writing is more than just presenting words neatly on a page, and much of a writer's time may be spent in gathering ideas, forming intentions, collecting resources, and producing plans. The task is recursive, in that the act of writing brings new ideas, which may lead the writer to revise goals and to embark on a new phase of planning and translation.

But a writer is more than a disembodied mind, and recent studies of single-person writing have moved beyond an examination of mental processes to consider the writer as a member of a community of practice, holding attitudes and approaches to writing derived from a long apprenticeship, and in constant interaction with other writers, who give a context for the task and who may provide direction, support or criticism. These studies have included investigations of authors' approaches to writing (Hartley and Branthwaite 1989), the use of external representations (plans, notes, drafts and annotations) to structure the task and share understanding (Neuwirth and Kaufer 1989), the characteristics of different writing tools and media (Eklundh 1992; Sharples and Pemberton 1988) and the social and organizational context in which the writing occurs (Flower 1989b).

Some of these recent studies have suggested how writing research might inform the design of computer systems, indicating how software might be developed to support a range of writing strategies (Sharples and Pemberton 1990; Smith and Lansman 1989), to provide appropriate views of the document (Eklundh 1992), and to support the production of written syntheses (Neuwirth and Kaufer 1989).

2.3.2 Small-Group Working

Not looking at gp dynamics

Small-group interaction has long been studied by sociologists and social psychologists (e.g. Bales 1950; Cartwright and Zander 1969). More recently, there has been a marked growth in interest in "task-focused" groups, with the issues of leadership, satisfaction, effectiveness, cohesion, conflict, task and group organization, communication and affective ties all set in relation to the performance of a common group activity (Bass 1980; DeStephen and Hirokawa 1988; Deutsch 1973; Gemmill and Wynkoop 1991; Wall et al. 1987; Zander 1979).

These studies tend to be relatively coarse-grained analyses concerned with how roles are negotiated, the relationships between group members, and so on. Some recent studies have used ethnographic and interactionist methodologies to gain more insight into the microstructure of interaction, to find out more about how, precisely, people work together on a task (Heath and Luff 1991; Hutchins 1991; McGrath 1991; Tang 1989).

Investigations of group work mediated by technology indicate that video-mediated communication has so far proven a poor substitute for face-to-face communication (Clark and Brennan 1991; Heath and Luff 1991), partly because of the difficulty of sharing and communicating reference to the group's artefact. McCarthy et al. (1991a) report difficulties with using synchronous text-based communication to reach consensus in a problem-solving activity, and Finholt et al. (1990) suggest that written text is more suitable for coordinating work than for substantive discussion.

2.3.3 Collaborative Writing

Very little has been researched on how people write together. Much of the available material considers collaborative writing as a pedagogical tool, either to teach the writing skills themselves (a technique frequently applied in American college composition classes) or to assist a group to explore a topic collaboratively (Bruffee 1983, 1984; Ede and Lunsford 1990). This process is perceived as both improving social skills such as negotiation and cooperation, and increasing subject domain and writing skills. This interest has extended to the use of electronic networks for interaction (ENFI) and other forms of computer-mediated collaborative writing (Hawisher and Selfe 1991; Spitzer 1990).

Some research has addressed, in more general terms, the process of collaborative writing and the production of a common document (Allen et al. 1987; Janda 1988; Plowman 1992; Posner et al. 1991; Rimmershaw 1992). Studies of collaborative writing episodes have indicated a need for close coordination during the idea-formation stage (Plowman 1992; Posner et al. 1991). Rimmershaw (1992) suggests that computer systems for collaborative writing should have facilities to make meta-comments linked to specific parts of the text and should provide ways of capturing informal notes. Observations of the use of prototype writing support tools have shed some light on the nature of the computer support required (Fish et al. 1988; Hahn et al. 1989; Neuwirth et al. 1990; Malcolm 1991).

2.4 Research Issues

There is no single activity that can be described as collaborative writing. An episode of collaborative writing may range from a few minutes taken to plan a joint memo, to many years for writing a co-authored book. Nor is there a clear distinction between writing and not writing; ideas gained from browsing through a library or talking to colleagues over lunch may be incorporated in the document. Given this diversity of activities, there is little hope of producing a simple all-encompassing account of collaborative writing. Instead, we take up some of the issues which appear to be central to collaborative writing and which need to be considered in the design of a new generation of computer tools.

2.5 Task Issues

One general way of categorizing collaborative writing is in terms of closeness of collaboration. At one extreme is the "shared mind", where the partners meet together for the entire writing episode and the text is developed around group discussion. At the other is "division of labour", where parts of the task are allocated to each partner, working alone. In practice, a collaborative writing episode will usually involve sessions of solitary writing interspersed with bursts of close collaboration between some or all of the partners.

Given these fluctuations in the closeness of working, it is important that any computer support should be flexible enough to enable face-to-face discussions to be mixed with other channels to allow the participants to get to know and trust each other, to decide on roles, and to resolve disputes before they escalate. Such meetings are particularly necessary in the early stages of collaboration.

2.5.1 Strategies for Partitioning and Coordination

Thompson (1967, cited in Bass 1980, pp. 475–479) describes three types of coordination in teamwork: pooled, sequential and reciprocal. Studies of writing groups (Sharples 1992; Rimmershaw 1992; Kaye, this volume) have, independently, identified similar types of coordination strategy for writing, which we shall call *parallel*, *sequential*, and *reciprocal*. They are shown in Fig. 2.1. A writing group may move from one strategy to another as the task demands.

Parallel working divides the writing into sub-tasks, either corresponding to parts of the document, or jobs that can be accomplished in parallel, such as checking spelling along with tidying references. The collaborators all work simultaneously and send their products to each other. For example, Kaye, in this volume, describes the writing method of Open University course teams, in which there is an initial stage of goal definition and work planning, followed by an execution stage during which work may be divided among individual team members or small sub-groups and carried out relatively independently, followed by an integration phase to merge the individual contributions into a finished product. (These stages may be repeated in an iterative manner a number of times to produce successive drafts.)

Sequential working is where the collaborators divide up the task among the partners so that the output from one stage is passed to the next writer in line. Each stage may be a section of the text (the next person in line then writes the next section), or a complete draft (the next person revises the text to produce a new draft). Timmers (1986, cited in Kaye, this volume)

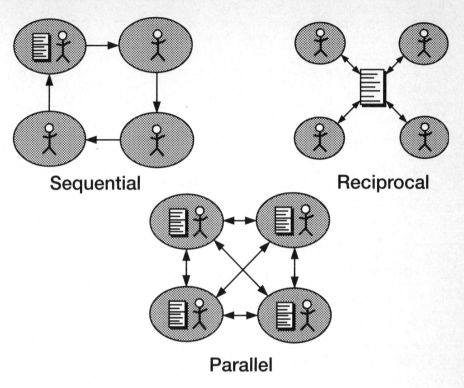

Sequential

Reciprocal

Parallel

Fig. 2.1 Strategies for coordinating collaborative writing.

describes the production of a chemistry course, involving drafts passed in the sequence:

writer → consultant → writer → editor → writer → editor

In *reciprocal working*, the partners work together to create a common product, mutually adjusting their activities to take account of each other's contributions. The technique of brainstorming (Osborn 1957) to produce a list of topics is a familiar example, but reciprocal working may be used to produce a complete draft of a text, either by the writers composing together out loud, with one person writing down their contributions or, if all the partners can access a common computer, by setting up a central file to which they contribute text or revisions. Rimmershaw (1992) gives a quotation from one writer who used this method:

> We developed a technique where nobody quite knew who we were writing with because we used to leave things on the machine and people would just add in and take out. Nobody really knew who'd done what. (Rimmershaw 1992, p. 27)

There are many issues related to task partitioning and coordination that need to be researched. A first step is to study how the work is divided and merged in practice, and what devices (such as calling meetings, setting deadlines, and circulating drafts) the partners use to keep the tasks roughly coordinated and to move from one strategy to another.

Although there have been attempts to prescribe standard sequences of activities and their coordination (see, for example, Kaye 1973) there has been little attempt to evaluate the effectiveness of different task sequences, or how these interact with individual styles of writing. Research on single-person writing (see, for example, Bridwell-Bowles et al. 1987) has identified quite distinct approaches to writing, broadly characterized by "planning first then writing", and "drafting first to discover ideas". It is not clear how such very different approaches can be accommodated in the coordination of collaborative writing.

The different methods of coordination have their advantages and limitations. For example, Riley (1984, cited in Kaye, this volume) refers to the "out of step" phenomenon in parallel working, where the partners may have different perceptions of what they should be writing, and what their colleagues are producing, based on earlier plans and drafts. This suggests that collaborators need ways to agree on the purpose as well as the structure of the proposed document, and then the means to communicate any changes of purpose during writing.

Sharples (1992) indicates some of the implications for computer support of the different strategies, including managing coordination, handling constraints, and specifying intentions. The addition of computer tools may well change the patterns of task coordination by offering ways to schedule activities and monitor progress, and by supporting some types of activity (such as revision) at the expense of others.

2.5.2 Interleaving Tasks

Collaborative writing occurs in the context of other interleaved activities. Some of these, such as writing other documents, may be closely related to the task, but others will overlap with it, or impede it. Beck's survey of writers of collaborative papers (Beck, this volume) indicates that writing groups may well be unstable, with people joining and leaving, and members waxing and waning in their commitment to the task.

This suggests a need for support of interleaving, allowing a writer to suspend the task in such a state that others can see the results and can continue it if necessary, and to resume it in a way that allows the context to be re-established quickly. There is also a need to support substitutability, making it easy for one writer to substitute for another and understand the intentions behind the writing and the context of the part-completed text. Methods of annotating text with the writers' intentions, of providing "filters" to show the contributions of particular writers to the joint text, and of rapidly switching between writing and other related tasks, such as reading electronic mail (email), are all ripe topics for investigation.

2.6 Group Issues

2.6.1 Substitutability and Interdependence Between Group Members

It is important for the performance of a task-oriented group that members should be working towards similar goals. The members judge success by the achievement of the interdependent goals, and assess the contribution of each individual in terms of how that member contributes towards a goal of interest to the others, supports the other members, and promotes the well-being of the group.

With pure promotive interdependency, each person's action is potentially substitutable for that of another (Deutsch 1973, p. 22). In terms of the writing process, this would mean each member of the group writing the document with and for the others, and acting as a proxy for the other members of the group in producing all or part of the document. In practice, actions are never perfectly substitutable, because people differ in their background knowledge, interests, skills and general abilities. Although the participants may be promotively interdependent in the pursuit of their main goal of producing a document, they may simultaneously be in competition to, for example, establish leadership of the group or claim credit for any success.

An important characteristic of collaborative writing is the need to find appropriate ways to divide up the task so as to satisfy the group members while maximizing productivity (whether in terms of quality or quantity of work). There may be activities within the writing process where high substitutability is possible, for example in shared editing, where it generally does not matter who types a character. By contrast, idea generation is usually associated with individuals, and needs to be treated as such: at times an idea can only be properly interpreted if its originator is known.

Issues which need further research include what promotive interdependence means in terms of designing computer systems for collaborative writing (for example, should partial products of less interdependent activities be stored, marked up, etc. in idiosyncratic ways by the individual co-authors?), and, following from that, which activities in collaborative writing are more promotively interdependent than others.

2.6.2 Roles

Roles clearly exist within writing groups. They may be general social roles, such as "facilitator" or "manifest leader", or more task-related, such as "scribe" and "reviewer". It is far from clear what significance a collaborative writing support tool should give to roles. Quilt (Leland et al. 1988) uses role information associated with each of its users to determine which actions they can perform. This is quite comprehensive: for example, it is even possible, on the basis of a participant's role, to restrict or even completely deny access to the system's group communication facilities, such as directed annotations and email.

The "role inertia" which systems like Quilt introduce may well interfere with experienced writers' "excursions" into other roles, which are better suited to the task at hand. Leland et al. cite the example of a "reviewer" who decides that the most effective way to suggest a revision is to add alternative text to the document: this would not be possible if the system were to embody a strict notion of the "reviewer" role. The challenge is to develop software that allows participants to take on defined roles to make their tasks and responsibilities clearer, without stifling flexibility and interdependence.

2.6.3 Management of Conflict

Conflict pervades group working (cf. Easterbrook et al. 1992) and can be either a constructive or a destructive influence on the performance of the task. The potential for disagreement may be latent in a group for a considerable time before it is expressed implicitly as a clash of perceptions or explicitly as an argument. Conflict management involves the realization that conflict is present, the identification of its source (conflict is often transferred from a personal to a task-related source), and the appropriate resolution of the conflict (Baxter 1982; Wall et al. 1987). Common sources of writing-related conflict include authors having differing perceptions of the audience for the document, or differing understandings of its rhetorical purpose.

Conflict may be implicit in the emerging document itself (through alternative drafts to a particular section, or through inconsistency between sections), or it may be explicitly discussed between co-authors. One possibility is for a computer system automatically to extract some of the conflicts embedded in the document and present them to the co-authors for discussion and resolution.

Highly cohesive groups are prone to suppress task-related conflicts, resulting in poorer solutions to the common group activity, a condition known as "groupthink" (Janis 1972; Mudrack 1989). In some circumstances, active elicitation of task-related conflict can improve the quality of a group's product. A CSCW system for collaborative writing could be designed to elicit conflict, perhaps through mechanisms for enhancing anonymity in idea-generation phases, through mechanisms to allow alternative documents to be developed (and thus for conflicting viewpoints to be expressed), or through notations to present arguments in a pictorial or graphical form.

Although some conflict may be desirable to stimulate creativity, there is a level at which it would consume too much attention for the group to progress, or would prevent it from creating a single coherent document. The optimum level of conflict will differ between groups and tasks, and product-related conflict (about the structure and content of the emerging document) may well be very different to process conflict (about how to organize and schedule the work) or social conflict (power struggles and differences of interest) in its development and resolution. A great deal of work is needed to investigate how CSCW systems can support sensitive and productive management of conflict.

2.6.4 Sub-Groups

The ability to break off from the main group, and work with selected members of the group can be very productive: sub-groups, formed of like-minded individuals, may make rapid progress when freed of the immediate need to justify their ideas to more sceptical group members. However, if coalitions are formed in response to a conflict expressed in the group these may simply entrench the different positions, hindering their development into an integrative solution.

Designing computer systems that encourage or discourage the forming of sub-groups for writing should be relatively easy. The Diplomacy game from the Theories of Multi-Party Interaction project (Hewitt et al. 1991) actively encourages coalitions, and Quilt (Fish et al. 1988) provides tools that support the formation of sub-groups of writers. There are also systems that make it impossible to share communication between some participants without making it available to all, thereby making it more difficult for coalitions and sub-groups to form within the system (Newman and Newman, in this volume, describe a system which was designed on the assumption that as drafts were written by individual departments within an organization they would be immediately saved on a central file server and thus made available to all the other participants. In practice, departments delayed putting their contributions onto the system, concealing them until they had thought through the issues and risks of making them public).

The difficulty comes in determining when there is a need for a group to fission into sub-groups and, once formed, how the requirements of each group differ. Some task-related subdivisions may occur regularly and naturally (for example, parallel partitioning of the task into groups working on individual sections), while others may be unstable, or against the interests of the team as a whole. Could a computer system be constructed which successfully intervenes to subdivide the task or to create coalitions among the authors? If so, could (or should) it be designed to distinguish between those coalitions that entrench the collaborators' positions or work against the interests of the group, and those coalitions that develop constructive new lines of thought or promote efficient working?

2.7 Communication Issues

Collaborative writing requires effective communication between group members, to establish a shared understanding of the task and the group product (Gere and Abbott 1985; Plowman 1992). However, it is not obvious that a collaborative writing tool should itself support the communication between authors. Shared editing tools, such as ShrEdit (CSMIL 1991) and GROVE (Ellis et al. 1990), provide no direct support for communication, with the assumption that collaborating writers will be able to coordinate their activity by other means such as by telephone or simply by conversing face-to-face over the top of their computers. Since the computer itself does not mediate the communication, it cannot guarantee the availability and adequacy of such channels to their users, and so does not provide a general solution to the problem of how to support communication.

The questions, then, are what kinds of communication between authors are required for successful collaborative writing, and how should a collaborative writing tool support them? Evaluation of the use of shared editors, in particular those situations where the tools fail to support the authors, may provide some answers to the former.

2.7.1 Identifying the Purpose of a Communicated Representation

Collaborative writing differs from other group activities in that written language is both the group's artefact and a means of communication between the writers. This may introduce confusion as to the intended purpose of a communication from a co-author. Is the text of a written message intended to form part of a draft document? Is it a modification to the plan of the document? Is it part of a more general discussion about the direction of the document? The scope for misinterpretation is broadened by differences in individual writing practices (cf. Carey et al. 1989). For example, one author may make very detailed notes, which have the appearance of fully worked out text, and pass these to a co-author in the expectation that the notes will be further developed; however, if the receiving author is in the habit of making sketchy notes, then the received communication may look like a completed part of the document, and be treated as such.

Technological mediation adds an extra twist, since text may be communicated in a printed form which resembles part of a finished document. This tends to add more weight and authority to the communicated text, perhaps contrary to the intention of its originator. More research is needed on the communicative effect of different media and forms of representation: which methods of computer-mediated communication are regarded as formal, informal, authoritative, tentative, personal, anonymous and so on.

2.7.2 Communication in Context

The successful interpretation of a communication often depends critically on the recipient of the communication understanding the context in which it was created and sent. In particular, ideas generated while drafting may be so related to the writer's train of thought (perhaps as expressed in the document at that point), that a brief note made of them can only be comprehended by re-reading the document to that point, reconstructing the train of thought. Within a group of collaborating writers, notes arising from ideas during drafting, detached from their originating context, are often going to be misunderstood, reducing the quality of communication in the group, and perhaps the quality of the document, as the group's shared understanding is muddied (Clark and Brennan 1991). If the writer then alters the part of the document that gave rise to the ideas, this may exacerbate the problem by actually providing false contextual information (the document in its changed state).

Designers of computer tools will need to know which types of communicated representations most need contextual information. More problematic is how to record and access the context of a message, once it has been established that contextual information is required. Possibly, findings from research in knowledge elicitation and transfer, the capturing of design rationale, and requirements analysis (Conklin and Begeman 1989) may be helpful in determining what contextual information can automatically be recorded, what has to be requested of the sender, and what can be reconstructed by the recipient.

2.7.3 Deindividuation and Media Effects

There seems to be a correlation between the amount of social communication in a group, and the effectiveness of that group in performing its task (Root 1988). However, the anonymity of communication mediated by technology can deindividuate group members (Jessup et al. 1990; Lea and Spears 1991), reducing each individual's perception of herself as a member of a group, which in turn undermines the cohesion of the group.

Even when steps are taken to counter this sense of anonymity, new media for communication can distort the conveyed meaning of messages. For example, studies of audio/video communication links have shown that users' attempts to deploy their normal conversational controls (cf. Brown and Levinson 1978) are stymied because the new medium is subtly different from the face-to-face context (Heath and Luff 1991).

Careful analysis of the factors contributing to the sense of anonymity can help designers to reduce the extent of deindividuation (Mantei et al. 1991), but addressing the subtle distortions of new media for communication is likely to be a more difficult task. If new communication channels are designed to appear as natural as possible, then they run the risk of appearing normal enough that they do not alert users, yet be different enough from everyday communication to distort the meaning of messages. If the new channels are designed to be different, then users may not be able to use sophisticated and well-tried social protocols to control the perception of their communications. The best hope is that users will develop appropriate social protocols given sufficient experience of the new media.

2.7.4 Structured Communication

Task-orientated dialogues do not occur haphazardly; they form regular patterns of interaction, enabling the participants to exchange information, solve problems, and resolve conflicts. Groups and individuals have such proficiency in maintaining these patterns of communication that they tend to be invisible to the participant and only become apparent when the regularities are broken or the communication breaks down.

Various encoding schemes have been derived to analyse the structure of conversations in terms of the purpose of each conversational act, and the commitments and responses engendered by its performance (Habermas, cited in Dietz and Widdershoven 1991; Searle 1969; Schegloff and Sacks 1973). It has been suggested, notably by Winograd and Flores (1986), that a computer-mediated communication system should require its users to observe a set of rules governing conversational structure, in the expectation that this would increase the productivity of their interaction.

An obvious problem with such rigorous structuring of conversation is that it relies on the structural rules to be complete and accurate, but Deitz and Widdershoven's critique of Searle's linguistic theories as embodied in the Coordinator system (Winograd and Flores 1986) shows that this is far from trivial. Further, the assumption of increased productivity disregards the effect that the imposition of such rigour on a collaborating group might have on the creative potential of "quick associations from group members" (Olson et al. 1990), let alone the impracticality of imposing such a regime without the consent of the group.

Malone et al. (1987b) propose to support conversation by allowing additional information to be attached to each message, describing more systematically what is the content, purpose, intended audience, etc. of the message. The intention is that these "semi-structured messages" will be more readily understood than unadorned text (both in terms of content and function), without being significantly more of a burden to generate, and without curtailing the freedom of expression of the parties to the conversation.

In collaborative writing, conversations of many diverse types occur, from far-ranging discussions which define the subject of the common document, and detailed negotiation to divide the task between group members, to rapid-fire, flowing exchanges to generate ideas for the substance of a section, and occasional comments intended to draw others' attention to particular facets of the text. It is far from clear, given the research so far, how the communication requirements of each of these different tasks should be supported by a collaborative writing tool. We need to analyse the patterns of interaction which emerge when writers pursue such tasks, to determine where rigour may be appropriate, where additional information in messages may best assist writers, and where the priority is for minimal interference in the speedy exchange of messages.

2.8 External Representation Issues

Single-author writing can be aided by the externalization of intermediate states of the writing task, such as writing plans and outlines, sets and organizations of ideas, and constraints on the document and task (Neuwirth and Kaufer 1989; Sharples and Pemberton 1988). The use of external representations helps to free the writer from the burden of mentally representing the state of the task, and serves to communicate that state over time.

When writers collaborate, they are much more likely to externalize the intermediate states, and communicate these to their co-authors (Neuwirth et al 1990). For the design of a writing tool, this raises the issues of what kinds of external representations need to be captured, and how they should be communicated between authors.

2.8.1 What To Represent?

The meta-textual information most commonly externalized by writers includes:

- collections of ideas, possibly with an organization imposed by the writer;
- outlines, which represent a document's structure;
- plans, which associate descriptions of purpose with parts of a document, e.g. "this section should discuss the role of folklore in Brazilian pottery";
- annotations, which associate additional information with a piece of document text, e.g. "this section isn't finished", or "the discussion of these two points needs to be more balanced".

These representations are common to writers, and many writing tools already have them incorporated into their designs (e.g. Leland et al. 1988; Neuwirth et al. 1990; Sharples et al. 1989; Smith and Lansman 1989). It would seem natural to include them in the design of software for collaborative writing, if writers are expected to coordinate their activities through such a system. More abstract information such as constraints on the document, conceptualization of audience, and allocation of work to individuals or sub-groups, is also communicated among collaborating writers, but it is less often formally represented. It is therefore at issue how a tool might capture and represent such information, and whether making this information explicit would benefit the writers.

Whatever meta-textual information is represented, a clear distinction should be made between it and the actual text of the document. A trivial example of the problem that may arise from confusing document text with meta-text is the annotation of a paragraph with an alternative wording. If the alternative wording is sent to the original author without a description of its purpose, i.e. that it serves as a "suggestion revision" annotation (Leland et al. 1988), then it may be misinterpreted as additional text.

Representing such a distinction is not too difficult: it is less obvious how the distinction should be presented to the user.

2.8.2 Constraints

Writing involves the manipulation of many simultaneous constraints (Flower and Hayes 1980). By setting out explicit constraints the partners can cut down the coordination needed during writing and provide a framework within which to create the text. Constraints arise from a number of sources (Sharples 1992; Sharples and O'Malley 1988):

1. The task set by the writers: topics, intended audience, purpose, the text structure, and specific boundaries such as the maximum number of words or the readability level.

2. External resources, such as reference books, papers, and notes.

3. Cognitive resources of the writers: their stock of ideas, mental schemas, and remembered text.

4. Textual resources: the material that has already been created in draft form.

There is more need in collaborative writing than in single-person writing to specify the constraints explicitly and in advance of writing, to avoid a writer getting out of step and writing text that does not mesh with the intentions of the others.

There are well-established ways of creating task constraints for the structure of a text (by producing an outline plan), its style (by agreeing to conform to a style guide, such as the *MLA Style Manual*, Achtert and Gibaldi 1985) and topics to be included (for example, by brainstorming for ideas and then allocating a cluster of topics to each writer). All this can be done face-to-face, or at a distance using textual communication. Sharing external resources is more difficult, but on-line access to databases and bibliographies (for example, it is now possible to access the library cata- logues of many UK universities via the JANET network) should make this much easier. The most difficult problem is in sharing the cognitive resources of individual writers. Tools such as ideas organizers, which allow people to externalize their ideas and intentions, and to communicate them to others, may be valuable in supporting shared cognition between writers at an early stage, before they commit themselves to text.

It is never possible to specify all constraints in advance, since the act of writing itself imposes constraints. Each piece of text must be integrated with the others and the document as a whole must provide a narrative flow, with each section forming a basis for the interpretation of the next. If the work is progressing in parallel, then as explicit constraints arise they need to be communicated to the other partners. There also needs to be judgement of how long a session of parallel working can continue before the implicit textual constraints become too great. There has been little research on the specification and communication of constraints and inten- tions among writers.

2.8.3 Communication of Representations

There are two basic issues here: first, the practical issue of how changes made by one author are propagated to other members of the group; and, second, the more psychological problem of how an author's meaning can be communicated.

Solutions to the first issue depend largely on the strategies for work coor- dination supported by the collaborative writing tool, and employed by the writing group. For example, if the group uses a sequential strategy, with each author working in succession on the whole document, then the changes are propagated when the entire draft of the document is passed between each pair of authors. In parallel working, different sections of the same document may be allocated to different group members to work on simultaneously. This raises the issue of what the other members of the group should see when an author is making changes to a section of the shared document: should the effects of every action be propagated, should only unitary changes be visible (e.g. the complete edit of a paragraph or addition of a comment), or should the previous version of the section be presented until the author signals that the change is complete? (For exam- ples, see respectively: Tatar et al. 1991; Rein and Ellis 1991; Malcolm 1991.)

Matters are made even more complex with reciprocal working, when more than one author can modify a section at a time. This requires an analysis of the semantics of such behaviour, within the context of the task: the authors may be aware of one another and intend to cooperate on chang- ing the text (e.g. CSMIL 1991), or they may intend to make separate revisions of the text (e.g. Malcolm 1991).

The interpretation of the represented document is a deeper problem. For example, if ideas are represented as fragments of text linked together to form a network, then it is entirely possible that two authors will place different interpretations on the network by ascribing different meanings to the links in the network. Attempts have been made to address this particular problem by adding "type" information to network links (Trigg 1983), but this only shifts the problem to one of differing linguistic interpretations of the link type names.

It is essential that the external representations proposed for systems to support collaborative writing be studied with a view to determining how adequately they capture the singular meaning of an author. Where serious problems of ambiguity exist, either the representations should be modified, or the systems which use them should be made aware of the problem, and constructed so as to actively help authors to express themselves clearly.

2.8.4 Effects of Media on Representations

External representations can be stored on a variety of different media. For example, notes can be recorded on a document processor, a sheet of paper, a series of file cards, sticky notelets, a dictaphone, or a whiteboard. The medium imposes particular constraints and influences the course of the writing process: for example, a writer who sets down notes on file cards is free to create a spatial plan by spreading them around the desktop, whereas notes taken on a dictaphone are constrained to a fixed order (Sharples and Pemberton 1988).

The choice of medium not only affects what can be represented, but also influences how a representation is used and interpreted by members of the writing group. A good example of this is the differences in use and impact between audio and textual annotations (Chalfonte et al. 1991).

Each of the representations to be used in the support of collaborative writing should be studied in terms of which medium best supports it, and how each medium influences use of the representation and interpretation of its content. Then, designers would be in a position to, for example, weigh the benefits that an audio channel could provide in their tool, or to compensate for the loss of a video channel. It would be useful to know:

- which media are appropriate for particular functions in the development of the shared document (e.g. while audio communication may support certain forms of interaction, it is unlikely that recitation is the most effective means of communicating drafts);

- which media are overloaded, i.e. used for more than one function;

- how writers use the properties of different media to support certain functions (e.g. printed paper drafts support the transfer of annotations, because new text stands out by being handwritten, and writers can use differences in handwriting or pen colour to indicate different annotators).

2.8.5 Version Management

What does it mean to modify a component of a document? Is the document irretrievably changed, or can the previous version be accessed? The issue here is not about the provision of "undo" operations in editors, but instead about whether versions of documents created in previous sessions should be stored, and if so how they should be accessed, and when a new version is created. Should parallel versions of a document be supported, and if so how should the users be made aware of the alternatives, and what facilities for merging the different versions should be provided? Malcolm (1991) reviews some of the issues of revision control for collaborative writing, but does not address the questions of whether it is necessary, and if so how it interacts with the writers' perceptions of the document (for example, what constitutes a revision worthy of recording).

2.9 Conclusion

As should be clear from this chapter, collaborative writing is a complex task. We have covered the main issues raised so far by studies of collaborative writers in action, but others will arise, particularly when writers begin to use new computer-based tools and discover new ways of working and writing together. We have not addressed such topics as copyright and ownership of text, the publication process and relationships with publishers, intertextuality and reuse of existing material, document maintenance, multimedia and hypertexts, or distributed texts (where the finished document is kept on-line, spread among a number of sites) yet these are growing concerns for collaborating writers. The design of CSCW tools for writers must be based on a good understanding of the cognitive and social processes of writing. As an agenda for further research we have suggested investigation of:

- the means of coordinating and partitioning the writing task and the circumstances in which different strategies are successful;
- the dynamics of writing groups, including group formation, allocation of roles, and the maintenance of group cohesion;
- the management of conflict, including sources of conflict within groups of writers and the means of resolving conflict;
- communication among group members, to discover the contexts of communicative acts, the effects of media on communication, and the regularly occurring conversational patterns;

- the external representations used to communicate constraints, structural plans, intentions, drafts and annotations, and the suitability of different media, such as email, voice and video for different representations;

One conclusion that system designers may draw from this chapter is that there is little point in trying to build a complete general-purpose tool to support collaborative writing. There are so many different ways of coordinating, communicating and representing collaborative writing that a single piece of software, however complex, is unlikely to fit with the practices and work environments of a group of writers.

A more useful approach may be to develop a suite of tools which are designed to work with each other, and to integrate with existing computer-based and non-computer collaborative writing practices. These extender tools could furnish users with new functionality (such as new types of external representation, communication support, awareness support, external memory, and version support) without prescribing unfamiliar ways of working.

Acknowledgements   Our thanks go to Warren Evans and Yvonne Rogers, who have offered valuable ideas and suggestions as members of our Collaborative Writing Research Group.

Chapter *3*

Social Writing: Premises and Practices in Computerized Contexts

R. Newman and J. Newman

3.1 Introduction

In view of the central role that written text plays in many forms of professional collaboration, support for joint or multiple authorship is a significant issue for computer supported collaborative work (CSCW). Design of systems for collaborative writing will need to take into account an array of social factors and social practices that are commonly taken for granted and invisible in normal face-to-face collaboration.

Previous work in CSCW has tended to underestimate or neglect the importance of interests, power-relationships, control and counter-control in organizations (Kling 1991). Often the settings and activities available for study have been atypical, in that no important interests were at stake. CSCW research has also tended to overlook the social practices that form the taken-for-granted background to collaboration. Asynchronous CSCW has also ignored the significance of the social patterning of time in collective or organizational decision making.

At the technical level, the more sophisticated approaches to CSCW have not yet "taken off" commercially (Kling 1991). Perhaps the most widely used collaborative writing technology in the automated office is *networked word processing* using a standard PC package with a central file server; this provides functions appropriate to the secretarial support office rather than to professional work. An alternative technology, which has been commercially available for several years, is *computer conferencing*, which is more appropriate to the professional office than to secretarial support. However, conventional computer conferencing systems are restricted by network bandwidth and terminal display capabilities, and therefore provide only limited support for discussion and decision making.

This chapter discusses some of the ways in which social practices and organizational factors may affect collaborative writing, with reference to two case studies in which documents were written collaboratively, using computer and communications technology, as part of a decision making process. In one case, which involved the use of a computer conferencing system, the intention was to make a series of technical decisions, to be embodied in a specification. The second case involved the use of networked word processing in the writing of a multi-volume document which would become the basis of a large-scale budgetary allocation process within a high technology organization. These case studies illustrate the relevance of four groups of factors:

1. Social practices

2. Organizational micropolitics

3. The purposes of writing

4. The patterning of time

The case studies also show the importance of interactions among the four groups of factors.

3.2 Background

3.2.1 Perspectives

Practices, time patterning and shared reality　In face-to-face interaction, a sense of coherence and common definition of reality and purpose is mutually accomplished as a result of practices that speakers are obliged to employ because of the inference of the oral medium. These practices have been extensively investigated in conversational analysis (Cicourel 1972, 1973; Garfinkel and Sacks 1969; Schegloff 1971). Not only do participants monitor responses and spontaneously initiate "repair" on signs of misunderstanding, but they frequently "gloss" the discussion, thus formulating and reformulating the common understanding that is being built up: so, for example, parties will know clearly which part of a joint plan each has promised to undertake. The practices whereby a common understanding is built up and sustained are those that render social reality accountable, and hence have become known as "accounting practices". Other conversational practices manage the time-course of the conversation, governing both turn-taking by participants (Sacks et al. 1978) and the initiation and termination of conversation (Garfinkel and Sacks 1969).

Where a face-to-face group is too large for conversational practices to work effectively to regulate turn-taking, recourse is commonly to the social institution of control by the occupant of a formal role, the "chair". While the manifest function of the chair is to control access to the "floor", many practices of "chairmanship" such as summarizing, taking the sense of the meeting, and so forth, compensate for the fact that in a large, formal meeting members cannot readily employ the same accounting practices that they use in dyadic or small-group interaction. The typical physical setting of the meeting, in which the chairperson is facing the other members, and sometimes above them, not only constitutes symbolic support for meeting practices but provides opportunities for the exchange of non-verbal cues between the chairperson and the membership. The chair, as part of social reality, is socially constructed by the meeting, using the resources of the current situation. These resources are inevitably affected by technical interventions such as computer conferencing that alter the concrete meeting situation.

Both conversational accounting practices and meeting practices maintain a shared sense of reality, and they do so by the formulation of edited accounts of the discussion. Where meetings are recorded by written minutes, this text is also typically an edited account and not a verbatim record. The close parallel between minutes and accounting practices may be seen from the following observations:

> Minutes, once they have been agreed, are not just one person's story of what happened; constitutionally they *are* what happened. Minutes are often an improvement on what was actually said. (Locke 1980)

Both in conversations and in meetings, the editing process plays a central part in the achievement of a shared reality; and the acceptance of the editing process is closely connected with the "local management" of members' time. It is only possible for both glosses and minutes to be an "improvement" on the actual, because members are willing to overlook small discrepancies: members implicitly recognize that insistence on perfect accuracy would be, literally, a waste of time. Interaction, in conversations and in meetings, takes place within a context of the social patterning of time which affects the appropriateness of actions and utterances. This social patterning plays an important part in decision making within face-to-face meetings, since it typically constrains the amount of discussion and argument that members will tolerate; as it becomes late and members have other commitments, there will be increasing pressure to arrive at a satisficing decision quickly, rather than to pursue optimality at the risk of delay (on "satisficing" decisions, see, for example, Simon 1981). One purported advantage of computer-mediated communication is that it makes collaboration possible without constraints of time and space. Our first case study suggests that the existence of such constraints is bound up with the practices that achieve effective local management of decision-orientated meetings, and that freedom from temporal constraints and temporal patterning in particular may actually pose a risk that decisions will not be taken.

Writing and decision making   Collaborative writing takes place in many different contexts, for many different purposes. Context and purpose influence appropriate strategies and modes of collaboration, which may range from close discussion and joint text production at one extreme, to a relatively fragmented division of labour at the other (Newman and Newman 1992a; Rimmershaw 1992; Sharples et al. this volume). The text may be intended as an end product, either for external publication (e.g. as a paper, a book or a technical manual), or for delivery to a client (e.g. a consultancy report), or it may be a step towards a further goal (e.g. a speci-fication, a standard or a syllabus).

Documents whose purpose is to represent a stage in problem-solution are particularly important where many different sources of expertise must be brought to bear. Text is also important as a formal apparatus regulating interaction: formal committee meetings are commonly regulated by a writ-ten agenda and recorded in minutes, which often include a note that specific members have been "actioned" to undertake given tasks before the next meeting. (Thus the locally-managed business of a meeting takes place within, and provides outputs to, a globally-managed project; Seel et al. 1990).

As well as minutes and agendas, more extensive written texts may play a part in structuring interaction for decision making; for example, written pleadings, proposals, recommendations, referees' reports, etc. In all these cases, there are practices of impression management that constrain the terms in which arguments can be put; certain issues are placed in the fore-ground and others are backstage. Moreover, where decisions are prepared through extensive sifting and reporting of information, the writing process may to a large extent determine the eventual decision by what it makes available and by what it conceals: as Bachrach and Baratz (1962) have shown, what is not made available for decision ("non-decisions") is an important facet of power.

Within formal organizations, action is typically orientated towards roles and statuses that constitute a structure of authority and power. Decisions are generally presented as the result of a formally rational process, in accor-dance with terms of reference provided by a higher authority; "formal rationality" is defined by the observance of a rule-governed procedure, by contrast with "substantive rationality" which is defined in terms of concrete outcomes (Weber 1947). Rationalization, in this sense, has characterized the growth of large bureaucratic organizations as the dominant economic form in the twentieth century.

The observance of formal rationality is therefore central to the legitima-tion of organizational decisions. At the same time, since outcomes differentially affect the interests of participants within the organization, the decision process is a focus of conflict among organizational units, and between individual members:

> Information in an organization, particularly decision-related information, is rarely innocent, thus rarely as reliable as an innocent person would expect. (March 1991)

The orientation to formal rationality thus becomes a rhetorical resource for members in defending their interests or in attacking decision options that would promote competing claims on organizational resources. Where text is written as part of an organizational decision process, its manifest content may be purely technical, but conflicts of interest will influence writing strategies so that material favourable to preferred outcomes may be highlighted. Thus, apparently technical choices in writing may have a micropolitical dimension related to the power and interests of different groups within the organization. Our second case study illustrates the importance of interest groupings within the organization, and the way in which this can not only affect the text but lead to manipulation of the time pattern of the writing process.

3.2.2 Technology

As Kling (1991) has pointed out, there has not yet been a widespread commercial uptake of the more technically sophisticated approaches to CSCW; the personal computer (PC) is widespread in the office environment, and preference is generally shown for systems which run on either networked PCs or on a host that can be accessed from a PC emulating a simple text terminal. While graphical user interfaces such as Microsoft Windows are available for PCs, many of the PCs currently in use in offices are, for a variety of reasons, restricted to using text displays.

Perhaps the most widely used collaborative writing technology in the automated office is the use of a standard PC word processing package, with files stored on a network file server which appears to the user to be an additional disc drive on the PC. The network software will normally provide password protection to guard against unauthorized access to files, and will ensure that a file is edited by only one user at a time, but such a system gives little support to discussion, formulation and adjudication of issues, professional roles, the distinction between text and comment, and so forth. Thus the technology of *networked word processing* appears more appropriate to the secretarial work of the support office than to the contract-orientated and information supply functions more typical of professional office work (cf. Newman 1987).

An alternative technology, which has been commercially available for several years, is *computer conferencing*, in which software running on one or more host computers, accessible through a network from PCs, terminals or workstations, supports the structuring of information as text "meetings", with open or closed membership, and with communications linked in a "discussion-orientated" structure such as the topic reply group or the comment tree (Hiltz and Turoff 1978; Shackel 1985). Computer conferencing provides explicit support for aspects of professional collaboration, and is more orientated to the information supply office than to the support office. Corporate computer conferencing systems have been in use for some time by companies such as DEC (Wicks 1988) and Hewlett-Packard (Rodden 1991).

Our case studies each involved the use of one of the above technologies; computer conferencing was used in the specification case study, while the budget allocation case study was based on networked word processing.

3.3 Case Studies

Both case studies are concerned with writing for decision making. The first case emphasizes the consequences of removing the face-to-face context. In the second, major organizational interests were at stake.

3.3.1 Case Study 1: A Specification

A group of human factors specialists, located at various institutions remote from one another, used a computer conference to develop the specification for an improved user interface. (Further details of the technical context are given in Newman and Newman 1992b.) Members contributed to this project on a voluntary basis, came from a variety of backgrounds and offered complementary skills. The group as a whole had a task remit, but the roles of group members were emergent from the group process. One member was initially appointed moderator.

A large number of "topics" were created within the conference; the moderator did not attempt to impose a definite structure upon it. The moderator produced an initial specification on paper; this document was never entered into the conference system, but was passed to another member who used it as the basis for coding a prototype of the interface, which was made available to other members, who were asked to evaluate it. Few responded in terms of overall evaluation of the design: most responses consisted either of reports of bugs, or of requests for additional functionality, most of which were agreed.

At this stage, therefore, the initial specification as a text document had not been inspected or formally critiqued by the team, but team members had access to a working model of the specified system (i.e. the prototype).

One team member had particular expertise in relevant international standards and their underlying scientific rationale. He made suggestions for redesign of the interface in order to make it conform to these standards. These suggestions were entered in the conferencing system as a "topic". Some characteristics of his proposed design were technically impossible to implement with available resources, and were disputed within the computer conference, particularly by the moderator. In order to clarify the issues at stake, the standards expert then entered, under the same topic group, a formal description of the prototype as currently implemented (with the intention that members could contrast this with his proposed design). He also made brief modifications to his proposal, and the moderator then expressed herself satisfied with the general principle he was now proposing. However, nobody undertook the task of producing a new version of the specification incorporating the additional functionalities and the standards expert's revised proposals.

The moderator then left to take up a post abroad, and several weeks later a new member was added to the team, as moderator, with the brief from the system manager to "get things moving". The new moderator took over under the impression that the prototype that had been implemented was a design that had already been validated by the team, and that the essential task was to ensure that its implementation was completed. He mistakenly assumed that the description of the prototype, entered by the standards expert, was a description of an approved design, and therefore took all steps to ensure that it was implemented and that user documentation was prepared.

When the interface and user documentation were released for beta-testing, the standards expert complained bitterly that his proposals, although agreed, had not been implemented, and demanded that extensive revisions be made. The completion of the new interface was ultimately delayed for a full year.

The difficulty the design team experienced in using computer conferencing to document technical decisions appears to have several causes. Some have to do with the perception of the role of different text items, while others have to do with decision taking as such.

The team failed to distinguish between formal documentation (the specification, or drafts of the specification), comments on the formal documentation, and informal discussions. The system did not provide any way of distinguishing between expressions of opinion and actual decisions. This might have been overcome, at least to some extent, by the adoption of clear conventions similar to those suggested by Sharples (this volume) for distinguishing text from extra-text. But confusion was also increased by the fact that the system kept old "discussion" material permanently available. The fact that the whole "discussion" remains present on the system suggests that computer conferences do not need minutes. In practice, the volume of material is generally excessive, and does not assist participants at a later

date to carry the business forward. The assumption that minutes are unnecessary in a computer conferencing system ignores one of their main
functions: by providing an edited account of the meeting, minutes create an
accountable reality to which future action can be orientated.

The team therefore lacked both software support and established
conventions for tracking discussions and decisions. They also suffered from
the difficulty of making any decisions at all using computer conferencing as
the medium. Previous studies (Dubrovsky et al. 1991; Kiesler et al. 1984)
have shown that one characteristic of computer conferencing is a relative
absence of normative pressure, at least partly as a result of lack of position-
al cues for status. Experimental groups take longer to reach consensus in
computer-mediated communication than face-to-face.

Where real decisions have to be made, the lack of normative pressure
becomes a serious drawback. Unlike the chairperson in face-to-face meetings, the moderator does not receive non-verbal social support (or pressure)
for an active role in guiding the meeting towards decisions. The freedom of
computer conferencing from time constraints on participation has the unin-
tended consequence that meetings held in this medium lack the social
patterning of time that creates pressure for resolution of differences
through explicit decisions in a face-to-face meeting: meal times, train
timetables, other engagements, and so forth. In computer conferencing,
decision time can only be determined by an explicit scheduling process
actively implemented by the moderator.

After the problem had come to light, the new moderator adopted a
changed method of working, which involved extensive active moderation
to impose explicit structure upon the conference. A new topic was created
for each unresolved issue; in this topic, the issue was stated, together with a
mini-agenda and timetable for discussion and decision. Once an issue had
been decided, the headnote stating the issue was replaced by one stating
the decision, and all discussion relating to that decision was placed in an
archive note, the original notes being deleted from the conference. The
guiding principle was that the conference would be perceived as a structure
of issues and decisions, rather than a chronological record. In other words,
the conference at any moment in time should be an edited account, rather
than a verbatim record (although the full history could in fact be retrieved
from the archive notes if necessary).

3.3.2 Case Study 2: A Document to Support Budget Allocation Decisions

A large group of writers in a high technology organization prepared a
multi-volume document as input to a decision making process which
would determine the allocation of a large budget. Writers had access to PCs
running a standard commercial word processing package, which were

networked to a central file server. On this file server, standard files had been pre-created into which all text for the decision making process should be entered, and a master document had been set up which would allow the whole multi-volume final printed document to be created by merge-printing.

Different parts of the final document were the responsibility of different departments, and only staff in those departments were supposed to possess the passwords that would enable them to enter text into their files, or alter them. However, other departments had the right to comment on drafts and to be consulted about them, and their passwords permitted them to read what had been entered on the file server, even though they could not alter it.

The whole decision process was to take place in a tight time-scale, and a large number of individuals had to provide inputs to the writing process, either as co-authors or commenters. The outcome of the decisions would materially affect the budgets of the different departments, and hence the power and prestige of their managers and senior staff.

The approach to distributed collaborative writing in this case constituted a mixture of the strategies presented by Sharples et al. (this volume). The overall exercise involved *parallel production* of the *whole* multi-volume document of several hundred pages, within a predetermined overall *document structure*. The extrinsic constraints were:

- the prior plan of the whole report, already implemented as a set of standard word processor documents on the file server;
- a set of instructions to authors regarding the approach to be taken, types of issues to be addressed, etc.;
- standard word processor "style-sheets" to be used by authors when preparing their drafts.

These constraints were supplemented by feedback from management during the writing process, generally aimed at ensuring a uniformity of treatment throughout the report. This might be at a detailed level (e.g. punctuation standards or the prescription or proscription of certain phrases), or might be of a more general nature (e.g. the type of evidence that should be adduced to support statements).

Intrinsic constraints derived from the organization of the document at three levels of treatment (detail, volume summaries, executive summary), which required some sections to be written after others: a volume summary must reflect the content of sections within the volume, and the executive summary must be consistent with the contents of all other volumes. Generally, volumes were written in parallel by different groups of authors.

Within volumes, sections were written in parallel, but the writing of an individual section (of up to 1500 words) would be undertaken on a sequential or reciprocal basis. Generally:

1. Subsections that were expected to be uncontentious were parcelled out for rapid drafting.

2. Meetings were held (within a department) to exchange information and decide policy; each person attending had been asked to prepare a statement on all the main issues, which would be tabled at the meeting; minutes of these meetings, together with the papers produced for the meeting, were retained as a basis for drafting the remaining subsections; this might involve selection of material from tabled papers, rewriting, or writing anew.

3. Potentially contentious subsections were written either on a sequential or a reciprocal basis.

4. In a proportion of cases, meetings were held with other departments; at these meetings the different departments might table or read out their own drafts, or give an oral account of the results of the department's internal meeting.

5. In some cases, the department with main responsibility for a section would adopt another department's draft as the basis for a contentious subsection, and then rewrite it; in other cases a draft from another department would be treated as a "comment" or additional list of points to be incorporated; in no case was the reciprocal mode adopted across department boundaries: since different departments were located in different buildings, reciprocal writing would have been difficult without much more sophisticated information technology support, such as multimedia desktop conferencing; but since much of the discussion in reciprocal writing sessions turned on the micropolitical implications of alternative phrasing of content, it seems unlikely that cross-department reciprocity would have been adopted even in the absence of geographical constraints.

The system had been designed on the assumption that as drafts were written they would be immediately saved on the file server, and would thereby become available for comment by other departments. In practice, much of the work of writing consisted of finding the appropriate selective emphases to support the outcomes desired by the writers' department, to maintain the general coherence of their departmental strategies, and to fend off potential criticism by other departments that could be used to divert budget allocations. Sensitive paragraphs and sections had to be carefully worked over within departments, either written on a reciprocal basis or by a sequential process of comment and examination. A department's output had to cover all possible threats and opportunities. This led to pressure for concealment of early drafts, so that the text would not become available to other departments until the political issues had been thought through. In order to maintain such concealment, sensitive drafts were often kept on floppy disc and not transferred to the network until the last moment.

A similar process occurred when it was necessary to incorporate the contributions of other departments. The short time-scale for the decision process made it advantageous to delay filing the final version until relatively late, but to use as much of another department's text as possible in order to maintain the appearance of collaboration. Thus text from other departments might be added to the file server soon after being received; but at a late stage a revised version of that text would be substituted, altering the sense to weaken criticism or otherwise further the policy of the department that "owned" the section.

The fact that this political game was played out on a system that had been built assuming consensus led to some considerable technical difficulties at the final stage of document production. The production-run assumed that all the text on the file server would have been entered directly into the standard files with their correct style-sheet settings for headings, table numbers, etc. In fact, because of the extensive cutting and pasting, substitution of files created on floppy disc in place of the standard files on the server, etc., considerable disorder had been introduced, so that much of what should have been an automatic final process had to be carried out by extensive human intervention.

3.4 Conclusions

Both the case studies discussed above involved using computer-mediated writing as a medium for the social activity of decision making. In both cases there was a mismatch between the computer support and the social practices represented by the writing activity; and this mismatch appears to derive from mistaken premises about the social process. In the specification case, the mistaken premises concerned the ways in which groups can reach agreement on complex issues: it was assumed that having a system that modelled a meeting as the discussion of a number of topics would be sufficient to permit a rational consensus to emerge. Members failed to recognize the need for practices analogous to those of formal chairmanship and minutes; the system also did not provide support for differentiating between different functions of text (regulative, substantive, extra-text, etc). The mistaken premises in this case mainly concerned the social practices of face-to-face meetings, and the role that the patterning of time has in bringing face-to-face meetings to agree decisions. In the second case, the mistaken premises had principally to do with the basing of a design on consensus and open access to information in the form of draft texts: the system did not provide for a draft document to migrate easily between public and private space. The only private space available (the floppy disc) was not sufficiently integrated into the overall system to permit such two-way migration over time. This example differed from the first case, both because important organizational interests were at stake and because there was strong time pressure for decision making; but once again the issue of the patterning of time arose. Here the problem was that the systems designers' premises did not allow for the social manipulation of time as part of the interplay of organizational interests.

The evidence from these case studies is qualitative in nature and specific to writing for decision making. Nevertheless it provides indications of some components that should be present in a theory of computer-mediated collaborative writing: social practices, organizational micropolitics, the purposes of writing and the patterning of time.

Chapter 4

Computer Networking for Development of Distance Education Courses

A.R. Kaye

4.1 Introduction

This chapter takes the case of teams planning and writing distance education courses as an example of the issues that need to be considered in using computer support through local and wide area networks for work groups engaged in collaborative authoring tasks. It outlines the main issues of a non-technical nature which seem important in influencing the successful use of various readily available software and networking tools by such groups, whether the groups are composed of authors from the same institution, or from different collaborating institutions.

The chapter concentrates on human factors, and focuses on the potential of the existing hardware and software facilities available to the average academic author in European distance teaching universities. It is based on a selection of relevant literature, informed by the author's personal experience of course team processes and of the use of computer-mediated communication for collaborative work and authoring. It takes as a basic premise the need for a progressive co-evolution of roles, organizational structures, and technologies (Engelbart and Lehtman 1988), if technology is to be successfully used for group work.

Various models for the development and production of distance education courses are described, with specific reference to the course team model widely adopted at the UK Open University (UKOU). A summary of some of the main findings from studies of traditional (i.e. non-technology-supported) course team activities is presented. Three successful cases of the use of computer-mediated communication for cooperative work which seem particularly relevant to the joint authoring of teaching materials are then reviewed. Finally, some questions are raised concerning the factors influencing the adoption (and rejection) of tools such as computer conferencing and electronic mail (email) for course team collaboration.

Although the chapter focuses specifically on networked computer support for teams planning and writing distance teaching materials, many of the issues raised are relevant to other group collaboration and authoring tasks, such as the planning and writing of reports, research studies and books.

4.2 Issues in Course Team Collaboration

The design, development, and production of distance education courses is a complex, multi-dimensional, group process, generally carried out over a relatively extensive time period (e.g. 18–36 months), and involving critical deadlines and milestones. Distance education courses of the type produced by the UK or Dutch Open Universities, the Universidad Nacional de Educación a Distancia (UNED) in Spain, or the Fernuniversität in Germany, can be considered as elaborate "products" with medium- to long-term "service requirements". The "products" (courseware) are the course materials, equipment, and software produced for, or integrated into, the course, and the "service requirements" are the sum of the institutional and other support services and infrastructure within which distance students and tutors use the course materials, over a period of 4–6 years of successive presentations of the same course.

As an illustration of the number and diversity of materials that go to make up an integrated multimedia distance education course, the following list presents a summary of the main components of a recent Open University course on which this author worked:

1. Twenty-four different print bindings of specially written self-study "course units", each binding including between 60 and 90 pages.

2. A printed course guide.

3. A booklet of seven tutor-marked assignments, and sets of examination papers, both requiring annual updating.

4. A 300-page course reader, co-produced with a commercial publisher.

5. Sixteen half-hour TV programmes.

6. Six C90 audio cassettes.

7. Media/broadcast booklet to accompany the audio-visual materials.

8. Various types of guidance materials for tutors.

9. Twelve diskettes of computer software.

10. Two computer software manuals.

11. A modem and connector cables, loaned to students taking the course.

The development and production of the range of integrated materials that make up a distance education course involves a far greater degree of complexity than does the design of a classroom lesson, or the preparation of a standard academic text, journal article or research report. This is because the authors of distance learning materials are required to attend to four different factors simultaneously, or iteratively, during their course development work (Henri and Kaye 1985):

1. Epistemological issues, concerning the conceptual structure and the selection of content.

2. Pedagogical issues, concerning the learning strategies which students will adopt, or which are to be promoted, and the approach to be adopted for evaluating students' achievements, based possibly on a particular theoretical perspective on learning.

3. Didactic issues, concerning the presentation, sequencing, and structure of the material.

4. Media issues, concerning not only the choice of which media will be used, but also the particular teaching and learning functions to be assigned to each medium.

The development and production of distance education courses, such that the end product appears to students and tutors as an integrated whole, sequenced over a study period of nine or so months, is a complex matter. It inevitably requires the combined efforts of both academic subject experts, and a range of media and production specialists.

4.2.1 Models of Course Development

There are, traditionally, two basic models of course development in distance education. The first is one in which an academic content specialist works with an editor, and there is a relatively clear separation of functions. The content specialist writes the initial draft of the material, whilst the editor is responsible for "the development of the materials and the quality of the text, (and) is also concerned with curriculum content, teaching methods, and quality of presentation" (Jenkins 1989), in other words, the pedagogical, didactic, and media issues.

Editors in this sense are also called transformers, educational technologists, instructional designers, educational developers, and course designers. For example, at the Open Learning Institute in British Columbia, the material for each (relatively short) course was typically prepared by one external course writer, who would work with an in-house "course designer" playing the role of course development manager, instructional designer and editor (Timmers 1986). In such cases, the editor also has progress-chasing and management roles to play, with overall responsibility for ensuring that materials get to the students on time. On more substantial courses which involve inputs from a number of different academic content specialists (writers) the editor will also need to ensure overall coordination, and maybe supervise the initial course planning processes. This model is one which is particularly common in traditional correspondence teaching institutions which rely on part-time and external writers as content experts, and in which the course materials are in general restricted to print, possibly supplemented with audio material on cassette or radio.

The second basic model of course development, mainly prevalent in university institutions with their own full-time faculty, is a course team approach, involving academics, media producers, designers, educational technologists and editors, working together in a relatively democratic mode. Such course teams are generally managed by an academic staff member, possibly assisted by a course manager. The planning and development of the course materials is a collective responsibility, and the process of discussion and refinement of successive drafts of the course materials by team members is claimed to be one of the main guarantees of the quality of the resultant course. The first vice-chancellor of the UKOU, Lord Perry, even went so far as to say that "the concept of the course team is, I believe, the most important single contribution of the Open University to teaching practice at the tertiary level" (Perry 1976).

External writers may be invited to contribute to a course team's work as consultants, and in this case their relationship to the team may be similar to that of the external writer to the "editor" in the model described earlier. In large teams, or in interdisciplinary teams with members from different academic disciplines, responsibilities may be subdivided between different working groups, each taking responsibility for a different part (block or module) of the course.

There are a number of variants of the course team model, and the use of large teams, typical of those set up for many courses at the UKOU (and which are discussed in some detail below), is not necessarily the most appropriate model in all instances. A number of experienced OU academics are critical of the large team model, and have proposed more streamlined structures, for example with "one or two individuals determining the curriculum, methodology, assessment and so forth, and then finding, commissioning, or directing others to produce materials as necessary, subject always to external evaluation" (Tight 1985). This approach, akin to the "transformer" model (Waller 1977) represents a halfway house between the "writer plus editor" and the large, democratic, multi-skill course team.

4.2.2 Course Team Work: An Instrumental Perspective

Course team work, like many other group writing or design projects, typically involves three main stages:

1. An *initial* stage of goal definition and work planning.

2. An *execution* stage during which work may be divided among individual team members, or small sub-groups, and carried out relatively independently (parallel partitioning).

3. An *integration* stage during which individual inputs are brought together to create the final product.

These stages may well be repeated in an iterative manner two or three times during the course design and development process, as first, second and final drafts of the course are developed.

The *types of task* carried out during course development can be divided into three main categories, each with specific communication needs and characteristics:

1. Project coordination and decision making tasks (e.g. allocation of authoring tasks, scheduling of work, setting of deadlines, allocation of budgets, organization of meetings, liaison with production services).

2. Research and information exchange tasks (e.g. identification of relevant course ideas, content material and matter experts; library-type research tasks such as finding suitable illustrations, video material, recordings, software, and publications).

3. Authoring tasks (e.g. drafting and re-drafting course materials, and commenting on other team members' drafts; developmental testing and rewriting of course materials; editing of materials to production handover stage).

One approach to organizing the complexity of the course production task has been that of itemizing all the activities carried out by the different members of a course team, and arranging them into an activity network or flow chart. Detailed examples have been produced at the UKOU, where course development is formally organized into three main phases (Lewis 1971a):

Phase 1: Planning

  1A: Course Planning

  1B: Unit Planning

Phase 2: Writing

  2A: Unit Writing

  2B: Developmental Testing

  2C: External Assessment

Phase 3: Editing and Printing

The complete network itemizing the activities which need to be fulfilled during each phase, by the various different course team members, specifies

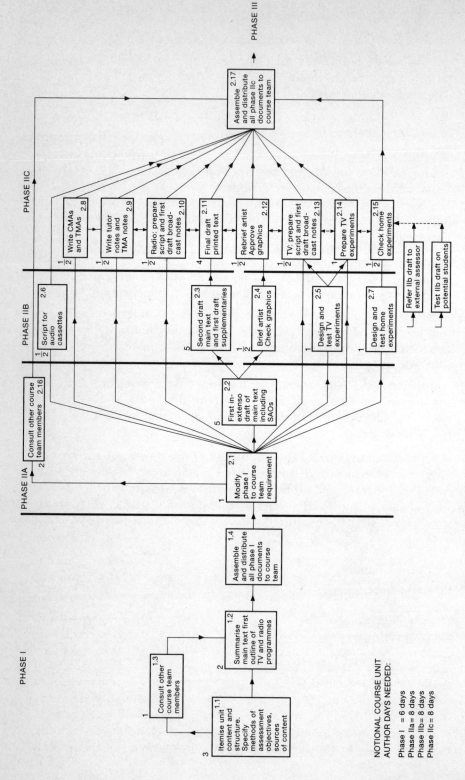

Fig. 4.1 Course production flowchart showing course unit author activities (Kaye 1973).

over 130 discrete activities. A simplified version, specifying only the major categories of activity to be undertaken by course unit authors (in this case, academics in the Science Faculty), once initial course planning has been completed, is reproduced as Fig. 4.1. It should be noted that, although this formalization of course team work at the UKOU, as represented in such diagrams, occurred nearly two decades ago, the procedures have remained relatively unchanged since then.

The main advantages of displaying the course development process in the form of a flow chart are that an optimal sequencing of activities is presented, that no activities are missed out, and that coordination of activities between different team members (e.g. authors, editors, producers) and/or working groups (e.g. a block or module working group, an assessment subgroup, a broadcast working group) with different responsibilities is facilitated. In reality, of course, it may not prove possible to sequence different team members' activities in exactly the way specified in the network, and in this respect any such chart presents an idealized situation. Although the network as such may not be used itself as a planning or scheduling tool, the specifications of outputs required at the end of each phase, and the dates of various deadlines, each derived from it, can be used in practice to keep a team's activities on track.

Although such apparently rational subdivision of the group writing task into a carefully scheduled chart or network of pre-defined activities might seem to be a useful tool in organizing academic team work, there are a number of major limits to its value. As outlined by Lewis (1971b), these include:

1. There is no unique way of specifying the network activities and sequence, and each course team tends, often quite justifiably, to conceptualize its activities and their detailed sequence in a different way.

2. It is often impossible to assign meaningful time estimates to many activities, especially those concerned with the writing of original material.

3. Mistakes and/or reappraisals may occur at any point, requiring individual authors, working groups, or maybe the entire team, to "return to the drawing board" and re-think aspects of the course.

Finally, and perhaps the most difficult aspect of all to cope with in trying to use flow chart techniques to plan and schedule course development activities, is the elasticity and uncertainty associated with the principal task of the execution phase: the drafting and re-drafting of the course materials. Regardless of the level of detail in a Phase 1 specification for a written unit, more often than not, the author's ideas only become clear when the extended (Phase 2 draft) is being written. As a result, colleagues' perceptions of what is being written (based on an earlier draft) may not be an accurate reflection of what any individual team member is in fact writing. Riley

(1984) refers to this as the "out-of-step" phenomenon. Clearly, if this phenomenon occurs in a course team on any major scale, serious problems will arise at the final, integration, stage of course production, when the various authors' contributions need to come together as a coherent whole. In practice, various informal tactics are used to minimize the likelihood of such problems arising, and this is obviously fairly straightforward when course team colleagues work in adjacent offices, and see each other regularly, both formally and informally, in between the course team meetings. In the case of distributed course teams, it would seem to be necessary to provide alternative channels of communication to substitute for physical proximity.

Other problems in the course development process can arise as a result of:

- lack of consensus over the content and structure of the course which do not – or cannot – get resolved in the initial design phase, and which may result in major disagreements and needs for redesign at a later stage;

- differing expectations held by different team members as to the precise scope and nature of other individuals' roles and tasks, and differences in the perceived trustworthiness of different colleagues;

- different working patterns (e.g. between team members who prefer to prepare their contributions in advance of schedule, and others who delay task completion until the last minute);

- varying preferences in the use of technology, such as academics who use word processors, and those who prefer to draft in manuscript prior to word processing by a secretary (note that those in the former group, *de facto*, obtain later deadlines for themselves, and might end up being behind schedule compared to those in the latter group).

4.2.3 Course Team Work: What it's *Really* Like

Far from being earnest collectives, most course teams are erratic, anarchic groupings, learning by trial and error in an area where educational technology usually has precious little to say, working by mutual adjustment rather than unitary consensus, bending and battering the system until it more or less fits. (Martin 1979)

If some course teams work smoothly, some collapse completely; if some deliver the goods on time, some are hopelessly late. In between there are perhaps the majority, which produce a course, but a little late, and less integrated and imaginative than could have been the case. Course teams can be likened to families. Happy families do exist, but others fall apart when rebellious children leave home or when parents separate; most survive, but not without varying elements of antagonism and resentment. (Crick 1980)

> What seems to happen in course teams … is that they start with promise. People, on the whole, are enthusiastic. Then there develops a destructive environment which by the end of the life of a course team has become a punitive one. Course material is produced, but usually by a very small residue of the original team. … people tell us that the most threatening aspect of a course team is the criticism that has to be taken and what seems clear is that it is felt to be an attack on the person and not just about competency. (Lawrence and Young 1979)

A number of experienced distance educators (Crick 1980; Drake 1979; Martin 1979; Mason 1976; Newey 1975; Nicodemus 1984; Riley 1979, 1983, 1984; Tight 1985) have provided insights into the ways in which academics live the course team experience. These insights are often in marked contrast to the impressions obtained from the traditional educational technology literature on instructional design, or from the apparently pre-determined and structured set of procedures laid out in networks such as those discussed above.

Riley (1984) stresses that the writing of distance teaching material is a complex, individual and emotional process. The "out-of-step" phenomenon already alluded to is one factor contributing to the complexity of the process. Of course, any writing process is complex in itself, but drafting materials for distance students is inherently far more complex than, say, writing an article for a journal or producing a research report. The potential student readership is likely to be heterogeneous, with differing levels of prior knowledge and of interest in the subject. In drafting the material, the author needs not only to consider links to colleagues' material, but also must pay careful attention to factors such as style, clarity, provision of student activities and self-testing opportunities, integration with other media (tapes, software, broadcasts etc.), ease of access to the text, links with formal assessment and examination material, and so on. Many of these factors will take on an increasing importance in the author's mind as the deadline for the final draft of the unit approaches. This may reflect a shift in the audience that is being written for as successive drafts are developed. Many authors essentially write their first draft for themselves – as a way of sorting out their initial ideas. The second draft is more likely to be aimed at course team colleagues, while the final draft is likely to be written explicitly with the student reader in mind. However, the "audience" dimension is further complicated in some instances, especially if the course materials are likely to be read and used by peers in other universities: this can lead to conflict between writing for one's own student audience, and writing for one's academic peers.

The process is individual to the extent that different authors may adopt different strategies for preparing their material, corresponding to different images or perceptions of what they are doing. Riley (1979) refers to three different images of the course unit writing process, derived from interviews conducted with academics at the Open University:

1. *Packing a box*: the author's primary concern is to "squeeze as much as possible into his box, and to do it tidily, so that ... there won't be any bits left sticking out".

2. *Producing a play*: the author's "first task is assembling his cast of players, the articles and quotations he has collected on his topic, balancing individual quality against the need to get a group that will work well together and the whole against his own conception of the characters".

3. *Designing a railway line*: this author "plans out his route before he starts, to take the students, or trains, from one point to another, through difficult mountains".

Different tactics adopted by authors at different stages of the course development process vary depending on the corresponding image. For example, "box-packers" are likely to start off by drawing up a list of contents for their unit, "producers" will collect and arrange possible resources, and "railway engineers" may start by drawing a diagram tracing an optimal study route. And, again, they may respond in different ways to suggestions for adding material to the unit – the "box-packer" trying to squeeze the extra material into his existing plan, while the "track-layer" may decide to re-structure his entire argument (route). And, in general, different authors use different tactics to cope with the anxiety generated by the process of receiving colleagues' comments on their drafts. These tactics include trying to defuse criticism in advance, playing for sympathy, agreeing to leave others' drafts alone if this is reciprocated, use of insider knowledge to counteract criticism, and simply going on the defensive.

Riley (1983) tries to interpret the reasons for the strategies and tactics she observed among OU academics, throughout the various stages of course

Table 4.1. Factors influencing course preparation (factors in **bold** are rated as being of major significance) (from Riley 1983)

Public factors

  1 **The subject of the course and academic tradition**
  2 **The characteristics of the students**
  3 Open University policies and resources
  4 The official size of the course team
  5 The spread of the course team (across different disciplines/faculties)
  6 **Momentum and precedents** (in course team decision taking)

Private factors

  7 **Individuals' beliefs** (about course content and/or teaching approach)
  8 **Individuals' commitments** (total or partial, time available)
  9 Office locations and working habits
10 Individuals' writing styles
11 Individuals' desire to enhance their status
12 Individuals' insecurities and fears
13 **The chairperson's personality and experience**
14 **Team interactions** (quality and nature of)

preparation, in terms of individuals' underlying intentions, which she classifies into public and private factors. These are listed in Table 4.1. Public factors are those which are openly acknowledged and discussed, while the private factors were only raised, if at all, in one-to-one conversations with trusted friends.

Of these factors, those that were rated as being the most important by the academics interviewed by Riley were individuals' beliefs and the personality and experience of the person chairing the course. Riley points out that the differing nature of individuals' beliefs about what they want to do in the course (and, specifically, what they want to see included and how it is to be taught) explain the wide variations in the ways in which different people comment on their colleagues' drafts, and in the ways in which individual authors react to comments. Again, the experience, leadership style, personality, level of efficiency, and temperament of the course team chair (and of the course manager) were seen as crucial in determining the success of the course preparation process. Newey (1975) stresses the importance of the chairperson's role in the course team in combining the responsibilities of an academic editor (in ensuring appropriate academic standards for the course), a production manager (in making sure that deadlines are adhered to), and a student advocate (in ensuring the teaching effectiveness of the course as a whole).

Such factors do not feature as significant variables in course production flow charts, nor are they mentioned in the typical educational technology literature on course development. Yet it is clear that they are of fundamental importance, as are the two other highly rated private factors (in bold in Table 4.1): the individuals' level of personal commitment to the course and the quality and nature of the interactions among course team members.

There is evidence to suggest that course team processes can become pathological if the factors listed by Riley (particularly, it could be argued, the "private" factors) are not properly addressed. One experienced course team chairman (Drake 1979) goes so far as to say that "the course team is a menace to the academic output and reputation of the Open University", because it provides a framework for protracted (and exciting) academic discussions about possible options for course content and structure, but that when the real deadlines are imminent, many academics are unable to come to definite decisions and produce satisfactory material. In extreme cases, pressure of deadlines can even indeed induce a variety of pathological behaviours for coping with the situation, including handing in one's work so late that there is no time for anyone to comment on it, adopting bullying tactics at course team meetings, shifting blame onto scapegoats, dropping out of the team and leaving others to cope with the extra workload, and even falling physically ill.

Large teams producing multimedia courses also include media producers as well as academic authors, and problems can arise in the relationship between academic staff and radio or television producers – especially when

a professional BBC producer might have different criteria for what constitutes a "good" programme from the academic subject expert. Confusions
can arise over individual responsibilities for different aspects of a programme, and different work schedules may make it difficult for a producer
to attend all course team meetings, thus leading to further coordination
problems and misunderstandings of who is doing what. Nicodemus (1984)
points out that the resultant anxieties can cause "a lot of flight behaviour
which simply delays and dramatizes the eventual confrontations".

A study carried out by the Tavistock Institute of Human Relations with
course teams at the UKOU (Lawrence and Young 1979) points out the difficulty in getting large groups of people to work together, because the larger
the group, the more people become influenced by unconscious social
processes. The strategy of splitting a large team into sub-groups under the
coordination of a chairperson does not necessarily improve the situation, as
individual participants may then feel that they have lost responsibility for
what is finally produced, and this may lead to other forms of anxiety and
distress, especially to feelings of dependency (which contrast with the
public myth that academics should be independent). The use of sophisticated technology by the OU in its teaching, and the constraints imposed by
production scheduling and deadlines, leads to an apparent emphasis on
rationality and instrumentality in relations, which prevents the unconscious
being acknowledged in the work environment. This conclusion has implications for the provision of networked computer support for team work in
general, if such findings have any applicability outside the institutional
context of the UKOU.

A brief review of studies of course team processes and instructional
design in distance education from other institutions, for example in India
(Gupta 1989) and Australia (Crick 1980; Nunan 1990) would suggest that
the UKOU experience is far from being unique in this respect. In fact, social
science research into other types of group task shows that the problems that
have been observed in distance education course teams also appear in other
large work groups carrying out complex intellectual tasks. For example,
Brooks (1982) has observed that when complex tasks are shared among
individuals or small working groups, the extra burdens of coordination and
communication often counteract the productivity gains expected from division of labour. In addition, problems arise from social psychological
processes: for example, pressures to conform in a group might cause people
to behave less effectively than if they were working alone, and diffusion of
responsibility and lack of ownership of a group product can lead to group
members contributing less effort to a group task than they would to a personal, individual project. General conclusions of this nature, from studies of
a variety of group projects, demonstrate that the working problems faced
by distance education course teams are far from being unique.

To conclude this section on a positive note, we could say that the course
team approach, when it works constructively, results in the progressive

refinement and improvement of the academic and pedagogical quality of the course materials. And conflict and tension within a team can, of course, have positive outcomes: "the cycle of integration–disintegration is, after all, also known to be important in creativity" (Nicodemus 1984). However, the processes involved in successful and "healthy" course team work can be problematic, even within a single institution, and with teams made up of colleagues from the same department, who are familiar with each others' expertise and working methods. In the case of distributed course teams (e.g. those working on interdisciplinary, or co-produced courses), where, *a priori*, a strong case might be made for networked computer support for collaboration, it would seem important to pay even more attention to the underlying dynamics within a team.

4.3 Technology Support for Course Team Work

In principle, distance teaching organizations seem to provide an ideal case for the use of computer networking as an effective support for course development activities. Many distance teaching organizations rely partially or mainly on external consultants and authors as key contributors to courses, so it is often the case that members of a course team are not co-located. In the European context, current initiatives to promote inter-institutional collaboration in development of distance education courses will increase the number of teams with members drawn from several institutions working on co-production projects.

However, networking support could also appear relevant to course teams where most of the members are from the same institution. Even in a single-discipline course team at the UKOU, where the majority of course team members are located in neighbouring offices, there are often some key members based in regional offices or on other parts of the central campus. Furthermore, preferences for the locus of course writing activities vary, with some academics preferring to concentrate on this aspect of their work at home, while others prefer to use their offices; so, even when members of a team have adjoining offices, they are not necessarily available for consultation on a daily basis.

At a technical level, the UKOU in particular is well furnished with the necessary infrastructure for collaboration in authoring of materials:

1. A large proportion of academics now write their teaching materials on a word processor, and the university has adopted Microsoft Word as the standard package for course teams, as part of an overall electronic publishing strategy.

2. The VAX cluster run by the university's Academic Computing Service provides standard VMS mail and access to external academic email

networks, and also hosts two computer conferencing systems (CoSy and VaxNotes).

3. Network access from offices (both on the central campus and from regional offices) is readily available, as is related technical help.

4. Access from home is available at local telephone call rates via a large number of dial-up nodes throughout the UK (these dial-up nodes currently serve over 2500 students and tutors on courses using the CoSy conferencing system and other on-line facilities, and the Academic Computing Service provides help services for such home-based users).

Although the UKOU may currently be somewhat more advanced in these areas than some other European distance teaching universities, similar levels of infrastructure support are fast developing elsewhere (e.g. at the Dutch Open University, and at UNED in Spain).

However, it is clear that, even at the UKOU, the use of networked support services for course team work has not yet developed on any scale, and use of email and computer conferencing for course team collaboration was never considered as an integral part of the development of a university-wide electronic publishing strategy. Some course teams, nevertheless, have tried to incorporate computer networking into their course development procedures, but there is little evidence that this has had any real impact on the ways in which teams operate. For example, a number of course teams in the Science Faculty use VMS mail as a convenient way of providing some of the comments on colleagues' drafts, but many team members prefer to reserve major comments for face-to-face discussion. In this faculty, although the combined use of electronic publishing technology and email has led to a compacting of schedules, and to changes in the roles and responsibilities of editors, the traditional three-phase course development procedure has basically remained unchanged despite these innovations.

In the remainder of this chapter, an attempt will be made to examine some of the factors that seem to be critical in determining the success or failure of the introduction of technology support for groups of "knowledge workers", such as academics developing written course materials.

4.3.1 Networked Groupware

Johansen (1988) defines "groupware" as a "generic term for specialised computer aids that are designed for the use of collaborative work groups. ... groupware can involve software, hardware, services, and/or group process support". In a review of different approaches to groupware, Johansen makes a distinction between those approaches designed to support face-to-face meetings, and those tailored to electronic meetings (when participants are not physically co-located). In the second category, which is the most relevant in this context, he differentiates groupware for synchronous communication from that for asynchronous communication.

Most preferred group usage of networked services in the course team context – in between periodic face-to face meetings – is likely to be asynchronous. Palme (1989) summarizes the three main advantages of asynchronous working as follows:

1. Participants do not need to find a set time when they can all be active simultaneously, and can contribute at times which suit them.

2. Participants are not forced into rash decisions because of the time limits of a simultaneous meeting.

3. The asynchronous mode allows participants to choose to spend the time they need to read and reflect on a problem – this allows for individual differences in the time needed to reach a decision.

The types of asynchronous computer and networked support available in the academic environment to facilitate course team collaboration activities are listed in Table 4.2, together with the roles which they might play in the course development process.

Table 4.2. Course development tasks and asynchronous services

Course development tasks	Asynchronous services
Course planning (including preparation of face-to-face meetings)	Computer conferencing Electronic mail (Voice mail)
Course research	Electronic mail Access to external databases and networks
Preparation of draft text materials	Word processing templates
Distribution of drafts	File transfer Course text databases Facsimile transmission
Commenting on drafts (of texts and other course components)	Computer conferencing Electronic mail (Voice mail)

For distributed teams where face-to-face meetings are difficult or expensive to organize, it would, in principle, be possible to complement these asynchronous services with a "pseudo" screen-sharing service, whereby team members could simultaneously hold a telephone conference call while they viewed the same draft of a document, called up from the conferencing system or from a central text database, on their office machines (few academics involved in such courses are likely to have the two telephone lines, or ISDN connections, which would be required for home based access). One member of the team (say, the unit author or working group convenor) could then modify the document and show revised versions to the other participants, in the light of their voice discussion.

4.3.2 Three Success Stories

Even when there is an agreed group task to be performed, and appropriate technological infrastructure to help in planning and collaboration tasks is readily available, there is no guarantee that the technology will be adopted by the target users. In an attempt to identify some of the variables determining take-up of computer-mediated communication for group work in the academic environment, brief summaries are presented below of three successful implementations that seem potentially relevant. Although only one of the cases specifically concerns the development of distance teaching material, the three examples cover the main stages of initial planning and design of a group product, execution of individual contributions, and the integration of individual contributions into a final product through commenting and re-drafting.

Electronic mail for group decision making at Hewlett-Packard (Fafchamps et al. 1989)   This study began with the question: "Why was one particular team of software engineers capable of conducting a systematic discussion over email when others had stopped in mid-course?" It is an analysis of one of the few successful uses of email to support group decision making at Hewlett-Packard, and concentrates on the nature of the group processes involved. The team, a newly constituted one, was made up of five people, working over a three-month period in preparation for a major design decision, using an electronic bulletin board for group discussion, as well as private email.

The bulletin board messages were analysed using the coding scheme devised by Benne and Sheats (1974) for analysing face-to-face meetings, which distinguishes between "group task activities" (messages concerned with exchanges and elaboration of information and opinions, and with coordinating and evaluating), "group-centred strategies" (messages nurturing the group climate) and "expression of individual attitudes" (messages fulfilling personal needs such as domination, justification, etc.). Message mapping showed three basic structures: *islands* (messages that do not receive a reply or comment); *dialogues* (two or more messages with a common header); and *webs* (messages that build one on the other, but do not share a common header).

The results indicate that the discussions show similar group task activities to those in face-to-face meetings, but few of the group-centred strategies (possibly because group maintenance functions were accomplished through face-to-face interaction). The most important conclusion from the study is that the role of the team manager was absolutely crucial to the maintenance of the email discussion, in terms of the volume of the messages he produced (half the total), the range of group task activities that he assumed, and the timing of his contributions. This is consistent with other experience and research findings concerning the key role of the moderator or organizer in computer conferencing discussions. For example, Fanning and Raphael (1986), relating other experiences at Hewlett-Packard, suggest that this role is so vital that the definition of an organizer should be "the person who keeps the conference alive".

The team manager used email for posting all relevant information needed by the project team so as to build a common group perspective on progress, and for sharing the results of his individual discussions with team members. Neither he nor other team members used the system for "information dumping" – they rather took time to clarify their positions, and to give evaluative comments to each other, resulting in the development of message webs that seemed to provoke increases in interaction levels. Finally, just as in face-to-face meetings, there were marked individual differences in frequency and style of contribution between team members.

Collaborative discussion and group authoring (Kaye et al. 1989) Linda Harasim, at the Ontario Institute for Studies in Education, designed and hosted a three-month on-line conference workshop with the aim of collaboratively developing and discussing research perspectives for educational computer communications. The goal of the workshop was to bring together (electronically) leading scholars in the field of educational computer communications to share and develop research skills and insights and identify research needs related to educational computer communications. The intent was to facilitate a collaborative process and, through this, produce a set of end products in the form of papers, which were then edited into a book (Harasim 1990). Considerable attention was paid to the design and structuring of the on-line environment in order to facilitate interaction and promote useful exchange. This led to the structure of ten educators with research experience in the field being invited to "present" a paper on-line and to moderate a conference on that topic, using a collaborative process to discuss and develop the main ideas. Ten other educators with theoretical and practical experience were invited to participate as discussants in the process of refining and reworking the papers. Participants were encouraged to log on at least twice a week, and the three-month collaboration ended with a face-to-face meeting of the presenters, at which the drafts of each participant's paper, modified as a result of the on-line contributions, were presented and discussed further.

An evaluation of the workshop shows that the overall group process was active and interactive. A set of consistently active conferees emerged as a dedicated core; a minority had a less consistently active role or followed along as readers rather than by actively writing comments. Harasim notes a distinct correlation between the level of input by the moderator and the level of activity in the conference: the more active the moderator, the higher the level of activity in the conference. There was also some correlation between the state of the paper entered into the conference system, and the level of on-line discussion: the document that received the most comments was in fact a set of headings and notes, and the authors specifically encouraged other participants to comment on these notes as part of the process of drafting a final version. Other papers, entered as more or less finished products, received far fewer comments.

The benefits of this on-line workshop were expressed as follows:

1. The discovery of new colleagues and new ideas: participants reported that they appreciated the surprisingly interesting contributions from previously unknown individuals.

2. The opportunity to update knowledge in the field: research, issues and activities.

3. The value of collaborating as a stimulating, rewarding process for articulating ideas.

4. The opportunity to interact over a period of three months encouraged a far deeper and wider exploration and analysis of issues than is possible in any face-to-face activity.

The difficulties highlighted by this kind of interaction were identified as follows:

1. Finding or making time to participate: on-line work is an add-on to existing academic activities.

2. Adapting habits of work to the on-line process: learning to make small inputs regularly, rather than indulging in crash preparation just before deadlines.

3. Contributing to discussions which wander or do not have a clear task or which diverge from expectations.

4. Moving from exchange of ideas to managing and drawing together the range of disparate perspectives.

The implications of this example of scholarly collaboration are, first and foremost, that it is possible for scholars located in three different countries and two continents to use a conferencing system for active collaboration and discussion, pursuing and deepening common interests. It highlights the need for increased institutional recognition of on-line work as part of academic job specifications. There are also issues to be resolved in the copyright and ownership of the ideas developed on-line. Finally, while excellent for brainstorming and expressing divergent views, conferencing is awkward for moving beyond synergy into organizing and managing the information generated by a synergistic encounter.

The process of producing the edited book from the various participants' contributions was facilitated because the documents were already available in electronic form, and the process of final editing was very much accelerated because it was easy for individual authors to make their final corrections and transfer the draft back to the editor.

Distance education course authoring: the "writer plus editor" model (Timmers 1986)   Earlier in this chapter, reference was made to the "writer plus editor" model of distance education course development. This model, which avoids some of the problems associated with team work, is particularly amenable to technology support, as it essentially involves only a limited number of exchanges of drafts between two, or at the most, three people, each of whom has clearly defined and proscribed roles.

The Open Learning Institute (OLI) in British Columbia (now incorporated into The Open Learning Agency) used microcomputers, modems and telecommunications links in 1984 and 1985 to augment the work of a small course team in writing an introductory chemistry course. The team in question was made up of an external writer, an external academic consultant, and a full-time OLI editor. OLI courses are traditionally made up of a set number of specially written study units which accompany an already-available commercially published textbook. Study units contain objectives, notes on the textbook material, theory and examples, self-assessment questions and answers, and a homework assignment. These study units are prepared by a contracted external writer, and checked by an external academic assessor or consultant. The OLI editor (or course designer) assigned to a course helps the writer in overall planning and design, which is embodied in an agreed course "blueprint". Writers new to OLI are required to prepare a draft of the first, prototype, unit, before being contracted to proceed with the rest of the course writing.

In the case of the introductory chemistry course described by Timmers, the first three units were prepared with traditional methods (a typewriter, and use of the postal service for exchanging drafts and comments between writer, consultant and editor), while the remaining units were written on a PC with a word processor, and exchange of drafts was by modem and the telephone network (a linear sequence of: writer → consultant → writer → editor → writer → editor). A standard "template" was prepared for the units on the word processor, which contained all the standard layout, design, typeface and component specifications, and the writer wrote her material within the template. At the final stage, the writer and editor discussed by telephone all the editorial interventions, while simultaneously scrolling through the text on their PCs.

A number of advantages for this mode of working, compared to the traditional method, are cited:

1. The writer much preferred using a word processor to a typewriter, feeling that the relative ease of modifying her text helped her to produce an academically superior product.

2. The review process was stimulated: the consultant became more active, and made more comments.

3. Time was saved at the re-drafting stages (because of word processing), in between stages (because of the instant telecom links), and at the production stage (no need for re-keying): on average, total development time dropped from 120 minutes to 50 minutes per page.

4. Electronic communication lent a "sense of excitement and urgency" to the process.

5. The editing task was much simplified.

6. The writer/editor relationship changed for the better, the writer feeling more of an equal partner in the process.

OLI has helped to introduce similar microcomputer-based course development procedures at the Universiti Sains Malaysia and at Universitas Terbuka in Indonesia. Timmers points out that the storage of course text material on computers allows for easy "taking apart and recombination" of elements of a course, and that features such as this shed a new light on possible joint course development and co-production activities.

4.3.3 Factors Affecting Successful Implementation

The effective introduction of technological support for groups engaged in intellectual teamwork involves the interplay of a number of different social, psychological and technological factors. Several of these are apparent from the three examples given above.

Firstly, it is clear that the mere existence of easily accessible or familiar asynchronous communication systems does not necessarily mean that they will be effectively used for group tasks. The case from Hewlett-Packard is cited as one of the few systematically conducted examples of successful group decision making over email, even though the great majority of staff in the organization are regular users of email systems for other purposes. Conversely, several aspects of the communications technology used in the two other cases were initially novel to those involved: the external writer at OLI has used neither word processing templates nor file transfer facilities at the start of the collaboration, and many of the participants in the OISE on-line workshop had to sort out international connection problems, and learn how to use the PARTI conferencing system, before they could start any effective collaboration.

If it is not the ready availability of familiar technology that is the determining element in success, we must turn out attention to other factors. One feature shared by all three cases is clear leadership responsibilities. In the OLI example, where the group size is small (editor, writer, consultant), and the prime mode of interaction is telephone discussion of a shared document, the editor has clear responsibility for tasks such as progress-chasing and coordinating the work of the consultant and writer. The Hewlett-Packard and OISE cases demonstrate that effective use of computer conferencing or a shared bulletin board requires that one member of the group has the explicit role of managing on-line discussions, and that the richness and value of these discussions depends strongly on the level of on-line activity of that person. The technology *per se* is of little value without this human organization and management. In this respect, of course, the situation is little different from any team-based project: the experience and leadership style of the person responsible for coordinating the team's work is crucial (for example, as stressed earlier, in the discussion of factors affecting course team processes at the UKOU).

A second important factor is the importance of mixing face-to-face communication with other channels. There is evidence that the lack of immediate feedback in asynchronous conferencing and in one-to-one email exchanges can more easily lead to coordination problems and protracted decision making than is the case for face-to-face meetings (see, for example, Galegher and Kraut 1989). There is always a danger that this feature of computer-mediated communication could, in turn, lead to exacerbation of any underlying pathologies within a team (i.e. increase of mutual distrust, paranoia, "flaming" etc.). Hence the importance of reaching an early agreement about the specific roles of each communication channel, and about the phasing of face-to-face meetings. Such meetings are particularly desirable in the early stages of a collaborative venture, so that team members get to know and trust each other, and so that initial agreement can be reached over the broad outlines of the project, and at the end of a project, for reaching final agreement on the group product. These meetings can become more effective – as shown in the case from OISE – if preliminary discussion and commenting has already occurred on the network, so that each person at the meeting is *au fait* with progress to date, and comes with clearly considered proposals.

The level of commitment of the members of a team, both to the project and to the way in which the communications technology is to be used, is obviously extremely important, particularly when asynchronous communication channels are being used. Unless there are shared expectations and behaviour patterns among all members of a work group about frequency of logging on to collect email or read conference messages, group discussions are likely to founder. If take-up of a communication channel such as email or conferencing is differential within a group – some members checking the system frequently, some rarely, and some not at all – then the value of the on-line aspects of the group process is seriously diminished. With computer conferencing in particular, there also needs to be consensus about the appropriate areas (topics, branches etc.) for messages on specific topics, as well as an agreement on what types of messages are destined for the whole group, and what should be sent by personal email or to specific sub-groups.

For such commitment to exist, there need to be clear advantages for members of the group in using the technology. For example, use of computer networking should enable team members to save time over alternative communication media, or to conveniently intercalate work on the group task with their other day-to-day responsibilities (asynchronous media such as email, telephone answering machines or voice mail permit intermittent contributions to group tasks during otherwise "dead" moments of the working day). Use of the technology should permit levels of interaction, and the development of relationships among dispersed group members, that would not otherwise be possible (such as the computer conferencing discussions in the OISE case, or the rapid turnaround of comments on the drafts sent by file transfer in the OLI example). In other words, participants need to be motivated to take part, and one of the strongest such motivations is the receipt of interesting and positive comments on earlier messages contributed to a conference, or on drafts or outlines of material submitted to the group. In all three of the cases summarized above, the likelihood of finding useful or interesting evaluative comments on one's own contributions was clearly a strong motivating factor. The example from OISE suggests that, in the early stages of the collaborative authoring of a text, initial drafts in the form of headings and rough notes are more likely to receive useful comments than are drafts which appear more "finished". Initial agreement in a group task over what constitutes first and second drafts of materials, and on the responsibilities of group members in providing feedback and comments, is likely to raise motivation levels within the group as a whole, and thus increase the likelihood of the communication system being used effectively.

It makes sense for there to be a continuity between design and drafting of course materials, arriving at agreement on the final version of the text materials, and final production of those materials. Draft texts entered into conferencing systems, or stored as files in shared databases, can be transferred to electronic publishing systems (although the procedures involved are not always as seamless as one would like). At the final editing stage of course development, many of the advantages claimed for technology support for shared authoring tasks are obviously similar to those for electronic publishing. Bacsich (1990) lists the main potential benefits of electronic publishing of distance education materials as reduction of external costs such as typesetting, reduction of elapsed time, increase of authors' control, improved quality and consistency of the final product, greater staff productivity, and better re-usability of material. Most of these benefits were also cited by Timmers in his account of technology support at OLI.

None of the examples above involves the use of sophisticated joint authoring and editing software for distributed work groups, able to handle multiple annotations and the use of graphics and other non-text items, and compatible with electronic publishing standards. Such products (e.g. those systems described and analysed by Miles et al. and Jones, this volume) are not yet widely available in the normal academic environment. Palme (1989) points out that functional software for joint editing, if it is to be properly integrated into a conferencing system tailored for group tasks, needs to provide support for:

- synchronous and asynchronous working on the same document;
- merging of simultaneous changes into a new document, without any prior version being lost;
- discussion of specific parts of the document during its development, with comments being "tagged" to the relevant sections of the document, using tools and syntax matching those in the conferencing system;
- flexible access control on who is allowed to update the master copy of the document;
- easy availability of the document and comments to all participants during the editing phase.

It is likely to be some time before suitable joint authoring software with these characteristics becomes widely available within the academic distance education community.

4.4 Conclusion

What lessons for the implementation of networked computer support for academic collaboration in course development can be drawn from the earlier discussion of course teams, and from the examples of technology applications for collaborative authoring analysed above?

The social, psychological and institutional factors influencing the processes and outcomes of academic teamwork were stressed in the first part of this chapter, because these factors are probably of greater overall importance in determining success than is the nature of any technology support which might be made available to a course team.

That this is a general issue, relevant to many kinds of intellectual team work, is evident from even a cursory glance at the social science literature on group processes and computer supported collaborative work. For example, researchers such as Hackman (1983) and McGrath (1984) point out that the key measures of a group's effectiveness are its productivity, the extent to which group members obtain the social, material and intellectual rewards they are seeking, and the group's ability to sustain itself as a social unit over time. Completion of collaborative intellectual projects (e.g. a course development project) involves an extremely complex interplay of skills, motivation and organizational support. Cognitive biases and social constraints, as we have seen from the research into course team work at the UKOU, often prevent people from behaving in ways which theories of rational choice might predict. Hence it is not, *a priori*, evident that the introduction of new communication technologies (often designed on simplistic and instrumental assumptions about the nature of group processes) will automatically increase a group's effectiveness. In fact, just the reverse might happen, as an added dimension of complexity – a new and possibly unfamiliar technology, subject to differential take-up by group members – is being introduced into the situation. Initially, time spent learning to use this technology may well decrease the group's productivity, increase coordination problems, and be a frustrating experience for group members.

Even when the mastery of a new communication technology is complete, and group members can use it transparently, it is not necessarily the case that it will be used – at least for the purpose initially envisaged. The research conducted by Riley discussed earlier in this chapter showed that, at the UKOU, two of the factors influencing course preparation which were rated as being of low to intermediate importance included the team members' office locations and working habits, and the spread of the team (across different disciplines/faculties). Use of email and computer conferencing as an aid to collaboration in course teams might be based on an invalid assumption that team members actually *want* to increase the rate of commenting on drafts, for example by allowing dispersed team members to contribute more often than they might otherwise, without having to wait for fixed face-to-face meetings or other "milestone" events.

Observation of commenting patterns in course teams, however, suggests that level and amount of commenting varies significantly from one person to another, regardless of their physical location or working habits, as does the preferred communication channel for commenting. Some prefer to send annotations on paper copies of drafts (and annotations in such a form are technically much easier for the author to process than, say, email messages or conferencing comments). Others – especially for major restructuring suggestions – prefer an informal face-to-face discussion, where tact and persuasion can be deployed more effectively than through email messages or annotations scribbled in red ink on photocopied drafts. Others prefer formal round-table discussion at a course team meeting, especially when the course chair is able to run such meetings effectively and diplomatically. Such factors suggest that, even when well-designed joint authoring/editing software becomes available, with effective procedures for handling multiple annotations and version control, it is not necessarily the case that the software will be used by teams of academic authors.

At the UKOU, there is not a great deal of evidence that the simple but relatively functional tools for electronic collaboration currently available are being used to any great extent for course development work. For example, currently, the CoSy conferencing system contains only a limited number of conferences set up by course teams for discussion of course planning and production issues. Where these conferences do exist, they tend to be for the few courses where CoSy is part of the teaching system, and their use for course team discussion – in between the regular face-to-face meetings – is often desultory, and usually only involves a small subset of the total membership of a team. In principle, it would be possible for course teams to agree to keep current drafts of course units on a central file server, so that each team member could readily check the status of colleagues' drafts at any time. Such a mechanism could reduce the likelihood of the "out-of-step" phenomenon developing; however, few teams have adopted this procedure, possibly because many authors do their writing in concentrated bursts of activity prior to previously agreed deadlines, and, in any case, may not wish to make their developing drafts public.

There is evidence that, in some of the courses that use computer conferencing as an integral part of the teaching system, conferencing and email is gradually becoming an accepted tool for maintenance course team activities, and for involving regionally-based tutors in decisions over assessment and examination issues (Kaye 1992). In some cases, initial drafts of "supplementary" print materials (e.g. tutor briefing notes, marking schemes, and other items that are revised annually) have been discussed and prepared collaboratively on CoSy before being finalized. However, such instances are still relatively rare. As far as course development (as opposed to maintenance) work is concerned, eventual use of conferencing or of email distribution lists is likely to prove more useful and acceptable at the early stages of course design for brainstorming ideas, and identifying relevant sources of information, than in the later stages of drafting of materials. Within the university community as a whole – including regional and central staff, and staff who do part of their work from home – use of email is developing quickly, but mainly as a more efficient substitute for brief functional paper memos or telephone calls (e.g. for transmitting information about dates and agendas for meetings, for emailing messages to secretaries etc.).

There are undoubtedly a number of technical barriers to use of computer-mediated communication as an aid to drafting and rewriting processes in course teams at the Open University. The different interfaces to VMS mail, to CoSy, and to VAXNotes, and the often complex procedures for accessing external email are repugnant to many staff, who might, however, be more prepared to use the systems if there was one standard, preferably graphic, user interface (current trials with PathWorks are proving positive in this respect). But even supposing that more people were prepared to send and receive comments on drafts via email, there are still major technical problems to overcome. Specialist character sets are required in many subject areas (in science, mathematics, technology, music, language teaching etc.), and these are not adequately handled by current CMC software. The machines used by most academic authors have small screens, which are not ergonomically adapted to dealing with large documents with their associated annotations, even if suitable software for handling annotations was readily available. It is still much easier, and more pleasant, to revise a document on one's word processor on the basis of written annotations on photocopied drafts on one's desk, than it is to open a tiny "window" with the same comments on one's Macintosh "desktop"!

Clearly, the ultimate acceptance of new tools and procedures for collaboration depends on a mix of technical, social, psychological and cultural factors. Engelbart stresses that "some of the barriers to acceptance of fully integrated systems for augmenting groups of knowledge workers may be more significantly social, not solely technical ... [and that] most developers [had] limited their analyses to technical issues and ignored the social and organizational implications of the introduction of their tools" (Engelbart and Lehtman 1988). It is necessary for a "co-evolution of roles and organizational structures and technologies" to occur if new technologies are to be successfully incorporated into group working habits.

Galegher and Kraut (1990a) have pointed out that "the history of experience with telecommunications and computer-based information systems contains many instances of expensive technological failures that are at least partly attributable to designs that do not mesh well with the social and behavioral systems in which they are to be used". They instance the inability to support "rich communication" between individuals as being one of the reasons why take-up of computerized databases to facilitate information dissemination among scientists, and use of video conferencing for meetings, have both failed to live up to implementors' expectations. "Rich" communication settings such as face-to-face meetings are often preferred during the decision making phases of a group's work, because they allow participants to cope more effectively with dimensions of "equivocality, uncertain preferences, and conflicts over goals and values", and as far as casual users are concerned "benefits [of technology support] are likely to be diluted because of infrequent use, and the costs are likely to be amplified".

Such statements, if valid, have implications for the likely effectiveness of computer conferencing and other, more sophisticated, groupware products for team tasks such as course planning, allocation of work among team members, and commenting on colleagues' drafts. Most course teams at the UKOU (as with many other teams of "knowledge workers" in other organizations) operate on the principle of careful interpersonal negotiation of task allocations, followed by subdivision of authoring among individual team members, who then work in parallel, and in relative isolation. Hand-over deadlines and face-to-face meetings provide the milestones and the forums for signalling completion of a given stage of the task, and for discussion and often delicate re-negotiation of intermediate and final drafts. In many instances, face-to-face course team meetings are an important part of the social culture of the university, providing a form of catharsis, and a reason for coming into the campus, which acts as a counterpoint to the lonely –

and often home-based – process of writing. The effective integration of electronic groupware tools into such a complex process is problematic, and may require a re-examination of existing approaches to course team work.

Such a re-examination, in the light of the potential value of new and existing groupware technologies, is particularly important in the case of truly distributed teams such as those involved in inter-institutional collaborations, where group discussions will, of necessity, often have to be electronically mediated – or hardly occur at all. In any event, the likelihood of new patterns of course team work developing, with changes in roles and organizational structures in response to new communicative possibilities, is possibly greater in the context of relatively novel inter-institutional projects, than within a single institution which already has well-established working patterns and role models.

Acknowledgements   This chapter is based on a study carried out as part of the first phase of the JANUS project, funded through the DELTA Programme of the Commission of the European Communities. The JANUS project is a feasibility study for the implementation of a satellite-based voice and data network to facilitate inter-institutional collaboration among the member institutions of the European Association of Distance Teaching Universities (EADTU).

## Chapter 5

How Collaborative is Collaborative Writing? An Analysis of the Production of Two Technical Reports

A. Dillon

5.1 Introduction

Psychologists have been taking an increasing interest in the writing process over the last decade, and models of human cognition and task behaviour during writing are emerging (see, for example, Hayes and Flower 1980; Sharples et al. 1989). Though we are far short of a complete model of this process, several basic components have been identified and most theorists allude to these at some stage in their description. For example, it is reckoned (as much from common sense as from experimental analysis) that most writing proceeds through a basic sequence of actions from a rough plan through a draft to a revision stage, which may occur cyclically until the writer believes the document is ready. Plans can be considered as either detailed or vague, influenced by expectations of the reader's knowledge, the typical form of the document being produced and so forth. The drafts may vary from the extremely sketchy to the almost complete, depending on the writer's experience, knowledge of the subject, preferred writing style etc. and revisions include such acts as minor spell checking, proofreading or complete rewrites.

The issues involved in understanding how we write as individuals are complex enough but when it comes to explaining how several authors produce a written document then current models are more limited. Here, account needs to be taken of responsibility for production, intellectual ownership, need for consensus among authors etc. as well as the process of text production. These issues are of increasing importance for designers and producers of information technology who are seeking to support the writing process. The emergence of hypertext as a means of authoring as well as

storing documents means that knowledge of how documents are created
could usefully inform the design process of such applications.

Regardless of the limitations of current knowledge, there is no shortage
of advocates enthusing about the possibilities for exciting advances in collaborative authoring as a result of emerging technologies. Trigg and
Suchman (1989) report how they used NoteCards as a collaborative authoring environment in their work. They clearly saw the advantages of a
hypertext medium and were quick to borrow a rhetoric from communications theory and sociology in proposing issues worthy of examination, such
as "meta-discussions" and "convention adoption". However, their published account provides few insights that support the claim that
collaborative authoring is itself aided by hypertext or even information
technology. As they state:

> But in what sense is the (system) supporting collaboration? ... Most simply, the
> notefile provides a shared workspace so that when working independently we
> have access to the product of the other's work ... In addition to the usual
> commentary that takes place with any form of draft-passing, annotations in
> NoteCards can lead to dialogues within the medium itself. (Trigg and Suchman
> 1989, p. 52)

It is not clear how ordinary paper drafts prevent such "dialogues within
themselves" except by providing less support than hypertext for the storage
and retrieval of old comments and drafts. Access to others' work in a
shared workspace is ideal but it does help if you share a site and/or video
conferencing facilities like these authors and do not have to rely on transferring files through fax and electronic mail (email) where the concept of a
shared workspace is more difficult to maintain. Their own example
provides little insight into how their draft document progressed but does
show that they spent a lot of time discussing things on and off the system of
which they felt obliged to note and keep detailed records. In short, their
paper represents the positive views of advocates more than the critical
analysis of human scientists.

Other advocates (e.g. Hahn et al. 1991) concentrate more on how the
technology to support collaborative authoring is constructed rather than
used. While such issues are undoubtedly important, they rely on the
assumption that such tools are desirable. Even if they are (and it is not clear
to the present author that this is the case), their design is doomed to failure
if discussions of functionality and facility provision occur in isolation from
user considerations.

Wason (1980), in a call for greater examination of collaborative authoring, provides to my mind at least, a more realistic (though brief) description
of typical practices. Alluding to the production of Open University course
units that he was writing with another author he states:

> After a brief planning session we each wrote an independent draft and then met
> again to see how we could weld what we had written into a single text. (Wason
> 1980, p. 136)

In other words, collaboration in the form of verbal discussion existed, but only distinct from (i.e. before and after) the actual writing act. The use of the verb "weld" to describe the process of merging these two drafts also seems telling, i.e. they were joined together in a far from seamless fashion. Obviously distinctions between the act of writing (at the point when pen meets paper or finger meets keyboard) and the writing task (which must include such acts as discussing likely contents or reviewing subsequent drafts) are fuzzy but it does seem from the limited and often anecdotal evidence we have to date that the headlong rush into collaborative technology may be less than essential for many of the actions that constitute the writing task.

There is currently a shortage of firm evidence in the literature on how real-world collaborative authoring proceeds and how it feels to be involved in this process with existing technology. Only by appreciating such issues can we hope to develop appropriate technology for typical writers. This chapter tackles these issues by examining the production of two technical documents in current work environments. In so doing it is hoped to at least describe the collaborative authoring process on the basis of data and to identify where present technology is lacking in its support.

5.2 Background and Method

Studying collaborative authoring in a realistic fashion raises several difficulties. Not only must the task involve producing a document that has some meaning beyond the experimental scenario in order to ensure a reasonable level of commitment to the task by authors, but monitoring the writing process itself is likely to be intrusive. Furthermore, devising suitable process measures of writing performance and style can prove problematic, especially since guidance in the form of an established literature on these issues is virtually non-existent.

In the present situation it was decided to maximize the realism of the task by studying the production of real documents but to avoid or minimize intrusion by merely examining the document development trail in terms of growth and modifications. Where possible, any comments on the process made by the participating authors were noted. The advantages of this approach lie in the fact that the documents and their production are genuine cases of collaborative writing, therefore enabling one to see what really happens when documents are so produced. The disadvantages lie in the fact that the data one gathers are primarily behavioural (i.e. the record of human action) rather than cognitive (what the authors are thinking) since cognitive data collection would require participation in the investigation on the part of all authors, possibly with consequent deleterious effects on performance.

Two brief accounts of collaborative authoring are presented. In each case the author was a member of a team of three writing a technical document. In the first account, a final consultancy report was being produced following several weeks of work on an interface evaluation. In the second example, two authors from one site and one from a partner on a project produced a document for a large multi-partner project. The partner at the remote site had never written collaboratively with the two single-site authors before. The latter two themselves had not collaboratively written more than two documents prior to this and were located at opposite sides of a large building. The texts and writing scenarios are typical of the authoring work routinely performed by the participants.

5.3 Document 1: The Consultancy Report

5.3.1 Authors

Three authors participated in the full knowledge that the process was being monitored. They formed an established project team involved in producing a consultancy report for a client at the time. Each was an experienced writer of human factors technical reports. These authors all worked on the consultancy project and shared office accommodation.

5.3.2 Document and Facilities

The report was a final deliverable for a short consultancy project and dealt with interface design issues for a computer-based purchasing system. This document had to be written to a deadline and the authors allowed themselves a fortnight to produce it. During this time the project team performed other work duties, both together and individually on different projects. All authors wrote using Microsoft Word 4.0 on their own Apple Macintosh machines linked together on the site network.

5.3.3 Design and Procedure

No formal design or procedure was employed. Authors merely performed the writing activities as normal except that each author used a unique font or text style to enable subsequent analysis, and all hard copies were collected. The authors had total discretion regarding when and where they wrote (all had terminals at home) within the natural time-frame allowed for completion.

5.3.4 Results for Document 1

Data analysis involved two general forms: quantitative and qualitative. The former examined each version of the text in terms of numbers of words, lines and paragraphs they contained. This provided a simple overview of the changes in document size over its development. The second examined the type of alterations that occurred as the document moved from first draft to final copy.

5.3.4.1 General Writing Style

The three authors have worked together for several years and during this time have evolved a stable procedure for report or article generation. Usually one of the team assumes responsibility for producing a first draft. Though a hierarchy exists in the team (one of the team is a project manager to the other two "equals"), responsibility for first drafts usually emerges from a consensus view of whose area of expertise is most appropriate for the task or which researcher had the greatest involvement in the work to date. In the present case it was determined by the fact that one researcher had most experience of interface evaluations and also had the most time available to produce a first draft.

In this group, one person typically writes the first draft on his own. Once produced, it is circulated among the other team members. Usually this means one copy is given to a second author (often electronically) and he modifies it as he sees fit and passes it (with modifications) on to the third author. The manuscript then returns with all modifications to the original first author. This cycle is repeated as necessary until all are satisfied with the document, whereupon it is formatted and considered finished.

This general procedure was maintained for the present document. For further analysis and reference, such a cycle will be termed a draft, except for Draft 1 which refers to the output from the primary author alone. Therefore, Draft 2 refers to the responses of the other authors to the first draft and Draft 3 refers to all the authors' comments on and inputs to the second draft, and so on. For each draft, an author's contribution might be trivial or major, depending on the time available. Thus, if the third author had time to spend on the document but it was being held up by the second author, who was busy with other work, the second author might just make a few passing comments on the manuscript and pass it quickly on to the third author, realizing that he would have a chance to modify it in more detail next time around.

All notes from meetings with the client and site visits to inspect existing systems were originally produced by hand on paper. The authors had compared and discussed notes on a meeting and site visit basis throughout the consultancy but, as usual, had not made electronic copies. These notes and subsequent points made in discussions served as inputs to the first draft.

The primary author had easy access to any of the others' original notes if he desired, but this was not deemed necessary in the present case. Previous reports both from earlier stages of the consultancy or from other similar consultancy projects were available electronically and accessed when needed by the relevant author. Indeed, the primary author incorporated several sections in a cut/paste fashion from earlier reports in the final report to the client (a procedure agreed in advance with the client, who requested a final report that drew all previous findings together in one document).

5.3.4.2 Document Size and Development

By the time the report had been completed, it emerged that the authors had produced five versions from first draft to final delivered document. The sizes of the various versions were calculated in terms of word, line and paragraph frequencies and the data are presented in Table 5.1.

Table 5.1. Text details for all versions of the report

Version	1	2	3	4	5 (final)
Lines	149	187	242	236	269
Paragraphs	50	64	70	63	72
Words	1422	1808	2485	2457	2592

As can be seen from these data, the major changes occurred in between the first and third drafts, during which time the document grew by almost 75% from 1422 words to 2485 words. A further growth of less than 5% occurred between the third and the fifth (final) draft. Interestingly, a slight trimming occurred in document size between the third and fourth drafts, countering the idea that documents inexorably grow in size until the authors cannot think of anything new to write.

5.3.4.3 Modification Types

In order to gain insight into how the document developed beyond issues related to size, the various contributions made by each author were examined. This process was enabled by the previously agreed restriction on authors to identify their contributions by a unique font or style. In the present instance, the primary author used plain Times 12 point, while the second and third authors used bold and italic versions of this font, respectively.

Each modification was attributed, noted and listed. Then they were grouped according to similarity in terms of how they altered the document. This classification created major categories for text addition, deletion, correction, ordering and queries, most of which are self-explanatory. It is

Table 5.2. Text modifications for all document drafts

Modification type	Version			
	1–2	2–3	3–4	4–5
Addition of new text:				
Signposts	1	0	0	1
Extensions	1	3	0	0
Generations	2	5	0	1
Examples	0	1	1	0
Wording	0	0	1	2
Error correction:				
Spelling	0	0	1	0
Re-ordering	0	0	1	0
Queries:				
Details	1	3	0	0
Objections	0	3	0	0
Clarifications	0	4	1	0

assumed that the primary activity in an authoring task is the creation or addition of text and this category is further broken down into types of addition. Those noted in the present study were the addition of signposts (e.g. headings or sentences aimed at orientating the reader), extensions (e.g. more detail or elaborated workings of existing sentences), generation (i.e. the creation of text based on new ideas or issues without altering the existing text, at least one paragraph in length), examples and wordings.

Each grouping was then assessed in terms of occurrences across drafts. The final classification of modifications is presented in Table 5.2.

As can be seen, the majority of activity occurs as addition of new text. This is hardly surprising in itself; the real interest lies in the type of addition and its time of occurrence across the document development cycle. The most frequent additions were generations of new points and extensions of existing ones.

A generation, by definition, must be at least a paragraph in length, although it could be much more; i.e. it must represent an independent text unit covering or dealing with a particular issue. Extensions, on the other hand, may be only a line or two in length and include only material that is an elaboration of the exiting text, with insufficient detail or length to justify describing it as a "generation".

As indicated in Table 5.1, the largest change in size occurred between versions 2 and 3. This cycle is obviously the major growth period for the document. This size growth is matched by the modification details presented in Table 5.2, where it can be seen that five generations and three elaborations occur. Also interesting at this point is the number of queries that the authors have. Questions of detail, clarifications and objections are raised with more frequency here than at any other stage. Why should this be?

The most likely explanation lies in the fact that the cycle that started with the second draft represented the primary author's first chance to respond to the other authors' comments on his preliminary draft. So the modifications termed "1-2" represent all authors' first inputs, modifications termed "2-3" start when the first author alters the text on the first draft (with comments) and circulates it to other authors, and ends before he responds to the others' subsequent comments on these modifications. Thus, this cycle is the first truly interactive cycle where all authors can comment on all other authors' inputs.

The lack of deletions is also interesting and is probably best explained by the fact that the authors are all familiar with each other's ideas and writing style, were writing up a report on a subject with which they were familiar and had discussed their views prior to the first draft. Even so, it is surprising that no deletions were marked in any versions of the text (the drop in size between versions 3 and 4 reflects a major rewording that reduced two lengthy sentences to one). The absence of spelling errors in the main results from the use of spell checkers.

Discussions among the authors afterwards indicated that they all felt the writing process to have been typical of their normal style and had not found the idea of using unique text formats or the knowledge that the production was being monitored intrusive. This team has used hypertext to produce an academic paper (using GUIDE) and are keen to try the process again. Like Trigg and Suchman (1989) they found that the centralized workspace and single working copy of a document was useful but they still used paper print-outs to work on and created some text for that document on their usual machines with word processors before copying it into the centralized hypertext document. Their experiences using a shared workspace had not encouraged them to write in this fashion subsequently.

5.4 Document 2: The Project Document

5.4.1 Authors

Three authors all working on a CEC-funded multi-partner project contributed to this document. Two were human factors specialists working in academia, the third was the project manager, working for a management consultancy company, who had a background in software engineering.

5.4.2 Document and Facilities

As a result of a perceived need for a policy document on issues associated with the project, two authors agreed to write it (including the present author). By the time the document was finished the author list had grown to three (two from academia, one from the partner site). The academic authors used equipment identical to that mentioned above. Situated in different offices, they could pass files over the network (using Public Folder on the Macintosh) and had the services of a project secretary using identical equipment. The author at the second site had IBM PCs but normally opted to use WordStar on a portable Toshiba. He also had the services of an on-site secretary.

5.4.3 Design and Procedure

Unlike the previous study, this was the first time the authors had written together. Furthermore, two of the authors did not realize that this process was to be analysed by the third author, therefore precluding the use of font type and size as identifiers of author's inputs. Both authors have subsequently been informed of this and have not objected to analysis or publication of the data. To maintain the possibility of input identification, the "experimenter" kept copies of each author's drafts and noted alterations by direct comparison of drafts. As it turned out, this process was simplified by developments in the authoring process.

5.4.4 Results for Document 2

5.4.4.1 *General Writing Style*

A pre-draft meeting between three potential authors was arranged to discuss the document and identify the key points that it should include. Those present were two participants from academia and the partner from the remote site. Of the academic participants, one became the primary author of the document, and the other failed to play any further role in text production and will be discounted from subsequent analyses. Her place on the authoring team was taken by another academic at a later stage in the writing process. The structure of the final authoring team was: primary author (senior researcher), second author (consortium project manager, based at remote site) and third author (local academic team manager).

The initial meeting resulted in the development of an outline in the form of section headings and likely issues to cover. These were agreed by discussion and resulted in a sketchy framework, indicating four major sections and suggesting the type of material to be included in each one. Crucial issues at this stage were the identification of audience requirements and acceptability criteria, matters to avoid discussing and the perceived purpose of the document. Central inputs were written comments made by project reviewers and knowledge of accepted views on such policy matters.

The time-scale was agreed by reference to project demands and existing deliverable and work package deadlines, taking account of annual leave plans and likely future project meetings that would require this document as input. This gave a time-scale of 10 days for the first draft and 40 days to completion. Then, as before, one person was charged with writing the first draft. In this case, the primary author (the most junior of the final three authors) volunteered for the task. No information technology was employed at this stage: all planning occurred on paper and whiteboard.

When this draft was produced by the primary author (using his word processor, Word 4.0 on the Macintosh) it was sent by fax to the second author, who worked at the remote site. The use of fax was requested by the receiving author as he had no reliable email connection, and email was felt to be of uncertain value by both authors who, believed that it might "lose" some of the text and/or require too much re-formatting of the document each time it was sent. Since this meant he had only a paper copy of the document, he chose not to modify the text electronically. Instead, he scribbled some comments on the fax paper itself and produced several pages of text on his portable computer, outlining all modifications he wanted to make. These pages along with the original but marked-up first draft were faxed back to the primary author. This, as before, will be referred to as the 1-2 modification stage.

The document was then modified by the first author, again in the light of the second authors' comments using the fax as a marked-up manuscript with which to modify the original electronic version. This will be referred to as the 2-3 modification stage and consisted of including and reacting to the comments of the second author. In other words, the activities of text correction and creation occurred together at this stage. After this the document was given to a third author (the local project team manager), who had not yet been involved, to modify and make suggestions. He commented by using a pencil to edit the print-out from the previous stage. His comments were accepted by the first author, who gave them in the form of the marked-up manuscript to the project secretary to add to the final document, which was then formatted. This represented an unusual political inversion in that the final say in editing lay with the most junior (in organizational rank) member of the authoring team.

5.4.4.2 Document Size and Development

As before, each version was measured in terms of line, paragraph and word numbers. For the hand-modified versions, this involved typing the modifications into the electronic version before calculation. These data are presented in Table 5.3.

Here we can see a major growth between versions 1 and 2, followed by a trimming of the document by its third version and another major growth again by version 4. Unlike the previous document, each version here

Table 5.3. Text details for all versions of the policy document

Version	1	2	3	4
Lines	271	273	267	274
Paragraphs	25	21	23	25
Words	2125	2311	2155	2351

represented the efforts of only one author in that the first draft was produced by the primary author, the second version was one author's responses and suggestions to this, the third was the primary author's reaction to these modifications and subsequent rewrites, while the fourth version was the product of the third author's comments and modifications to version 3 as approved by the primary author. These labels are the participants' own referencing system.

5.4.4.3 Modification Types

As before, all drafts were examined and all modifications noted. These were then grouped according to general type, whereupon it soon emerged that

Table 5.4. Modifications types for second document

Modification type	Version		
	1–2	2–3	3–4
Addition of new text:			
Signposts	4	1	0
Extensions	3	2	8
Generations	0	2	2
Examples	1	0	0
Deletions:			
Large	1	0	0
Medium	0	3	0
Small	1	0	0
Re-wordings:			
Large	5	0	0
Medium	2	0	0
Small	17	2	3
Error correction:			
Point/wording	1	3	1
Typos	0	5	2
Queries:			
Discussion points	2	0	0
Questions	1	0	0
Answers	3	0	0
Objections	1	0	0
Suggestions	4	0	0

the range of modifications was greater in this document. The classification system was therefore adjusted to take account of this, though where similar activities occurred the same labels were used to aid comparison. It should be noted that it is not the intention of the present author to produce a robust classification to support all such analyses; those used here represent first attempts at each data set, and much more work is required to produce a reliable and valid classification for all such data. The modifications made to this document are shown in Table 5.4.

It is immediately obvious that this report was subject to more modifications than the previous document. Particularly noticeable are the large number of rewordings, classified here according to size, with "large" referring to at least a paragraph, "medium" to anything more than a sentence but less than a paragraph, and "small" to rewording at the sub-sentence level. In particular, the modifications from version 1-2, when the author at the remote site modified the first draft, involve 24 rewordings of all sizes. Yet this author did not produce a single text generation (i.e. new text unit of at least a paragraph in size), indicating a more reactive than generative writing style on his part. Only small rewordings occurred in subsequent drafts.

The most frequent additions are extensions (i.e. elaborations of existing ideas, up to a paragraph in length). Interestingly, the largest number of extensions come from the final author, who provided eight extensions as well as two generations. The bias towards extensions over generations runs counter to the trend in the previous document study, highlighting, perhaps, an unwillingness/inability on the part of the less cohesive team to create original text (an unfortunately speculative hypothesis that might be explicable in other terms, such as perceived lack of time or high agreement between authors on the sufficiency of the first draft).

Deletions were also more frequent in this study than in the previous one. Classified into large, medium or small, according to the same criteria as the rewordings, these occurred mainly in version 2-3, i.e. were largely the work of the primary author in his response to the modifications of the remote author. However, it must be noted that some of these involved deleting text that originally asked questions or sought extensions from the remote author on the first draft that he had failed to supply or answer adequately.

The number and type of queries in this document were also greater than the first. The primary cause of this seems to have been the inclusion of many questions or suggestions for points to be covered in the first and second drafts, which were either answered or removed by the subsequent author. By the time the third draft was produced all such queries were resolved. Typical queries were of the form:

"Need to state something about X's role in this work?"

"Is it worth saying this here, could we leave it out? The decision is yours."

Not all issues were resolved. In two instances a failure to elicit a response from another author to a question resulted in the original author dropping the point altogether.

5.5 General Discussion

Three interesting issues emerge from these analyses:

1. The extent to which there are similarities and differences between the two authoring teams.

2. The extent to which collaboration existed and could be supported in these writing scenarios.

3. The extent to which these results can be generalized.

This section addresses these issues in turn.

The general sequence of activities involved in producing these texts was similar for both groups. First, there was the identification of the need for such a document (either imposed, as a project requirement in study 1, or agreed, on the basis of ongoing group discussions in study 2). This led to pre-draft discussions. These discussions included various inputs in the form of other documents, notes, views, knowledge, data and so on. A primary author was "identified"; a complex process influenced by group politics, ratings of others' intellectual strengths and weaknesses, time availability and willingness of participants to take a leading role. The primary author produced a draft according to an agreed plan, others responded, and the task was completed when agreement or time limits were reached.

Both teams relied heavily on the first draft and, in each account, the producer of this draft acted as a type of "gatekeeper" to the document's contents. In other words, the primary author had the ability to make certain adjustments to the suggestions and modifications of the other authors by virtue of his position in the cycle. Though no formal editorial position was granted to an author in either team, the "gatekeeper" largely controlled inputs and modifications. For example, the first team passed all their modifications cyclically back to this person, who modified each draft and re-released it. In producing a second draft, he had to respond to any queries raised by other authors and incorporate any suggestions they made that did not neatly slot into the existing text. In the second team, the "gatekeeper" acted as a collection point for other authors' comments, with the net effect that the second and third authors never actually communicated directly with each other, and the second author never directly received the third author's comments. Under such circumstances it becomes increasingly difficult for non-primary authors to monitor the progress of their own inputs as the cycles progress, and technology may offer a solution to this potential problem.

The quality of the first draft in each case was determined largely by the quality of the preceding discussions between the authoring team and the ability of the primary author to reflect these ideas and points in his initial draft. In both case studies such discussions resulted in an explicit proposal for the document's structure and likely content type for each section. For the first team, the subject matter and structure resulted from shared consultancy experiences and pooled interpretations carried out over several weeks, as well as the contents of earlier reports, therefore ensuring that most disagreements between participants had been ironed out by the time the first draft of the final report was produced.

In the second team, the contents of the first draft were determined by discussions between the authors at the initial meeting. As stated above, this meeting did not involve all three of the final authors of the document. Lasting the best part of a working day, the meeting ranged over numerous issues that were irrelevant to the task of document production or to the report's contents. The decisions taken at this meeting meant that the primary author had a large degree of autonomy in producing the first draft. It is perhaps surprising, therefore, that more generative modifications were not made at all stages for this document.

The first team were very familiar with each other's work and writing styles. Having produced numerous reports and papers together they have evolved a production style that appears "efficient" (however that is measured) and allows all authors to have several opportunities to influence the development of the document. They produced more draft versions but made fewer modifications than the other team. The second team, less familiar with each other, both personally and in terms of writing, spent more effort rewording and deleting text from each other's versions. Drafts were not circulated among everyone at all stages and the resulting document was altered stylistically more than content-wise by the time it was completed.

It may be tempting to assume that these differences reflect the familiarity levels of the authoring teams more than anything else. However it is possible that increased familiarity would not alter the general style which may result from the characteristic writing method of individuals or combination of individuals making up the collaborative team. Issues pertaining to subject matter, individual knowledge, the political structure of the team (who has the final say? who can criticize whose ideas? whose inputs are most important? etc.) and time availability are almost certainly all contributory factors here. Obviously such dynamics are worthy of further investigation and would need to be accounted for in any proposed model of collaborative authoring.

The second interesting issue and probably the most important one from the perspective of authoring environment design is the precise nature of collaboration that can be seen from these document records and what this tells us about designing writer-compatible technology.

What is most striking is the apparently little collaboration found in the document records. The first case certainly reveals the querying of details, objections to certain points and requests for clarification by all authors on several issues at the start but these are virtually absent from the final two drafts. Similarly, with the second document there are several suggestions and discussion points in the first two drafts but these become non-existent after that. What has happened to the suggestions and counter-suggestions, discussions and arguments, agreements and disagreements that one would assume to be part and parcel of the collaborative authoring act?

It seems that debate about content and issues was largely concluded prior to the production of the first draft and subsequently handled verbally among the relevant authors. For the first team at least, the present technology in its current socio-technical environment (shared office, compatible technology, high integration of established work practice) offers an acceptable medium for text production (it should be noted that their method of text production was chosen by them despite the opportunity to use a supposedly more supportive hypertext environment for this task). Two of the second team also discussed the contents of the first draft of their document in advance but had to handle all subsequent debate through the medium of the document or, if need be, via telephone. These authors did communicate via telephone on several occasions during the production of this document but as they had parallel issues to address not concerning the document, the only noted conversation about it dealt with issues such as deadlines and circulation rather than content.

The extent to which these results may be generalized is debatable, and caution must be exercised. The authoring teams consisted in total of five different authors but four of these worked in the same organization. From the perspective of the author involved in both teams there were noticeable working practice differences that impinged on the task and such differences must be seen as major determinants of collaborative style. How research should tackle this issue is difficult to envisage.

The reliance of both teams on a primary author to generate a first draft may be interpreted by some as indicating that these studies do not really address collaborative authoring but reflect the process of a single author seeking feedback. This would be flawed reasoning, however. Both teams set about with the intention of collaborating, chose to work this way and concluded that the documents were collaboratively written. These data, coupled with the findings of Beck (this volume) that less than a third of collaborative authors she surveyed produced documents without a primary authoring role emerging or being agreed, suggest that such a role is the norm rather than the exception.

The text type could also be a factor influencing the nature and extent of collaboration witnessed here. Both documents were relatively technical and had to be produced to deadlines. Elaborate discussion and debate would hardly have been acceptable to the authoring teams, particularly through the rather constrained medium of text. Cohesion and adherence to a single view was brought about through pre-draft activities and discussions. Remaining debate seems to have been taken care of in the first couple of drafts. Certainly the document creation processes described here were typical of the participants' professional authoring activities and they are examples of real-world collaborative authoring, but it remains the case that studies in other domains may reveal distinct patterns of activity.

The investigative method used in these analyses also deserves comment. It is clear that the analysis of document records is a far from ideal method of studying collaborations among authors, and the present studies would have been improved with more information on the nature of all discussions between authors, especially as it is these aspects of authoring that seem to reflect the greatest collaboration according to these data. Certainly this is an issue to address in further studies. Participation in the studies by the investigator, particularly without the prior knowledge and consent of all parties throws up ethical as well as practical issues. Given the nature of the material, the direct involvement of the investigator in the main aim of the text production task and the agreement of all participants to proceed with the analysis, it is not seen as a major concern here but potential investigators should be wary of attempting such analyses without preparation. However, the method does provide a reasonably unobtrusive account of what happens when more than one author attempts to produce a document. To date, such accounts have been thin on the ground.

5.6 Conclusion

If we accept a definition of collaborative writing as the activities involved in the production of a document by more than one author, then pre-draft discussions and arguments as well as post-draft analyses and debate are the collaborative components. However, such a broad definition will always embrace activities that are not necessarily directly relevant to the task of writing and render the quest for a technology to support the collaborative writing task partially indistinguishable from other collaborative technology designs. This is no bad thing. In a very real sense we do not need a collaborative writing tool *per se*, we need better technology for collaboration, e.g. better communications facilities enabling people to contact each other and transfer documents, graphics, audio and video images easily and reliably. Given this, many technology-mediated tasks will be better supported. Writing will be just one of these (see, for example, Baydere et al., this volume, for details of multi-author writing with a CAD/CAM system). The search, therefore, for a dedicated collaborative writing environment is too narrow because in itself, collaborative writing is a misleading term.

We are in the midst of a trend that emphasizes collaboration as the dominant theme in advanced work technology design. Whether this results from a justifiable, if under-critical, reaction to the standard information process-ing view of human activity espoused for the last twenty years by most psychologists and ergonomists or from a desire to keep up with the current emphases in cognitive science is not clear to me. While I hope it is the for-mer, and cannot find fault in the view that all work is in some sense a collaborative act, I would advocate a more realistic view of collaboration that doesn't insist on it being the major factor to concern ourselves with in ergonomic system design. Certainly it has a place; it is a component of most tasks, but it is not necessarily the most essential component, which we must address to the relegation of all others (for a more balanced view of the relevant system design issues see Eason 1991). The major problem with much of the literature on collaboration remains the translation of its unde-niably valid perspective into applicable design advice (see Newman and Newman, this volume, for example).

Certainly in the authoring situation there appears to be a meaningful dis-tinction between the act of writing, which is intrinsically an individual activity, and the writing task, which may involve all types of collaborative acts, in much the same way as traditional task analysis breaks jobs into tasks into actions. However, such collaborative acts are not necessarily unique to the writing situation, but reflect the manner in which most human activities proceed. In collaborating in this fashion, authors may expend considerable effort dealing with issues that are not even contingent on the writing task, but deal with related subjects and work activities. The stages of document production outlined at the start of the discussion demonstrate the fact that before actually drafting a document, the partici-pants were involved in activities that could not be deemed uniquely "writing" work. The role of the technology surely is to support people and to this end designers should not try to control or manipulate collaboration but just concentrate on providing the most transparent media possible and let the naturally occurring processes of group working take care of them-selves. To concern oneself directly with supposed collaborative authoring environments is to risk losing sight of this and hyping up what may only be another technological solution looking for a problem.

Acknowledgements   The author would like to thank all participants in these investigations for their permission to analyse and publish the data. Thanks are also due to Mike Sharples, Eevi Beck and an anonymous referee for their encouragement and sound advice on improving this paper.

The work on collaborative writing was funded by the British Library Research and Development Department and carried out at HUSAT as part of Project CHIRO.

Chapter 6

A Survey of Experiences of Collaborative Writing

E.E. Beck

6.1 Introduction

This chapter reports on a survey of the experience of collaborative writing of twenty-three largely academic co-authors. It was found that discussions took place during writing more than before (or after) writing, and that adherence to an initial plan was not seen as an important determinant of success. Different leadership types existed in the writing groups reported on in this survey, including self-appointed leader and no leader at all. Fluctuating membership and commitment to the writing group were shown to be common. The emerging picture of the collaborative writing reported on by these respondents is one of a dynamic process with continuous negotiation and re-negotiation of questions relating to both the contents of the document, and to a range of other issues, such as leadership role and sharing of responsibilities between the co-authors. Implications for the design of computer systems for collaborative writing, such as the necessity for support of the dynamic structure of writing groups, are discussed.

Writing is an activity engaged in by many people whether they are professional writers or not. To provide appropriate computer and other tools to support group writing, there must be an understanding of the process of group writing, or co-authoring. Respondents to a large survey of collaborative writing reported that, by their own estimate, 44% of their time was spent "in some kind of writing activity", and 87% reported that they sometimes wrote as members of a team or a group (Ede and Lunsford 1990).

There is little in the way of an established literature on collaborative writing (Ede and Lunsford discuss reasons why this may be so). However, the interest has recently been increasing, both among humanists and literary critics, where it forms part of a concern to question the concept of (single-person) authorship (Ede and Lunsford 1990), and in human– computer interaction/computer support for collaborative work, where the purpose is to develop better computer systems to support collaborative writing. Surveys of collaborative writing have been conducted in the United States (Couture and Rymer 1991; Ede and Lunsford 1990; Mackler 1987) and some recent authoring surveys in the UK have included aspects of writing in collaboration (Chandler 1993; Dorner 1992; Hartley and Branthwaite 1989).

Ede and Lunsford (1990) report on a large survey of about 700 respondents who were members of seven professions in the US; a second, more in-depth survey, which followed-up about 80 of the original respondents; and finally case studies of six of those individuals. Their research took as its starting point the pedagogical issue of whether the writing education in the US should incorporate more collaborative writing, and to this end demonstrated the pervasiveness of joint writing activities in the work situation of the persons they surveyed, as reported above.

Couture and Rymer (1991) briefly report the results of their study of about 400 professionals in the US (the rest of their paper reports on case studies). This survey found that 24% of respondents reported contributing to a team-authored document sometimes, often, or very often; 76% sometimes or more often talked over their writing with others before drafting. Couture and Rymer also make a distinction between "routine" and "special" writing tasks, reporting that the amount of collaboration is less for routine writing.

Hartley and Branthwaite (1989) describe a questionnaire study of 88 productive academic psychologist writers and, whereas most of the study is not about writing in collaboration, report that the writers who were most productive "sometimes collaborated with long-standing colleagues when they wrote" (p. 440). (No data is reported on how frequent such collaborations were.) They also found that for respondents with high productivity with books (defined, in this case, as writers who had written 2–5 books over the preceding three-year period), one of the three most predictive factors was that when they collaborated with others in writing, "they were more likely to work on separate parts of text and then to put the parts together" (Hartley and Branthwaite 1989, p. 436 and Table 7). Hartley and Branthwaite do not elaborate further on aspects of collaborative writing.

Mackler's 1987 study is one of the earlier ones of collaborative writing. A preliminary study of the process of collaborative course work writing among 49 US undergraduates is reported. It concludes that "the majority of respondents felt that the group produced a stronger, higher quality paper than one that they could have produced alone" (p. 71).

Chandler conducted a survey of mainly single-person writing among 107 academics at a university in the UK. One of his most significant findings relates to patterns of co-authoring among respondents from different subject backgrounds. Chandler found a statistically significant difference between the prevalence of co-authoring in arts and sciences.

A full account of the process of writing must include an understanding of the context of writing (Flower 1989a). Therefore, in order to build co-authoring support systems on a full understanding of the process of collaborative writing, there must be an understanding of the context of group writing. This should include an appreciation of the dynamics within writing groups and of the process of collaborative writing itself, so that a broad platform of understanding of the process can become the basis for the design of its technological support. For example, in the survey below, when it was found that the groups split evenly between having an agreed leader, a self-appointed leader, and no one taking the lead, this immediately raises the issue, as discussed below, of how a computer system might be designed to provide the flexibility necessary to handle these different organizations of writing groups.

One approach to obtaining the desired understanding of salient contextual issues in collaborative writing would be to look at how co-authoring is experienced. The most direct route is to ask the co-authors themselves. In the study reported on in this chapter, the experiences of non-fiction co-authors is collected through their responses to a questionnaire. The survey is part of a project on the context and dynamics of collaborative authoring which advocates the use of both qualitative and quantitative results for informing the design of computer-based tools for collaborative writing. The project as a whole spans more quantitative and more qualitative methods of investigation, ranging from this survey to case studies of collaborative writing groups. This range is also reflected in the survey itself, in that it aims to study in some detail the respondents' experience of collaborative writing, and in that there are open-ended questions as well as more restricted questions. The case studies and survey were designed within a conceptual framework of non-task-focused aspects of co-writing (see Beck 1991).

The main objective of the survey described in this chapter was to gain an initial insight into aspects of dynamics within, and the context for, non-fiction writing as it takes place in writing groups in the UK. Further, it was envisaged that the work would provide pointers to interesting areas of investigation for co-writing in general, and obtain preliminary implications for computer support for collaborative writing. In so doing, it sought to combine the need for predictability arising directly from systems design issues with a concern for the importance of the contexts in which writing in collaboration takes place. The survey thus intended to elicit, in quantifiable terms, descriptions of individual collaborators' subjective experiences of writing with others. The survey also includes some contextual, including qualitative, questions.

The results are presented as completely as is practical, so that the readers have access to much of the original data and can, if appropriate, draw their own conclusions about its meaning. An attempt has been made to present the results in such a way that the specific statistics can be skimmed by those for whom they add little or no information. It is hoped that this will contribute to making the results meaningful to readers from a range of backgrounds.

Finally, the terms "collaborative" and "cooperative" are treated as synonymous, as are "writing" and "authoring". Co-writing and co-authoring are used as shorthand for collaborative/cooperative writing and authoring.

6.2 Method

A survey with 27 questions about experiences of non-task-focused aspects of co-authoring was designed. The questions were developed from an initial set of 1–2 hour interviews with ten academics about collaborative writing projects they had taken part in. The survey was distributed to participants at a conference (the fourth Computers and Writing conference), and to members of two university departments, all of whom in their own view had co-authored a document. The respondents were asked to think of one instance in which they had taken part in collaborative/group authoring and answer the questions with respect to their personal experiences that particular time. (Respondents were encouraged to choose their last such project.) As far as is known, each respondent was reporting on a different writing group (this is the case for at least 87% of the responses).

In the instructions which accompanied the questionnaire, the confidentiality of the data was assured. There was also a form asking for volunteers for a further study, which required the respondents' names; however, these were detached from the questionnaires upon collection.

Question formats were:

1. Multiple choice: 14 questions, 3–5 choices in each.

2. Statements to be ranked on 7-point scales (Likert Scales): 11 questions, 3–17 statements in each.

3. Other formats encouraging expression of further comments. These were one open-ended question and several smaller supplementary questions.

Respondents were asked questions centred on the document being written (e.g. audience, publication); on the group writing it (e.g. group purpose, membership); on organization of the work (e.g. leadership, discussions in the group); on individual experience of working in the group (e.g. satisfaction with own and colleagues' inputs); and on individual orientation (e.g. motivation for joining group, conceptions of success, perceptions of collaborative writing).

6.3 Results

The number of responses was twenty-three; six (26%) from women and seventeen (74%) from men. Twenty-two (96%) described an academic writing project. Prior experience with collaborative authoring among the respondents varied from zero to, in one case, "hundreds".

6.3.1 Document

6.3.1.1 Document Purpose and Current State

The content of the co-authored documents described in the survey was mainly academic (19 of 22, i.e. 86%). In eighteen cases (82%) the purpose was external publication. The majority were to become papers or articles submitted to conferences or journals (15 of 23, or 65%), two (9%) were to become books, another two grant proposals, one (4%) a report and one a paper or article for part of a book. Two replied "other".

Fourteen of twenty-one (67%) were reporting on a project which was finished. Of the five that were still ongoing at the time the survey was filled in, four indicated that they were still taking part in them, one that he did not know whether he was taking part or not.

6.3.1.2 Audience

In reply to the question "who do you understand to be the audience of your document", respondents were asked to rate each of eight potential audiences on a 7-point scale (1 = "least important"; 7 = "most important"). The results are summarized in Table 6.1. The respondents overall agreed that of the choices, the most important audience was "the research community / academic peers". The analysis of this question shows fairly high standard deviations, indicating a high spread of responses; in other words the

Table 6.1. Perceived document audience
(1 = least important; 7 = most important. The s.d. is the standard deviation; the range is the highest and lowest scores; N is the number of respondents who replied to the question)

Statement	Mean	Range	s.d.	N
The research community / academic peers	5.8	1–7	1.9	22
Reviewers of the document	4.8	1–7	1.9	22
Attendees at talk or conference	4.1	1–7	2.6	22
Our writing group collectively	3.3	1–7	2.3	22
Buyers of book or conference proceedings	3.3	1–7	2.5	21
Bosses / managers / funding bodies	3.0	1–7	2.0	22
One or more individuals in our group	2.6	1–7	2.2	21
The general public	2.1	1–7	1.8	21

Table 6.2. Perceived sources of influence on the document
(1 = not important; 7 = very important)

Statement	Mean	Range	s.d.	N
One particular individual	4.8	1–7	2.1	23
The whole group (group consensus)	4.3	1–7	2.2	23
The deadline (if any)	4.0	1–7	2.1	21
Persons external to the group	2.8	1–7	2.1	20
A sub-group	2.8	1–7	2.3	19

respondents differed quite a lot on how important they thought each of the suggested alternatives were.

6.3.1.3 Perceived Influences on the Document

Five potential sources of influence on the final document were given (see Table 6.2), and each rated on a 7-point scale of importance. Again, fairly high standard deviations indicate that opinions differed among respondents. (Two reported other reasons also being important in their projects; these were the need to follow the length and contents of a previous book, and "the geographical distribution of the group".)

6.3.1.4 Discussions on Document Content and Structure

Respondents were asked to report the frequency with which they discussed the content and structure of the document. They overwhelmingly reported such discussions as taking place most frequently during writing as opposed to before or after writing, and also reported feeling that their discussions had been adequate. The results are summarized in Table 6.3. (Note the low response rates for two of the statements. This was due to an error on some of the questionnaires whereby a dividing line between those two state-

Table 6.3. Reported discussions on content and structure of the document
(1 = not infrequently; 7 = very frequently)

Statement	Mean	Range	s.d.	N
We discussed content and structure during writing	5.3	3–7	1.3	22
At the time, I felt that our discussions on content and structure were adequate	4.9	2–7	1.8	21
With the benefit of hindsight, I now think our discussions on content and strucrure were adequate	4.8	1–7	2.0	20
We discussed content and structure before starting writing	4.6	2–7	1.7	10
There were group-wide discussions about content or structure of the document	4.5	1–7	2.3	22
We discussed content and structure after finishing writing	3.3	1–7	2.1	22
There were discussions in sub-groups about the content or structure of the document	3.0	1–7	2.6	8

Table 6.4. Organization of work between the co-authors
(1 = very infrequently; 7 = very frequently)

Statement	Mean	Range	s.d.	N
We discussed organization of work while writing the document	4.6	1–7	1.6	22
At the time, I felt that out discussions on how to organize the work were adequate	4.6	1–7	1.8	20
We discussed organization of work before starting writing	4.5	1–7	2.3	21
With the benefit of hindsight, I now think our discussions on how to organize the work were adequate	4.2	1–7	2.0	21
There were group-wide discussions about how to organize the work	4.0	1–7	2.2	21
There were discussions in sub-groups about how to organize the work	3.5	1–7	2.3	16
We discussed organization of work after finishing writing	2.4	1–6	1.8	22

ments was missing. The responses which did not distinguish between these have been omitted.)

6.3.2 Organization of Work

6.3.2.1 Discussions on Organization

Respondents were asked to indicate on a 7-point scale the frequencies of discussions on "how to organize the work" between the co-authors in their group at various stages in the writing process. The results are shown in Table 6.4.

The discussions were felt to be reasonably adequate, both at the time and with hindsight. Discussions on the organization of the work between the co-authors *after* finishing writing received the lowest score. Nevertheless, 50% of the respondents did report some such discussions (eleven rated this above 1). Note that this result may be confounded by interest in writing among about half the respondents (attendees at a writing conference).

6.3.2.2 Comparisons between Discussions

The reported frequencies of two kinds of discussions – discussions on content or structure of the document and discussions on the organization of work between the individuals – were compared to test whether respondents who reported frequent (or infrequent) discussions on content and structure in their group, tended also to report frequent (or infrequent) discussions on organization of work. A positive correlation, statistically significant at $P < 0.01$ (where P is the probability, out of 1.00, of the result being obtained by random chance) was found between reported frequencies of the two kinds of discussions. (Spearman Rank test for correlation;

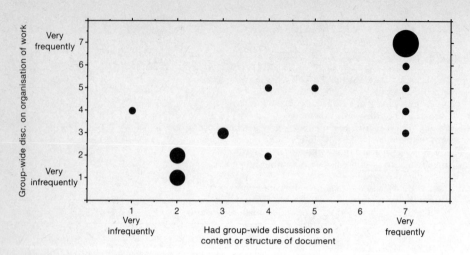

Fig. 6.1. Discussions on content and structure of document versus discussions on organization of work.

rho-value for correlation = 0.806; N = 21. This test for correlation between two variables uses rank order rather than the absolute values of the variables. The resulting rho determines, for a given N, the P for the correlation.) The scattergram in Fig. 6.1 shows the distribution of the combinations of replies. (Note, in the scattergrams an enlarged point indicates more than one response with that combination, and a high correlation in the data produces a clear diagonal in the scattergram.)

A further two such tests were made to examine correlations between reports on the frequency of discussion on the organization of work prior to writing with the perceived adequacy of those discussions, and between the perceived adequacy and the perceived frequency of such discussions while the writing was ongoing. Significant positive correlations ($P < 0.01$) were found in each case, indicating that those who reported that they thought their group had high frequency of such discussions also reported that they felt those discussions had been adequate, while those who reported that their group infrequently had such discussions also reported that they felt that those discussions were not adequate. (Spearman Rank test for correlation, rho for correlation between adequacy and pre-writing discussion = 0.664; rho for correlation between adequacy and during-writing discussions = 0.824; N = 20 and 21, respectively). Fig. 6.2 shows the distributions of combinations of replies.

Group-wide discussions on the content and structure of the document showed particularly sharp differences between the respondents. There were tendencies towards a binary split between respondents who reported having had such discussions very frequently, and those who reported having had such discussions very infrequently (mean 4.5; range 1–7; s.d. 2.3). Fig. 6.3 shows the frequency distribution of the responses.

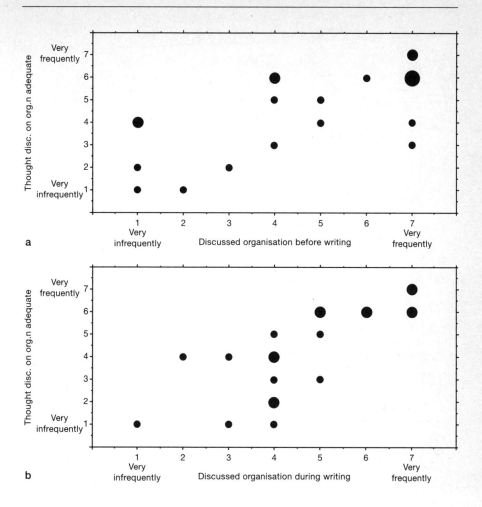

Fig. 6.2. a Reported frequency of discussions on work organization prior to writing versus their perceived adequacy. **b** Reported frequency of discussions on work organization during writing versus their perceived adequacy.

6.3.2.3 Leadership

Respondents were asked to choose one of seven replies to the question "who was it, if any, who in your opinion took the general lead?". Twenty-three responses were obtained. Seven (30%) indicated that a self-appointed leader or facilitator took the lead; six (26%) chose "no one took the general lead"; five respondents (22%) indicated that an agreed leader or project manager did; one (4%) that an agreed editor or editors did, and another one that an agreed group facilitator or coordinator did. Three (13%) replied "other" (these replies were "myself, the researcher"; "initially I took the lead [...] later my co-author"; and "one person wrote most of the text and the rest revised and added parts").

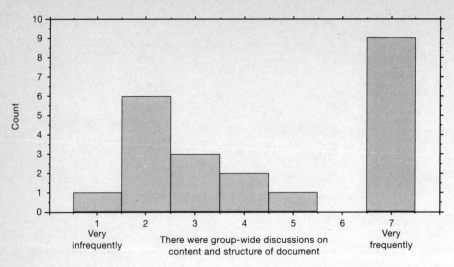

Fig. 6.3. Frequencies of group-wide discussions on content and structure.

6.3.2.4 Sharing the Responsibilities

In the respondents' consideration of four statements on the general distribution of work among the collaborators, a picture emerged of the sharing of responsibilities between the co-authors being somewhat complicated (see Table 6.5). Responses showed a spread of opinions on whether "a person or sub-group had primary responsibility for the production", and also, with a similar, though lower, mean, "we were all collectively responsible for the whole document". Respondents were also asked to rate statements on overlap between areas of responsibility, and indicated that they infrequently felt responsible for their own part only, or that there was little or no overlap between areas of responsibility. In other words, responses indicated a mixture of perceptions of how the general responsibility was shared among co-authors. Areas of responsibility were not clearly delineated (they felt responsibility for other parts than just "their own", there was overlap between areas of responsibility, they were divided on whether the co-authors were collectively responsible or not, and more divided on whether a sub-group had the primary responsibility).

6.3.3 Group

6.3.3.1 Group Sizes

Sizes of writing groups were small in this survey: when asked about the average size of their writing group, thirteen of twenty-three (57%) indicated two in the group (one plus themselves), with the percentage rapidly declining as group size grew.

Table 6.5. Perceived sharing of responsibilities
(1 = very infrequently; 7 = very frequently)

Statement	Mean	Range	s.d.	N
A person or a sub-group had primary responsibility for the production	4.8	1–7	2.2	23
We were all collectively responsible for the whole document	4.2	1–7	2.0	23
There was little or no overlap between areas of responsibility	2.5	1–6	1.5	23
I was responsible for my own part only	2.2	1–7	1.7	23

6.3.3.2 Changing Group Membership

There were also indications of transient group membership. In a multiple choice question (yes/no/don't know), respondents were asked to indicate whether there were any changes in the number of persons in their co-writing group while they were writing the document. Five replied "yes" (however, see below).

Respondents who replied "yes" to the first question were asked to indicate the nature of the changes by chronologically listing the numbers of members in their group. Respondents were asked to indicate coincidental arrival and departure of members by repeating a count. Six reports were obtained. Some of the reported changes in membership were considerable. The changes were decreases in two cases (from 9 to 1 and from 10 to 3), and increases in membership in four cases (three were from 1 and 2 to 3, and one from 4 to 10).

Cross-checking revealed that two respondents who had reported no changes in their group membership had nevertheless given reports of changing numbers, and that one respondent who had replied that the group membership had changed, had not provided such a report. There were, therefore, seven respondents of twenty-three (39%) who in some way indicated that the number of co-authors in their group had changed during the writing of the document.

In another "yes/no/don't know" question, respondents were asked "except for right at the beginning, were you at any point ever unsure about who were going to be the co-authors?". Twenty-two replies were obtained; five of these (23%) were affirmative. Here, one might expect that those respondents who had been unsure about who their co-authors were, had been so when changes in the membership were actually taking place. If this were the case, the five who reported unsureness would be a subset of the seven who reported actual changes. However, relating individuals' responses to these questions revealed that two respondents reported having felt unsure about who the co-authors were although they reported no actual changes in their groups. In this sample, then, feelings of unsureness about who the co-authors were appear to have arisen for other reasons as well as actual changes in group membership. Explanations may be that in these groups questioning of group membership occurred without it ever coming

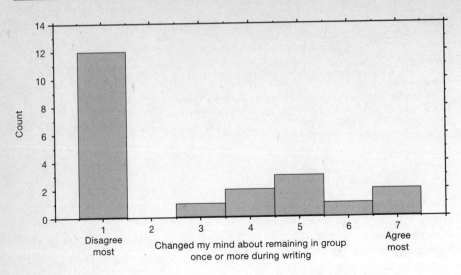

Fig. 6.4. Reported changes of mind about remaining members of the group.

to actual changes, or that for some groups, membership had never been clear. Either way, it is interesting to note that the question of who was and was not a co-author was not always clear cut, because of the implications for issues such as security and locking (who will have access to documents), decision making (who takes part in making decisions), and communication (who should be included in exchanges between co-authors) in designed support systems.

There were thus nine respondents altogether in this sample (39%) who *either* had been unsure of who the co-authors were going to be, or had actual changes in their groups (or both).

In another question, respondents were asked to what extent they agreed or disagreed with the statement "once or more during the production of the document I changed my mind about being a member", by indicating a number from 1 ("disagree most") to 7 ("agree most"). On this question there was a clear polarization between those who totally disagreed, and those who agreed with the statement: twelve of the twenty-one who replied (57%) indicated that they had never changed their minds about being members (these all chose 1, or disagreed most with the statement). Nine (43%) indicated that they agreed to some degree that they had changed their minds (these chose numbers between 3 and 7). Fig. 6.4 shows the frequency distribution of the replies to this question.

6.3.3.3 Discussions on Relationships between Co-authors

Respondents were asked to indicate how frequently their group had discussions on the relationships between the co-authors before, during, and after

Table 6.6. Discussions on the relationships between co-authors in the group
(1 = very infrequently; 7 = very frequently)

Statement	Mean	Range	s.d.	N
With the benefit of hindsight, I now think our discussions on the relationships in our group were adequate	3.9	1–7	2.5	21
At the time, I felt that our discussions on the relationships in our group were adequate	3.8	1–7	2.2	21
We discussed the relationships between group members while writing	2.7	1–7	2.3	22
There were group-wide discussions about the relationships between group members	2.3	1–7	1.9	22
We discussed the relationships between group members before starting writing	2.3	1–7	2.0	22
We discussed the relationships between group members after finishing writing the document	2.2	1–7	2.0	22
There were discussions in sub-groups about the relationships between us co-authors	2.1	1–7	1.8	19

writing their document, and in the group as a whole as opposed to in sub-groups. The results are presented in Table 6.6.

Note that when asked about the adequacy of those discussions, respondents appear to be split in two, and overall did not consider their discussions very adequate. Taken together with the low frequencies reported for these kinds of discussions, this indicates that the co-authors surveyed did not discuss the interrelationships with their co-authors much, and that almost half considered that they had fewer discussions on their interrelationships than they would have liked. The histogram in Fig. 6.5 shows the bipolar frequency distribution for the statement "with the benefit

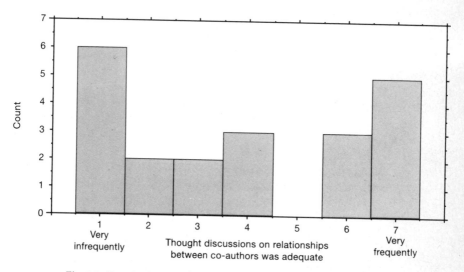

Fig. 6.5. Perceived adequacy of discussions on co-author interrelations.

Table 6.7. Perceptions of the progress of the work
(1 = very infrequently; 7 = very frequently)

Statement	Mean	Range	s.d.	N
I (personally) was doing too much	3.2	1–7	2.4	23
Others were contributing too little	2.7	1–7	2.3	23
We (the whole group) were doing too little	2.2	1–6	1.8	23
I (personally) was contributing too little	2.1	1–6	1.6	23
Others were contributing too much	1.6	1–5	1.1	23

of hindsight, I now think our discussions on the relationships in our group were adequate", indicating that the respondents were split in two on this question.

6.3.3.4 General Progress of the Collaboration

Respondents were asked to indicate how frequently they thought they had held certain opinions about themselves and the progress (or otherwise) of the writing project while they were writing. Some of the statements were about the perceived amount of work put in by the group and its members. One might have expected that academic writers in this survey would be feeling some pressure towards being prolific and successful writers (because of the importance of the number and prestige of publications in their career structure), and that this might be reflected in conceptions of collaboration in writing, perhaps through apportioning blame on colleagues. Taking all respondents, there was no real trend among respondents generally to claiming that their colleagues were doing too little: the statement "others were contributing too little" received a mean which was only slightly higher than "I (personally) was contributing too little"; see Table 6.7.

However, the fairly high standard deviations for these two questions indicated that the respondents had varied opinions. A test was therefore made to examine a possible correlation between respondents thinking that they themselves had been doing too much and that others were contributing too little. A positive correlation, significant at $P < 0.01$, was found (Spearman Rank test for correlation; rho = 0.722; $N = 23$). Fig. 6.6 shows the scattergram for combinations of responses to these two statements. (Note that due to the possibility of bias from the high density of points at one end of the diagonal of the scattergram, a cross-check of the significance of the result was made by excluding all respondents who chose 1 for both questions and repeating the correlation test. The correlation retains its significance only at the less favourable probability of $P < 0.05$ (rho in this case = 0.727, $N = 10$).) Thus, in this sample of collaborating authors, feeling that they themselves were doing too much was closely related to feeling that others were contributing too little.

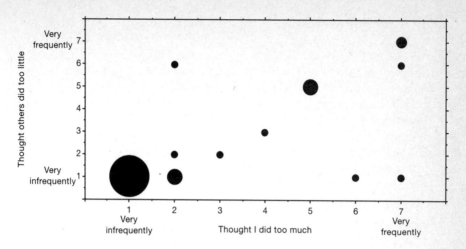

Fig. 6.6. Perceived own versus others' input.

6.3.3.5 Purpose of the Writing Group

In response to the question "in your *own* opinion, what was or were the purpose(s) of the creation of the writing group?" respondents were asked to rate 7 statements from 1 ("least important") to 7 ("most important"). Table 6.8 shows the statements, along with the responses obtained. The most popular reason was getting the document written; second was to work together. What the respondents agreed most on was that creating new cooperation on matters other than that dealt with in their paper was *not* important. It is perhaps also worth noting that maintaining existing cooperation or relationships relevant to the subject of the document was rated no

Table 6.8. Perceived reason for establishment of writing group
(1 = least important; 7 = most important)

Statement	Mean	Range	s.d.	N
To get this paper written	5.7	1–7	1.9	23
To work together	4.5	1–7	2.0	21
To enhance or maintain among the co-writers **existing** cooperation or relationships **not** relating to the subject of the paper	3.6	1–7	2.1	19
To enhance or maintain among the co-writers **existing** cooperation or relationships relating to the subject of the paper	3.5	1–7	2.1	21
To obtain funding for another project	3.1	1–7	2.4	19
To create among the co-writers **new** cooperation relating to the subject of the paper	2.9	1–7	2.0	19
To create among the co-writers **new** cooperation **not** relating to the subject of the paper	1.7	1–4	1.2	20

more important than maintaining existing relationships which did *not* relate to the paper.

Respondents were asked whether none, some, or all of the purposes listed in Table 6.8 were explicitly agreed in the group, and whether other purposes than those had been agreed. In twelve cases (52%), respondents indicated that none of the purposes they saw for creating the writing group were explicitly agreed by the whole group. This may be an indication that the purpose of the group was (or appeared to be) so obvious that it was felt no discussion was needed, though it is also possible that the purpose was not clear to the participants.

6.3.4 Orientation

6.3.4.1 Working in a Group

Respondents were asked to indicate their level of agreement with statements about working as part of their writing group. The responses are listed in Table 6.9.

Table 6.9a shows statements for which respondents were asked to indicate their general satisfaction with the collaboration through the frequency with which they thought they had felt a number of factors during the writing. They most frequently reported thinking that the collaboration was worth while, that they were in some ways very pleased with the collaborations, and that they felt the group worked well together. They

Table 6.9a. General satisfaction with the collaboration
(1 = very infrequently; 7 = very frequently); and **b** perception of collaboration versus writing alone (1 = disagree most; 7 = agree most)

Statement	Mean	Range	s.d.	N
a				
The collaboration was worthwhile	5.5	1–7	1.7	22
In some ways very pleased with the collaboration	5.4	1–7	1.7	22
The group worked well together	5.3	2–7	1.5	23
I think the cooperation of the writing group was enhanced as a result of the collaborative writing	4.8	1–7	1.8	22
In some ways very displeased with the collaboration	2.9	1–7	1.9	23
The group worked poorly together	2.8	1–7	2.0	23
I think the cooperation of the writing group deteriorated as a result of the collaborative writing	2.1	1–7	1.9	22
b				
It took less time to write with others than it would have taken on my own	3.9	1–7	2.0	23
I could not have done it on my own	3.8	1–7	2.4	23
I would have done it better on my own	2.9	1–7	1.9	23
I had to sacrifice too much for the collaborative writing of that document	2.5	1–6	1.9	23

were not sure that the cooperation of the writing group had been enhanced as a result of the collaborative writing, but only a few thought it actually had deteriorated.

Table 6.9b shows statements asking for a comparison between writing the same document on their own and writing it as part of a writing group. The respondents differed on whether they thought they could have done it (at all) on their own, and were less certain they would have done it better had they done it on their own. The respondents also differed on whether the collaboration had taken less time than if they had done it on their own. There was more agreement that they had *not* frequently felt that they had to sacrifice too much for the collaborative writing of the document.

Four of the statements in Table 6.9a were concerned with the frequency of respondents' general feeling of their groups' working well or poorly together, and feeling pleased/displeased about the collaboration. These statements were pairwise exact inverses of each other, and could be tested to indicate the general reliability of the data obtained in the survey. High scores were obtained for the positively phrased statements (feeling the group worked well together; feeling pleased with the collaboration), and corresponding low scores were obtained for their inverses, as shown in Table 6.9a. Tests found significant positive correlations ($P < 0.01$) between individuals' responses to the two statements on frequently feeling that the group worked well together, and frequently feeling pleased with the collaboration (Spearman Rank test, rho = 0.744, $N = 22$); and also between feeling that the group worked poorly together and feeling displeased with the collaboration (Spearman Rank test, rho = 0.698, $N = 23$). These results indicate that for the co-authors in this survey, feeling pleased about the collaboration was closely connected with feeling that the group worked well together. Furthermore, negative correlations were, as expected, found between the negatively and the positively phrased statements, giving another indication that the data were reliable with respect to these questions.

6.3.4.2 Motivation

The respondents were asked to indicate to what extent they agreed with nine candidate reasons for joining a writing group. The most popular were "I thought I would enjoy it" and "I thought it would be good for my future job or career prospects". Least agreement was obtained for the statements on not knowing the reason for joining, to establish new private relationships, and joining as a consequence of pressure from outside the group (see Table 6.10). In addition, five respondents (22%) ticked the box for "other reasons" for joining their writing group. Reasons given were that an existing group was continuing working/writing together (two respondents), because of an interest in seeing ideas published (two respondents), and joining to help ensure a deadline could be met.

Table 6.10. Personal motivation for joining writing group
(1 = disagree most; 7 = agree most)

Statement	Mean	Range	s.d.	N
I thought I would enjoy it	5.0	1–7	2.2	20
I thought it would be good for my future job or career prospects	4.5	1–7	2.1	22
Keep in touch with people I already knew	3.2	1–7	2.3	20
Establish new work relationships	3.2	1–7	2.6	21
Obtain funding for a specific other project	3.1	1–7	2.7	21
I felt some pressure from person(s) in the group to join (e.g. chairperson, colleague)	2.6	1–7	2.0	20
I felt some pressure from person(s)/body outside the group (e.g. manager, leader, funding body)	2.0	1–7	1.7	20
Establish new private relationships	1.7	1–6	1.5	19
I never knew why I joined	1.4	1–7	1.4	18

In a separate question, respondents were asked to what extent they had wanted to be taking part in the group writing project prior to joining it. Given that these all had in fact ended up joining those writing groups, one might expect that this statement would receive a very high mean. However, whereas eleven respondents (48%) did choose either 6 or 7 (7 being "agree most"), the other half of the twenty-one respondents were evenly spread between 1 ("disagree most") and 5. (Mean for all responses 5.0; range 1–7; s.d. 2.3.)

6.3.4.3 *Perceptions of Success*

The question of what constitutes success in collaborative writing has a number of potential answers. In this survey, respondents were first asked how confident they had felt during their collaboration that the group would succeed. Respondents appeared to have considerable confidence in the collaborative writing projects they were taking part in: they were united in quite frequently thinking the group would "definitely succeed" (mean 5.3; range 2–7; s.d. 1.4), whereas they reported that they were much less frequently "unsure whether it would succeed or not" (mean 2.6; range 1–7; s.d. 1.9). Finally, respondents reported infrequently thinking that the group would "definitely *not* succeed" (mean 2.4; range 1–6; s.d. 1.9).

Respondents were then asked to consider in more detail the nature of their conception of success by indicating the importance of eight potential components of success in collaborative writing on a 7-point scale. Table 6.11 summarizes these and the responses obtained. Respondents overwhelmingly agreed that the most important determinant of success was the acceptability of the resulting document to themselves (note that all twenty-three respondents replied to this question, and each one gave this statement a rating between 5 and 7). Opinion differed more on the next most highly rated component, acceptance by reviewers, although the mean scores were similar for these two statements.

Table 6.11. Perceptions of success
(1 = very unimportant; 7 = very important)

Statement	Mean	Range	s.d.	N
The resulting document is acceptable to you	6.2	5–7	0.9	23
The resulting document is acceptable to its reviewers	6.1	2–7	1.3	22
Everyone in the group considers the finished document a good one	5.8	2–7	1.3	23
The group members get on well personally	5.5	2–7	1.4	23
There was good communication between the group members	5.1	2–7	1.6	21
Group members will carry on working with each other	3.9	1–7	1.7	21
There was a close adherence to an initial plan	3.1	1–7	1.4	22
New work or personal relationships have been formed	3.0	1–6	1.5	21

6.3.4.4 Perceptions of Collaborative Writing (Open-Ended Question)

As outlined in Section 6.1, Ede and Lunsford (1990) and Couture and Rymer (1991) used different definitions of collaborative writing and obtained quite different results for the prevalence of collaborative writing. In this survey, the issue of definition was addressed in terms of the respondents' own perceptions of collaborative writing. Respondents were asked the open-ended question "what is, to you *personally* and in your own words, the purpose of taking part in collaborative writing/co-authoring/writing in a group?". A preliminary analysis of the responses has been conducted by the author.

All twenty-three respondents replied to this question, most indicating more than one reason. The responses cannot easily be partitioned into wholly unrelated issues. Some of the statements may fit into broader categories of concerns. The suggested categories are: concern with improved quality of the resulting document (more combined knowledge, more criticism); concern with faster process (increase in speed/decrease in work for a document); collaboration in writing as a consequence of collaboration on the reported work; concern with relationships with collaborators; and concern with sharing (statements which cannot reliably be attributed to one of the other categories). According to this categorization, improved quality of the resulting document was the most frequently stated purpose in taking part in collaborative writing. Thirteen respondents (57%) were considered to have in some way indicated this purpose. The next most frequently stated purposes for joint writing were as a result of joint work (6 respondents) and that the process of producing a document was faster (4 respondents). Quite different perspectives, in evidence from individual respondents, were that work and writing were fundamentally social activities, and that the respondent had no choice in whether to write collaboratively or not (managers decided). These responses are summarized in Table 6.12. (Note that, for ease of reading, responses or elements of responses with virtually identical phrasing have been collapsed into unquoted items. The number of

Table 6.12. Perceptions of collaborative writing; preliminary analysis (Numbers in square brackets indicate which respondent(s) provided each response)

Responses	Category of concern
"create something better than individuals could achieve alone" [2]; "produce a better paper" [5]; "I know better quality work results from collaboration" [12]; "the whole is greater than the sum of the parts" [13]; combining expertise/complementing each other [1, 5, 13, 14, 20, 21]; larger set of views/ideas [8, 10, 12]; idea creation/review [10, 22, 23]; co-authors' challenges/critical attention before submission [4, 12]	Quality of product (13 respondents)
"natural part of such a culture [of working in small teams within a sub-task]" to cooperate on reports, papers, etc. [6]; for work which has been undertaken collaboratively [17, 19, 22]; providing/representing a picture of the whole group doing the work by all being co-authors [16, 18]	Result of other collaboration (6 respondents)
"efficient process" [1]; speed of producing a paper [7, 13]; "doing more work in less time" [20]	Fast process (4 respondents)
sharing the load [2, 4, 10]; "sharing the problems, worries, decisions, work [from initial conception to layout]" [15]; "the pleasure of marriage of minds" [10]	Sharing (4 respondents)
"to get the work done" [9] "motivation" [21]; "less easy to be non-productive" [13]	Getting the work done (3 respondents)
"get to know people" [21]; "establish a working (and possibly also private relationship […] since a successful collaboration […] requires trust and a common world view" [23]	Relationships (2 respondents)
"I think I see work as inseparable from interaction with others. While I sometimes enjoy going off for a while to write alone, the work itself and writing seem to me to be fundamentally social activities, so I almost have to turn the question around and ask what would be the purpose o[f] not collaborating" (from a respondent who reported taking place in hundreds of writing projects of various kinds). [3] "I think individual writing is almost impossible" [12]	Necessarily joint activity (2 respondents)
"My experience of collaborative writing is restricted to the real world employment situation, in which I basically do as I'm told: if I'm told to work with others, I work with others. The purpose of collaboration is usually to ensure that dealines are met. Occasionally it happens in order to allow a trainee to work with a more experienced writer." (from the only respondent who indicated writing journalistic, technical or popular non-research prose, as opposed to academic research or other purposes) [11]	No choice (1 respondent)

respondents who included the category in their reply is indicated together with each category name.)

Finally, in their (voluntary) general comments on the questionnaire, three respondents made reference to how collaborative writing will change over different instances of co-writing even for the same person, due to factors such as different partners, writing goals, experience, group composition, or leadership (respondents 12, 15 and 17). One respondent wrote that he edits a lot, but does not himself generate the ideas in the text, and in that respect asked "what is collaborative writing?".

6.4 Discussion

6.4.1 Results

6.4.1.1 *Discussions in the Groups*

Any writing group must at some level agree on the content and structure of the text they are producing, if the result is to be a single document. One might expect that in academic writing groups, such discussions would be prevalent, whether in sub-groups or in the whole groups. It was therefore perhaps surprising to come across tendencies of a binary split among respondents to this survey with respect to group-wide discussions on content and structure. It is possible that those who reported relatively infrequent group-wide discussions reported relatively frequent sub-group discussions, but due to an error on some of the questionnaires on the sub-group issue, this cannot be properly investigated. Another possible explanation is that since the measures are to some extent relative to the respondents' own expectations, it may be that such discussions were frequent, but that some respondents felt that in their latest collaborative writing group, such discussions were somewhat less frequent than expected and therefore gave a low score. Perhaps more plausibly, it is possible that the responses describe a situation in which the collaborating writers have such clear notions of what the content and structure of the document is going to be that there is little need for such discussions. Finally, it is possible that discussions on the content and structure of emerging documents are so common that they are not being noticed and hence not reported in the survey.

Discussions were perceived of as taking place more frequently during writing than either before or after. This was the case for all three kinds of discussions addressed: content and structure of document; organization of work within the group; and the relationships between the co-authors (except perhaps for discussions about the organization of work; here discussions during writing were reported only slightly more frequently than discussions prior to writing and the result is not interpretable).

The correlations found between responses to statements about group-wide discussions on the organization of work, and discussions on the content and structure of the document, mean that the more frequent one kind of group-wide discussion was seen to be, the more frequent the other kind was seen to be. One explanation for this may be that the two kinds of discussion normally take place together, perhaps because they are causally linked, i.e. that one causes the other. If this were the case, then systems designers may need to know, for example, how close in time these tend to occur, and therefore how integrated with each other any support functions for the two kinds of discussions need to be. Another explanation is that some other factor causes the two to co-occur; in this case perhaps opportunity for having discussions at all. The implication of this view is that given the opportunity, co-authors will discuss such issues. Considering the correlation between the frequency of discussions on organization and how adequate they are considered to be, it might become an aim to the design to provide plenty of opportunities for such discussions.

The correlation found between perceived frequency of discussions on work organization and reported high satisfaction with the adequacy of those discussions also indicates that in this survey, respondents who reported infrequent discussions were less inclined to describe the discussions they did have as adequate. If this is a general tendency among collaborating authors, and if reports of adequacy means that expectations are felt to have been met, then this result could indicate a general expectation among co-authors that discussions on organization of writing will, or should, take place frequently. If co-authors feel that it is not adequate to have little discussion on the organization of writing, an environment for collaborating authors must at least provide spaces in which such discussions can easily take place; the question is also raised of whether discussions on the organization of the work could and should be actively encouraged.

6.4.1.2 Organization of Work

It seems as if there is an element of collective responsibility running in parallel with individual or sub-group responsibility for almost all of the instances of group writing reported on by the respondents to this survey, and that this responsibility is exercised in such a way that individuals' areas overlap during the joint writing project (respondents thought infrequently that there was little or no overlap between areas of responsibility, or that they were responsible for their own part only). This could be either concurrent overlaps, or overlaps arising from changing responsibilities at different stages. Either way, this would seem to be a pointer to the allocation of responsibility itself being dynamically – perhaps continuously – re-negotiated during the writing process.

6.4.1.3 General Satisfaction

Questions phrased positively in terms of belief in the group, enjoyment of participation, the group working well together, etc. scored consistently higher than those phrased negatively (e.g. "group would definitely not succeed"). Thus, respondents appeared to be quite pleased with the collaboration they were taking part in. This result is, however, somewhat paradoxical considering that almost half had at some point during the collaboration changed their minds about remaining in the group. One explanation for this apparent contradiction might have been that many respondents were reluctant to expose their (private) criticisms of their co-authors in this survey, or that respondents were "agreeing" with the statements as put. However, low means were obtained in this question for statements which were opposites, making it unlikely that the responses were mere results of the question design. An alternative explanation is that the reported low frequencies of the respondents having these opinions (low means and not-too-high standard deviations) could be interpreted as the respondents being fairly happy with the efforts of the writing groups they were members of (with the exception of a tendency among some to think they themselves were doing too much and others too little). This may be a product of co-authors believing, or presenting, an improved image of their collaboration. Finally, the apparent contradiction may be an indication of the process of writing together having involved periods of crisis in the groups which were later resolved and/or did not affect the overall impression of the joint writing effort as satisfactory. If this is the case, then co-writers may well benefit from support of some kind to get through the difficult periods. (The issue of what kind of support would be helpful in this respect is beyond the scope of this study. This may, however, be addressed in other studies, for example case studies, which could identify turning points and their causes during the co-writing process.)

6.4.1.4 *What Is Success?*

If the quality of collaborative writing technologies is to be evaluated, some answers to the question of what constitutes "good" collaborative writing must be found. In this survey, participants' conceptions of success were addressed in the question "how important are or were these factors to you in determining the success of the writing project?". High scores were obtained for statements addressing the acceptability of the finished document to participants and reviewers, i.e. the respondents considered it an important determinant of the success of the writing project that individuals involved in its production and its review found it acceptable. A notably low score was given to forming new work or private relationships, and to "close adherence to an initial plan". The latter may indicate that co-authors do not see following plans as important for successful collaborative writing, or that initial plans may be significantly revised (or are seen as being open to revision) during the writing process. This corresponds with Hartley and Branthwaite's (1989) recommendation that someone who wishes to improve their writing productivity in academia should make a rough plan initially, but one which "you needn't necessarily stick to" (p. 449). This preliminary study therefore suggests that computer tools which aim to support planning should also be designed to support the easy alteration of plans. It follows that any automatic enforcement of plans (for example, automatic reminders of work which is due) must be easy to override by the users.

6.4.2 Coverage

6.4.2.1 *Limitations of the Results*

The best understanding of individuals' experience can probably be gained through qualitative methods, such as participant-observation or interviews. This has the significant advantage of addressing in some depth the situation in which the task takes place. However, such an approach has limitations. The results cannot readily be quantified, thus making it more difficult to use as a base for generalizations. It can also be a time consuming way of gathering data. Finally, qualitative methods typically gain data from a small number of people, who may not be representative, or may not exhibit the range of styles and approaches to collaborative writing used by all collaborative writers. This may be a particular problem when the ultimate aim of a study is to serve as the basis for predictions on the behaviour of others in similar situations, as is the case with research for computer system design where the ultimate purpose is to make reasonable predictions about the behaviours, needs, etc. of the future users. There are also limitations inherent in the use of questionnaires (see Hartley and Branthwaite (1989) for a discussion of these). The most appropriate method for gaining an overall view is probably not one or the other, but a combination of the two, both for studying writing (Hartley and Branthwaite 1989) and in the design of computer systems (Wright and Monk 1991).

The results from this survey should be viewed as preliminary. First, the instances of collaborative authoring reported on by the respondents were almost exclusively academic writing. Therefore they do not necessarily generalize to collaborative writing as a whole. Secondly, there were some reports that a few of the questions were ambiguous, resulting in some questions being omitted from the analysis. Thirdly, the respondents were self-selecting on engagement in "collaborative authoring". There is no one definition of collaborative authoring which is agreed to be the correct one. For example, Ede and Lunsford (1990), in the study cited above, used a broad definition of writing which included "writing activities". Couture and Rymer (1991), on the other hand, made a distinction between writing in a group on the one hand and interacting with others during the writing process on the other, and obtained a different figure for the prevalence of collaborative writing in "the professions", as reported above. For the purposes of the survey reported in this paper this problem of definition was resolved by allowing, in effect, the (potential) respondents to apply their own definition of collaborative authoring (the survey was clearly labelled "co-authoring survey" and it is assumed that only those who, by their own definition, considered themselves to have written collaboratively with others replied). However, given the lack of an unambiguous definition of collaborative writing, and given that the purpose of this survey was not to establish the frequency of collaborative writing, but to examine some characteristics of collaborative writing when it is seen to be taking place, this is not considered a serious limitation.

6.4.2.2 Further Implications for Systems Design

The results reported above are tentative, based on a sample of twenty-three mainly academic co-authors, and should not be generalized too far. However, these findings already raise some design issues worth considering further.

A view is emerging from the data of the experience of collaborative writing as a process which is dynamically re-negotiated. It is necessary for designers of computer support systems for collaborative writing to take into account the need for some space in which co-authors can negotiate and re-negotiate not only the contents of the emerging document, but also their organization of the work that needs to be done, and the relationships between them. For example when the data show that the reported groups split fairly evenly between having an agreed leader, a self-appointed leader, and no one taking the lead, this raises the issue of how a computer system might be designed for, or designed around, the necessary flexibility to handle these different organizations. If one was envisaging a system that provided support for a person to take on a leader/facilitator role, it might be quite reasonable to include a computer system through which any person (or none) could claim leader status; this might remain in force until challenged. This would initially cover the case of three scenarios in which a leader had been agreed between the group members, a self-appointed person took the lead, and no one took the lead: in the first case one could stipulate that any discussion about who should be the leader would have taken place prior to invoking this function, such that the agreed leader subsequently could claim the computer system's "leader" role. (However, see below.)

Fluctuating group membership and commitment to the group implies that an environment in which co-authors are expected to work must allow for changing involvement in the task, and should allow people to join and leave a group with reasonable ease. The possibilities for supporting the smooth substitution of co-authors for others should be explored. For example, one might consider encouraging co-authors to store ideas, incomplete drafts, etc. in such a way that if the situation arises and permission is given, they could be made easily accessible to those who are to take over the interrupted task.

A secondary objective of the survey described in this chapter has been to serve as an example of a combination of strengths of quantitative and qualitative methods of research, in terms of their respective benefits for systems design. Wright and Monk (1991) advocate a combination of such methods for the evaluation of user reactions to early systems designs. Hartley and Branthwaite (1989) regard questionnaire approaches as "complementary" (p. 448) to other approaches in the study of writing. This survey has attempted one solution to the trade-off between the approaches: partial combination, by obtaining, in mainly quantified terms, perceptions on contextual issues, supplemented by qualitative responses. This has enabled the dynamic nature of the writing groups in this survey to be examined, revealing the necessity to take account of the dynamic structure of writing groups when, for example, designing computer systems to support them.

There are, however, still unanswered questions. Consider again the cases where respondents reported that their group had a self-appointed leader. The types of situations covered by this might range from there being very clearly a leader – this may even have been agreed between the rest of the group apart from the respondent – through a "natural" leader gradually emerging during the writing project, to, at the other extreme, a situation in which all (or both) group members are taking a share of organizational responsibility, but where, something (for example, a comment) makes the co-author(s) perceive one of the collaborators as a self-appointed leader. How is one to know which scenarios to anticipate? Unfortunately, this survey does not provide the answer to such questions. In particular it is not clear how one could ever get around the problem of designing for generic users on the basis of data from a limited number of cases. However, it is hoped that the results from this survey and the design issues extracted have demonstrated the importance of writing group dynamics as one starting point for finding answers to such concerns.

Acknowledgements   I am very grateful to those who took the time to fill in the survey, and also to those who have provided comments, discussions, advice and support during the development of the questions, the analysis of the results and the writing of this chapter: in particular, Paul Dourish, Radka Dvorak, Mike Sharples and Charles Wood, for useful comments on earlier versions of this chapter, and Steve Easterbrook, James Goodlet, Lydia Plowman and Yvonne Rogers, for general support in our research group.

Chapter 7

Multimedia Conferencing as a Tool for Collaborative Writing: A Case Study

S. Baydere, T. Casey, S. Chuang, M. Handley, N. Ismail and A. Sasse

7.1 Introduction

In this chapter we investigate the use of multimedia conferencing systems to support the process of collaborative writing. It is a case study in which we report on the production of this chapter as a team effort, with all interaction between team members taking place through the facilities provided by the CAR multimedia conferencing system (CAD/CAM for the Automotive Industry under Research for Advanced Communications in Europe (RACE)) supplemented by electronic mail (email) and a shared filestore.

7.1.1 Collaborative Writing

Problems faced in industry and science have become increasingly complex, often require multi-disciplinary expertise, and have to be solved in shorter time-spans through the interaction of geographically dispersed groups. Consequently, the number of collaborative projects in business and science is increasing, and many of them require documents to be produced as part of the activity.

Collaborative writing requires clear communication between group members at all stages of the writing process. The stages of the writing process can be described as planning, execution, integration, review and revision, but collaborative authoring of a document also raises issues of communication, coordination and social relationships which are irrelevant to solo authorship (Galegher and Kraut 1990b).

7.1.2 Multimedia Conferencing

In general, multimedia systems offer a range of different tools for collaborative work. These tools can be distinguished into those that support *synchronous* interaction and those that support *asynchronous* interaction between collaborative workers. Synchronous communication occurs when two or more people interact in real time, e.g. in a telephone conversation. Asynchronous communication occurs when two or more people interact in a non-simultaneous fashion, e.g. by sending messages in email.

Multimedia conferencing integrates a user's existing software environment with the audio and video communication traditionally provided by video conferencing systems, and allows users to exchange multimedia information in real time. During a typical conference, users will communicate through the audio and video facilities with each other in a way similar to a face-to-face meeting. In addition, users can share software applications, such as DTP and CAD packages, and data with other users. This allows the conference participants to work interactively, each from their own workstation.

7.1.3 Collaborative Writing with Multimedia Conferencing Support

The ease and success of a collaborative writing project depends partly on the communication tools group members used (Chalfonte et al. 1991). While communicating via a relatively static medium such as text (e.g. email) may be sufficient for the purposes of exchanging information, complex interactions involved in performing intellectual teamwork normally require high levels of direct, informal, face-to-face communication.

Indeed, Galegher and Kraut (1990b) found that collaborative writing is virtually impossible without face-to-face meetings: groups of students charged with writing a joint report only by means of computer conferencing (i.e. text messaging) and telephone did arrange some face-to-face working sessions, even though they were told not to. They found it especially difficult to cope without face-to-face meetings when they were trying to get the project launched at the beginning, and when trying to merge individually prepared contributions into a joint paper.

It can be assumed that collaborative writing could be improved if electronic means could be provided to support activities that normally take place in face-to-face meetings. Such support could be provided by a general-purpose meeting or conferencing system such as multimedia conferencing, rather than by a system specifically developed for collaborative writing (see Dillon, this volume). The reason that multimedia conferencing is currently not employed very often is mainly because very few collaborative writing teams have access to such a facility. Recently, however, ISO JTC 1 Special Working Group on Procedures has been instructed to investigate the procedural implications of conducting meetings via teleconferencing and electronic messaging, and a draft document for consideration by this group has been submitted (ISO/IEC JTC 1 1991).

Multimedia conferencing is an obvious candidate if we are looking for an electronic tool to take over the role of face-to-face meetings in intellectual groupwork, since it provides the necessary software tools as well as rich channels of communication. It should score high on both criteria defining richness: interactivity, i.e. quickness and appropriateness of feedback, and expressiveness, i.e. multiplicity of cues, language variety, and ability to incorporate emotional and social aspects into the communication (Chalfonte et al. 1991).

7.1.4 Case Study

We view this project as a first attempt to write a paper entirely through multimedia conferencing. The project should be seen as a case study in which the development, composition and editing of the chapter will be done via a multimedia conferencing system. In effect, this is a recursive writing project: the authors explored collaborative writing by multimedia conferencing by collaboratively writing a document, via multimedia conferencing.

The authors are academic or research staff at the Department of Computer Science at University College London (UCL) who have been involved in the CAR project.

The team agreed that all interaction between team members regarding the document should take place via the multimedia conferencing system and email only. From its inception to the final version, it was agreed we would attempt to write it without face-to-face meetings or individual discussions, as if team members were geographically distributed. However, on occasions we were forced to resort to face-to-face meetings because the conferencing system was not available. As the number of team members is larger than available multimedia stations, most of the time two people have shared the same multimedia station during conference sessions.

In the following section we describe the conferencing system and the mechanisms that supported this authoring effort. Next we describe how the document evolved within this environment. In the final section we assess the value of our methods and discuss some recommendations for future work.

7.2 Supporting Mechanism

In this section we describe our prototype conferencing system, which has been developed by the CAR project team at UCL, and other supporting tools used in association with the conferencing system. We also explain the method we employed to ensure consistency and concurrency control over our shared data.

7.2.1 CAR Multimedia Conferencing System

The CAR multimedia conferencing system (Schwartzlose and Penter 1991; Morgan 1991) provides an environment for geographically distributed participants to hold conferences by interchanging information through video, voice and multimedia documents.

This system, which is shown in Fig. 7.1, facilitates real-time conferencing between multimedia workstations. Each station consists of a Sun SPARCstation, a microphone, a video monitor and one or two cameras.

A conference is made up of a group of conferees each associated with a multimedia station and connected to an analogue audio/video network. Shared applications tied together via local area networks and wide area networks (LANs, WANs) and multimedia conference control software run on the multimedia stations. This has the capability of including other existing applications available on a conferee's workstation for interactive use by replicating the application display to all conferees' screens. The shared application can then be manipulated by all conferees. All changes made to the shared applications become visible at all stations immediately.

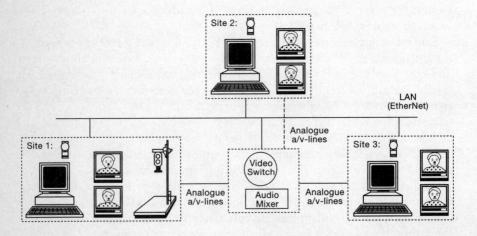

Fig. 7.1. CAR multimedia conferencing system.

Fig. 7.2. Photograph showing CAR multimedia workstation.

Though CAR conferences are unchaired, only one conferee can hold the floor at any one time. Any conferee can take the floor at any time. The floor holder controls all shared applications and the video broadcast channel. Fig. 7.2 shows the CAR multimedia workstation.

A conference session starts by showing video windows together with control windows for conference control and device control. A conference has one common video channel at its disposal. What is broadcast on this channel is shown on all conferees' monitors. The channel can be run in two different modes:

1. "Quad mode", in which the common video channel contains a composite image dividing the screen into four quarters, each one originating from one conferee's site.

2. "Single-image mode", where only the video signal originating from the current floor holder is broadcast on the common video channel.

The current floor holder can switch the conference channel between the two modes, affecting all screens in the conference. Each conferee can also switch their monitor into "preview mode", which enables them to check the output of their own camera. This has no effect on the other conferees' monitors. Audio is an open channel in which everybody hears each other at the same time.

7.2.2 Electronic Mail

A text-based electronic messaging system was used for asynchronous communications. Our email system is an X.400-based implementation developed at the Department of Computer Science at UCL (Kille 1988) with the MH user interface (RAND MH User's Manual).

7.2.3 Shared Filestore

This work was carried out with SUN NFS (Sun Microsystems 1989) shared filestore, in which a log of email messages, conference agenda, minutes and the partitions of the document was kept. Sharing a filestore facilitates collaboration and maintenance of the integrity of the document. We do not feel it is essential to the collaborative writing process, but in a non-shared workspace, issues such as integrity and revision control are likely to be of greater importance (see Section 7.4).

7.2.4 Consistency and Concurrency Control

In a collaborative writing environment, authors may work independently or jointly on separate sections of the document. From the early planning sessions we recognized the need for consistency and concurrency control.

7.2.4.1 Revision Control

While writing this chapter, each section was stored as a separate file. If two or more authors try to change the same section at the same time, a concurrency control mechanism is needed to coordinate the editing. A common method is to grant a lock to one of the authors. The others will be informed of who holds the lock if they try to change a locked section.

The other requirement that we identified was the ability to retain all previous versions in a structured manner with minimum storage overheads. Previous versions should be recallable and there must be a way to show the difference between versions.

We employed an existing revision control system in our experiment, the Source Code Control System (SCCS) for the following reasons:

1. It provided a basic mechanism of revision control.

2. It would be the best way to identify features required of such a tool.

SCCS is a maintenance and enhancement tracking tool that runs under the UNIX system. It takes custody of a file and, when changes are made, identifies and stores them in the file with the original document. It will allow only one person to check out a file for editing at any one time, thereby maintaining the integrity of a document section.

Retrieval of the original or any set of changes is possible. Any version of the file as it develops can be reconstructed for inspection or additional modification. History data can be stored with each version and provide an audit trail of changes made to the document. SCCS provides these facilities using a minimum of storage and processing.

SCCS was also used to monitor the progress of this collaborative writing project. The editing history is used to analyse the pattern of change made during the document preparation process.

7.2.4.2 Revision Control Protocol

SCCS provided us only with the mechanism to achieve version control. A set of protocols was still required to ensure seamless coordination. In our experiment, all sections of the document were under SCCS control. We agreed that each section would have a "manager". The manager was responsible for the version control when a section was freshly created, and put the first version under SCCS control before releasing it for comments.

To preserve integrity and prevent confusion, the aim was that all changes should be made under SCCS. Our convention for making on-line comments was:

1. If the change is very small, such as spelling, an omitted word, etc., make the change without marking that you have changed it.

2. Make any additions to the document in such a way that they stand out from the original text. (Our convention is [**TC: this is a comment**].) A more complete example looks like this:

   Synchronous communication occurs when two or more people interact simultaneously and in real time, e.g. in a telephone conversation [**TC do we need both examples**] or a video conference.

3. No text should be deleted by a commenter. Mark the text for deletion or replacement, but let the person responsible for the section include the changes as they see fit: [**MH 9/10/91 The above text should be replaced with: Text should not be deleted...**].

Commenters keep the modification history at the top of the file up-to-date. For example:

#	Modification History		
#	DATE	YOUR_NAME	REMARK
#	14/10/91	MH + AS	2nd attempt at draft
#	15/10/91	MH + AS + SB	Revised and edited
#	26/10/91	TC	Commented
#	28/10/91	MH + AS + TC	Discussed comments + edited

This is necessary because although SCCS stores the location of the changes, it is not immediately obvious from the actual text. This is because SCCS does not visibly mark changes in the text of the document, but stores their location as separate control information. When significant changes were made, it was considered polite to email the section authors, saying a comment had been made to their section. The manager of each section would then clear up all these marks at the end of the review.

7.3 Document Evolution

The evolution of this document is the result of the following kinds of activities:

1. The generation of fundamental ideas.
2. The management of the project.
3. Reviewing and editing.
4. Integration of sections.

7.3.1 Generating Ideas

The process of the generation of ideas for writing or for other collaborative work is a complex issue. Creativity is not something that can necessarily be ensured simply by arranging the right environmental conditions. However, it can be shown that the conditions under which ideas are generated in a collaborative environment can have a marked effect.

Conventional chaired meetings can have the problem that a participant with an idea may not be prepared to speak out for fear of stepping out of line, thus such meetings may stifle creativity.

To avoid this problem, many groups employ "brainstorming" sessions to attempt to stimulate new ideas. This involves allowing anyone to make any suggestion on the topic in question, however irrelevant, and not allowing any criticism of these ideas until later, when the promising ideas are selected. The premise is that even the most far-fetched ideas can be valuable, since they encourage participants to take a "fresh look" at the issue. Practice has, however, shown that there is less variety among ideas generated through a collective brainstorming session, than among ideas generated by the same people individually. The combined effect of interrelated ideas and an attempt to achieve consensus may be that a "group-think" (Janis 1982) mentality sets in, and good ideas are not found because they are outside the group's frame of reference. Our findings appear to confirm that "personal" and "group" brainstorming serve different and complementary purposes (see Section 7.4).

Due to its relatively high speed, inherent reusability, and multi-cast nature, email is quite suitable for the interchange of ideas during a development process, and is now widely used both in academia and in the commercial world. As it is an asynchronous interchange, the immediate feedback of face-to-face meetings is lost. During the early stages of the development of this chapter we relied heavily on the use of email. When it was used for the generation of ideas, both positive and negative effects were noted:

1. Consensus takes longer to achieve, if it is achieved at all.

2. Misunderstandings may remain unresolved for longer. Participants are less likely to question phraseology, and may retain a different understanding for longer.

3. Group-think takes much longer to set in, and may not be as all-pervasive. Consequently new ideas appear more readily.

4. People who would not express opinions face-to-face feel freer to do so.

5. Ideas are often better thought out when they are written down for email.

6. People who could not be in a meeting for logistical reasons may still express their views.

The contrast of styles was particularly noticeable when we discussed the same ideas synchronously. Many misunderstandings needed to be resolved. The synchronous discussions tended to produce few new ideas, but existing ideas were effectively combined and refined.

The implications may be that asynchronous discussions such as email throw up a wider range of ideas from a broader group of people. However, a consensus view and a common course of action may be much more difficult to agree.

Multimedia conferencing systems such as the one used for this experiment have similar consequences to face-to-face meetings for the generation of ideas. However they allow the sharing of data, text etc. in a much more immediate manner than face-to-face meetings. The multimedia conferencing system was used in many ways during this experiment. For idea generation and discussion, the preferred usage pattern that evolved was to discuss ideas one at a time verbally until some sort of consensus was achieved and then summarize the idea on-line, so that everyone could see, and comment if they disagreed. The advantages of this are:

1. Everything worth noting gets documented.

2. The resultant ideas are available on-line in a reusable form for anyone to use as the basis for further work.

3. Securing agreement is a continuous process.

4. Far fewer misunderstandings are carried around, due to the combination of the greater expressive richness of verbal communication (Chalfonte et al. 1991), and the interactive minuting of the interchange.

5. Latecomers and absent members can catch up relatively easily.

Table 7.1. Two opposing tendencies in multimedia conferencing

	Consensus	Originality
Electronic mail (asynchronous)	Decreasing	Increasing
MM conference (synchronous)	Increasing	Decreasing

This immediate minuting process is much more natural than the usual minuting procedures used in face-to-face meetings, and appears to be one of its major advantages for collaborative writing. However, this can be hard work for the person responsible for the minuting.

Unfortunately multimedia conferencing obviously suffers from the same potential group-think problems as face-to-face meetings. When it comes to consensus and originality there appear to be two opposing tendencies, as shown in Table 7.1.

This suggests that no single method of interchanging ideas is optimal. Rather, a cyclical process of *generating and discussing ideas asynchronously*, and then *developing and discussing them synchronously* is effective, and would strike a good balance between originality of ideas and consensus of opinion. Synchronous minuting of ideas and decisions is an effective technique in a multimedia conference, and helps to remove misunderstanding and ensure consensus.

7.3.2 Managing the Development

The development of this chapter was a creative activity that can be divided into sub-processes such as structuring, partitioning and task allocation.

From the beginning of the experiment, we adopted an open planning model, comprising cycles of sub-processes or events. Each cycle targeted a new draft of the chapter, and the phase of the events was changed after a careful "review–refinement–revision" process at the end of each cycle. This open model allowed us to review our approach during experimentation and revise it where necessary. The open model might be peculiar to this chapter – it was essential in overcoming the "bootstrapping" problem we faced in writing a chapter about writing a chapter. Other models might be a more appropriate representation for collaborative writing of documents on well-defined topics with a pre-determined structure.

7.3.2.1 Planning

The planning process started with decisions regarding the use of computerized tools, email, multimedia conferencing, revision control mechanism, the protocols we might need, commenting policy etc. Later, we identified the events which we thought would be repeated in each cycle of the development process. These are:

Structuring, in which we developed the topic items based on the contents of the chapter and our limitations determined by the state of the art, our environment, its relevance to the topic, time factor, etc. (There are two related concepts of structuring with which we are not concerned at this time, namely: the use of a structured document mechanism, such as a template; and the structured manner in which we deal with revisions via the SCCS system, as discussed above.)

Partitioning, in which we divided the topical items into sections and subsections, considering the fact that our aim was to modularize the document in such a way that each participant would have a well-defined subject area and the aggregate effort could be integrated effectively.

Task allocation, in which we allocated writing responsibility to a person or a group. Groups were free to choose their own working protocol as a subcommittee. For instance, they were allowed to have face-to-face meetings to discuss their joint partition if they wanted to.

These events started at different but related times and their outcome continued intermittently, until a draft was reached.

Fig. 7.3 illustrates the events of a cycle of the planning process. This open model also allowed us to employ some pre-events between cycles. For example, the first cycle started with "investigating the current state of the art" as a pre-event activity in which everybody took some published work in this area and reported on its relevance to our work in the following conference session. We should also point out that these events were tightly coupled with feedback between concurrent events in each cycle.

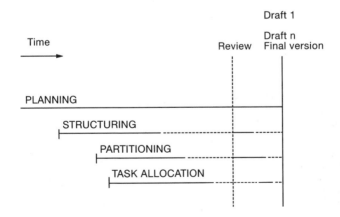

EVENTS IN ONE PLANNING CYCLE

Fig. 7.3. Open planning model.

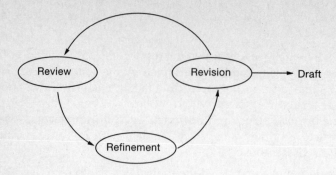

Fig. 7.4. Review, refinement and revision in the planning model.

After the completion of a draft, the activities and methods employed were reviewed and revised when necessary. The outcome of the events of a cycle became an input to the revision process and affected the identification of the events in the next cycle.

Fig. 7.4 shows the iterative nature of the model. The review, refinement and revision processes here apply to the *planning cycles* rather than to the actual document. The latter is discussed later in the chapter.

7.3.3 Review and Commenting

During the process of collaboration on a paper, there are inevitably many occasions when authors disagree with each other's emphasis, phraseology or content. The cyclical nature of the write–review–refinement–revision process requires feedback from the co-authors in order to be successful and worth while. What form this feedback takes depends on the nature of the environment, and the degree of disagreement between the authors. In a non-distributed environment, this is usually achieved by one of two processes:

1. Sitting down together and discussing the document, possibly annotating a paper copy as they go along.

2. Sending an annotated paper copy of the document back to the author for revision.

In a distributed environment, neither of these is a very efficient way of working. Sending an annotated copy back to the author can be speeded up by the use of fax, but as fax is a non-reusable medium, this is less efficient for making anything other than small changes.

The environment in which we composed this chapter (multimedia conferencing, email, shared filestore with SCCS), provided us with several ways of closing this feedback loop:

1. Email the author of the section.
2. Email everybody working on the document.
3. Telephone the author of the section.
4. Change the original document (under SCCS).
5. Raise the issue in a group multimedia conference.

Each of these commenting methods has a unique nature, and so affects the way we presented our comments, and the way the other authors treated it.

1. *Email the author of the section*   This is a subtle, private form of discussion. It does not affect the other collaborators until we agree on a course of action, or decide we can't agree and broaden the discussion. It is one-to-one, and therefore does not carry much force. Rather, it is a suggestive method, and tends to lead to discussion rather than conflict. People tend to be less immediately defensive when approached in this manner, but it is also possible they may ignore the commenter's views completely.

2. *Email everybody working on the document*   This is a very public way to air disagreements. It is useful when strategic issues are being addressed. It is also useful when more subtle approaches have failed to achieve any resolution, and a majority opinion is needed.

However there is a danger that this approach will be used as a way of attempting to achieve support for an idea without having attempted to agree the issue in private first. If this happens too often, a confrontational attitude may set in.

3. *Telephone the author*   We never used this method of commenting. It has the advantage that it is immediate, but as the two parties cannot see exactly what is referred to, it could all too easily lead to misunderstanding.

4. *Change the original document*   This is possibly the most controversial method of review and comment. There is a risk that rephrasing someone else's work will offend them, or change their meaning. To prevent this we agreed certain rules for change (discussed in Section 7.2.4.2). By conforming to these rules, commenting becomes an integral part of the writing process. This makes this approach the most genuinely collaborative, and leads to writing being a more continuous process.

5. *Raise the issue in a group multimedia conference*   This is the most immediate form of commenting. All conferees can see what is being referred to, and can change it if they wish. However if many issues are brought to conference, this can be extremely time consuming.

Multimedia conferencing is best used for higher level issues such as planning strategy, and for immediate resolution of existing conflicts. It has been noted that if email discussions do not solve themselves relatively quickly there is a danger of a divergence of views occurring. In a multimedia conference, as in a face-to-face meeting, there is a tendency for people to attempt to reach consensus, so this is a good place to resolve issues that have failed to be resolved elsewhere.

It has been noted (see Section 7.3.2) that the process of collaborative writing should be seen as iterative in nature. At each review stage, comments should be invited from all authors, whether involved with a section or not. Without this continuous feedback process collaborative writing ceases to be collaborative, and coherency may be difficult to achieve.

7.3.3.1 Comments on Review

Review of draft document sections was done in both synchronous and asynchronous modes. Early in the development, we made more use of electronic mail for asynchronous communication, and used only a few shared files as "idea stores". At this time we had no formal revision control protocol, and found that synchronous reviewing during conference sessions became concerned with rather trivial aspects of the document and was less concerned with the general or conceptual elements. This was not expected according to recent research (Chalfonte et al. 1991). This phenomenon changed as members of the group became more comfortable working with each other and the technology. In addition, approaching deadlines enforced a more focused way of working. As we made more use of shared files under SCCS, most of the detailed comments were added directly to the relevant files. We then found that we made virtually no use of email for commenting, and the amount of "detail" discussed in conferences also fell. The focus of attention during the conference sessions became directed to higher level issues of structure and content with a corresponding improvement in document content and style.

In the early stages of our document preparation process it seemed to be much easier to get all team members together for conference sessions. This became much more difficult to do as the writing progressed. At one time during the writing, half of the authors were abroad, which required that some of the work be done asynchronously. These circumstances forced us to become much more efficient in the allocation of our time.

7.3.4 Integration

Integration is the process that brings the various sections together to form a unified document. Individual sections were written and the revision process managed by the section author(s). Ideally, with proper planning and structuring of the document, the integration process would be straightforward and easily completed. This was not necessarily the case for this chapter because the planning and structuring of the document was an ongoing process, mainly due to the recursive nature of the subject.

7.3.4.1 The Integration Experiences

Two stages of integration were undertaken for this project. One, for the first draft; another for the final draft.

1. *The first draft*   Integration took place at a time when only half of the authors were present to participate in the multimedia sessions that were held to produce the draft. Those absent participated asynchronously by submitting section material via email or fax, but they did not take part in the decisions which reviewed, revised and integrated the sections for the first draft.

A different interactive technique was used by this small group during the "first draft" review, revision and integration process. The three authors sat around one workstation, with one of them attempting to document any decisions taken, which the others then disagreed with when necessary; thus consensus was quickly achieved. In this way it was similar to what was actually happening in a conference – usually one person did most of the typing on any one topic, attempting to summarize what everyone had decided. This technique worked very efficiently.

As noted earlier, individual sections were commented on, reviewed and revised as separate entities. The order of the sections was debated and for the most part agreed upon by the sub-group present. There was some disagreement on the placing of the section on SCCS, and no one was entirely happy with the integration of the first draft.

Some sections were written in a "generally discursive" style; others were more "descriptive". These sections did not fit well together, and for the first draft there was debate over whether we should re-order the document to reconcile this style clash, or whether we should ignore it, and order the sections according to their content. By a majority vote, it was agreed to accept the latter option, with the proviso that we would try to rephrase some sections for the final draft.

The resolution of this issue was undertaken during the integration process of the final draft, by re-ordering some sections, and rewriting other parts of the chapter.

2. *The final draft*   Integration was undertaken before complete revisions of specific sections were complete; some restructuring of the document was also undertaken, and an attempt was made to begin the preliminary formatting of the document. Two of the team now undertook to put the document in a form which would help us reach a consensus for the final draft. A printed copy of the document in its "rough" final format was provided to all members of the team for comments.

There was a feeling at this time that some repetition among the sections needed to be removed, that some renaming of sections might be helpful, and that a reorganization of the structure might be useful. Comments on the draft were solicited.

During integration, many misunderstandings about style and structure were dealt with; some inconsistency and repetition showed up only in this stage of the development process, when the entire document was read by the authors.

7.3.5 Decision Making and Conflict Resolution

Decision making is the process of choosing from a set of different alternatives according to a set of weighted criteria. In the case of collaborative writing, where more than one person is involved in the process, conflicts are more likely to be encountered. Different people can have different criteria and different priorities. Generally conflicts can be due to:

- disagreement on the set of alternatives;
- disagreement on the set of criteria;
- disagreement on the set of priorities;
- misunderstandings.

Most of the conflicts that we faced during the planning, writing and integration of this chapter were solved within conferencing sessions. This proved to be a very reasonable way of solving conflicts. The audio and video facilities provided by the multimedia conferencing system, plus the immediate interactive sharing of data, made it easier for people to be able to express their ideas and views clearly, thus decreasing the possibility of misunderstandings and, accordingly, conflicts.

For the different stages of the document evolution, different methods for solving conflicts were tried. The only general rule that we had was that majority voting would be our last resort.

1. At the planning stage conflicts were solved mainly through discussions. This usually lead to a general agreement on one of the alternatives. At this stage most of the decisions were about protocols, tools and strategies. It was not that difficult to agree on the criteria and priorities for such decisions. Most conflicts resulted from different understanding about the alternatives. Once these alternatives were fully discussed in a conference it was relatively easy to arrive at a general understanding. For example, when we were trying to find an appropriate mechanism for version control many ideas were produced via email and it seemed that there was a conflict. A conference was held where all ideas and mechanisms were fully discussed and an agreement was made to use SCCS as the basic mechanism for revision control.

2. When the writing of individual sections began, conflicts were controlled by assigning a section manager to each section, with editorial control. Comments were allowed but how conflicts were resolved was left to each

section manager to decide. The general rule was that the final say on any conflict was up to the section manager.

3. At the stage of integration, the role of the section managers was abandoned. It was everyone's responsibility to resolve conflicts. Due to the nature of the conflicts at this stage, they were sometimes difficult to resolve. A new dimension of personal and psychological issues began to appear, which made it difficult to agree on criteria and priorities. Again, it was decided to use different methods for resolving conflicts, depending on the nature of the conflict, and reserving majority voting as a last resort.

4. On issues concerning the rephrasing of a certain paragraph or some restructuring of the document, we tried to present some aspects of the different arguments in the document. An example of this is described in Section 7.3.4.1, where differences in structuring the document for the first draft could be resolved only via a majority decision, with a proviso that the issue would be dealt with further in the final draft.

5. In some instances, changing the context of the issue which created the conflict could help to solve it. For example, there was a conflict about moving a certain paragraph from a section where it did not quite fit. Simply changing the name of the section solved the conflict.

It worth noting that no decision making tools were used while writing this chapter. In a larger project, however, conflicts are likely to occur more often, and a formal tool or a "conflict resolution protocol" would be useful. Multimedia conferencing makes it possible to integrate and interactively use such tools within the system, thus rationalizing and formalizing the process of decision making for collaborative work.

7.4 Assessment and Evaluation

7.4.1 Using Synchronous and Asynchronous Modes of Communication

One of the key questions we faced was which mode of communication, synchronous or asynchronous, best supports the collaborative writing process. In this section, we consider synchronous and asynchronous communication in terms of effectiveness and efficiency. *Effectiveness* of communication is achieved if a task is completed as agreed (e.g. writing a summary). *Efficiency* of communication can be assessed in terms of a cost–benefit analysis of resources spent on completing a task (e.g. how many hours were spent on compiling a list of all papers referenced in the document).

Efficiency and effectiveness of synchronous and asynchronous communication will be examined with respect to issues connected with collaborative writing:

- bridging time and place gaps between collaborators;
- agreeing structure and content of a document;
- capturing, reusing and disseminating information.

7.4.1.1 *Bridging Time Gaps and Place Gaps*

In many work groups that have to produce documents as a team effort, group members are geographically distributed, and it costs time and money to bring the group together for a face-to-face meeting. Place gaps can be bridged by means of the synchronous facilities such as audio or video conferences. While these facilities save a great deal of travelling time, they are still expensive in terms of investment and use. We have used synchronous communication for most tasks that involved more than one person (e.g. idea generation, planning of chapters, integration of sections) in the production of this chapter, and all group members found their patience tested at some point. Even though some of us had plenty of experience with the "writing by committee" approach and its drawbacks, we found that the use of video conferencing sometimes seemed to make it worse. In every meeting there were situations where some members of the group became involved in discussion which was not of interest to all group members – for instance, two people would argue about a technical feature of multimedia conferencing which others knew nothing about, and thought not to be relevant to the document. There are fewer opportunities for the "waiting" members to cope with this situation than there are in a face-to-face meeting: first, body language cannot be used as effectively to signal lack of interest and impatience to the "talking" group members; second, "waiting" group members have little opportunity for "displacement" activities by communicating in an unobtrusive way, verbally (e.g. whispering) or non-verbally (e.g. grimacing, body language). The best way to cope with such a situation is for "waiting" group members to use other channels of communications (e.g. messaging) to have "asides" with each other, or use a non-shared application and get on with some work of their own. These problems are partly associated with the size of the authoring team, which was quite large for a group of authors working very closely together (see Beck, this volume).

Synchronous facilities require all group members to be available at the same time, which is difficult if group members are located in different time zones, or have busy schedules. Such time gaps can only be overcome through asynchronous modes of communication. Most of the current asynchronous facilities are text-based and therefore lack expressiveness – this severely limits users' abilities to deal with higher level issues in a document (Chalfonte et al. 1991). We used two such facilities – email for distributing messages (e.g. that a draft of a chapter had been finished and was available for commenting), and a revision control tool, SCCS.

We found that employing different modes of communication and different tools for work tasks and enabling tasks (see Denley et. al., this volume) to be very beneficial. This way, all comments are included in the actual document, next to the point to which they refer, and all members can be sure they see the latest annotated version. Text-only is a drawback – a similar multimedia-based tool (e.g. voice annotation of a written document) would help when making comments on higher level issues.

7.4.1.2 *Agreeing Structure and Content of Document*

Planning activities in collaborative writing, such as drawing up a structure and determining the content of a document, requires a rich mode of communication. Galegher and Kraut (1990b) found that it was impossible for groups to complete the planning phase in a collaborative writing project without face-to-face communication – groups instructed not to have face-to-face meetings resorted to "cheating". We had a series of synchronous multimedia conferences in the planning phase, and found them to be both effective and efficient. As with face-to-face meetings, synchronous communication helped group members to establish the different viewpoints, and converge on a document structure fairly quickly. Misunderstandings and differences of viewpoint were identified early in the planning process and resolved quickly through group decisions. In addition, having the emerging structure of the document typed out for all members to see helped to focus discussions in the planning phase, and made it easy to define and allocate activities for the execution phase.

It should not be overlooked, however, that the speed (i.e. efficiency) with which convergence of viewpoints is achieved also harbours dangers for the effectiveness of intellectual teamwork. Exploring a variety of divergent viewpoints, their origins and implications can lead to new and innovative insights – this is one of the main benefits of intellectual teamwork in general, and collaborative writing in particular. If group members converge too quickly on an outline of the document structure, ideas that lie outside this structure are not explored, and the solution space might be closed prematurely. Group-think (Janis 1982) can set in: people working in groups tend to work towards a solution that is acceptable to everyone, and once a consensus is achieved, group members are very reluctant to depart from it. Convergent thinking towards a group consensus can be the death of creativity and innovation. Group members are usually very reluctant to challenge fundamental beliefs and assumptions for fear of upsetting other group members.

We have adopted two techniques for beating group-think in the planning phase, one synchronous, one asynchronous. The synchronous one follows a suggestion by Janis (1982) for combating group-think in face-to-face meetings: appoint one group member in each session to play the role of a devil's advocate, and try to find as many arguments as possible against the consensus document structure. It is hard work for the devil's advocate if she takes her role seriously. The asynchronous technique is less spectacular: individual preparation, in writing. Group members are asked to think about a document structure before the meeting, and write it down. This allows the group to compare the consensus solution to the individual ones, and prevents the group from conveniently forgetting points which do not fit into the consensus outline.

7.4.1.3 *Capturing, Reusing and Disseminating Information*

In both synchronous and asynchronous modes of communication, there is an issue of *which* and *how much* information should be stored for future use. There is usually a trade-off between volume of information recorded and how easy it is to locate a particular piece of information. In a "total logging" approach, we decided to record all information generated by group members. With asynchronous communication (e.g. email or voice messages), we usually stored information in chronological order on a specific medium. We decided, for instance, to keep a copy of all email messages that were sent in connection with the writing project. The folder does grow quite quickly, and it becomes fairly difficult to locate a particular message. In a "selective logging" approach, one or more group members decide whether a particular message is worth keeping, and might decide to set up a number of folders for particular topics to make it easy to locate specific information. Text-based computer messaging systems allow limited access through keywords, by message author, or by dates. For text-based communication such as email, a free text storage and retrieval mechanism can be usefully employed to manage access to a "total logging" information store.

In a synchronous communication mode, with a "total logging" approach (in a multimedia conference, audio and video, and all information genera-ted in shared applications), we are storing an enormous amount of data. Any group members who have missed the conference have access to all information that the members who were present at the conference had. On the other hand, if we were trying to locate information within that log (e.g. all interaction related to a particular topic in the document), there is currently little support. Unlike text-based information, continuous media such as audio and video face a problem of granularity, i.e. how to partition the information into meaningful units that can be retrieved (Laurel et al. 1990). We opted for a "total logging" approach with respect to text-based asynchronous communication: all electronic messages were kept in one folder, and the use of the versioning software (see Section 7.2.4) made it possible to keep all annotations and changes made to the document itself. For synchronous multimedia conferences, we adopted a "selective logging" approach akin to minuting: all decisions and the rationale behind them were written in keywords. Some sessions were sampled on videotape.

Since four of the six authors were away for considerable periods of time, logging changes and decisions in this way seemed important. On return, these authors would read the current version of the document (which happened to be the first draft), and enquire about the rationale of changes to sections and new sections. Using the logs, we could show how other solutions had been tried and why they were discarded. It was quite interesting that the authors who were involved in the integration of sections into the first draft had different recollections about the conflicts which had to be resolved at that stage. "Evidence" from the logs and witness statements from the authors had to be pieced together to work out why the first draft turned out the way it did. It was important for all authors to share the "conflict history" of the document in order to avoid resurrecting those conflicts as work progressed.

7.4.1.4 Video

We found that video interaction is required as it simulates face-to-face communication. One of the comments we often heard during these conferences was "I cannot see you". This has shown that people want to see each other during communication, but local asides between the people at one station may be disturbing to the people at other stations. On one occasion we used a workstation that was not equipped with a monitor in a multiway conference. The conferees at this workstation found that they felt "left out": they contributed less to the conference than usual, chatted to each other, and started doing non-shared work. This shows that video is very important in terms of interactivity.

7.4.2 SCCS

SCCS has proved to be a powerful tool in our collaborative writing experiment. Together with the set of protocols that we devised, commenting and revision is carried out in a coordinated and efficient fashion.

However, we have also identified a few drawbacks in SCCS. Firstly, the granularity of the locking is at the file level. One of the problems that we have observed is the possibility of a co-author grabbing the file for too long. This problem is not unique to a shared file environment. When a document is passed in a "round-robin" for editing using email, document hogging can still happen when one author refuses to act quickly. To alleviate the problem, a mechanism to lock only part of a document, i.e. *record-level locking*, is required. Due to this limitation in the locking granularity, we have found SCCS works better with individual sections rather than the complete document.

In fact, with a record-level locking, a revision control mechanism can be incorporated into an editor to create a powerful collaborative editing system for a group of co-authors working asynchronously on a shared document.

The second shortfall that we observed with SCCS is the *visibility of changes* within the document. Even though SCCS preserves all previous versions and changes, these are not visibly marked in the document. A view feature such as the one provided by MILO (see Jones, this volume) would be very helpful. Again, we had to devise a set of protocols (see Section 7.2.4) to employ this tool in a useful and efficient manner.

7.4.3 Sharing Applications

Although we can share many applications in the CAR environment, most of them are not relevant for collaborative writing. We worked mostly with two shared text editors in windows on screen simultaneously. At times, we found it difficult to keep track of the structure of the document, so we contemplated using a structured editor similar to MILO (see Jones, this volume). The problem with using such an editor, however, is that they do not allow inclusion of any "disconnected" ideas (notes, etc.): everything has to be tied to the structure of the document. Ideally, we would like to use an editor that provides structure support, but still allows us to keep items in the document that are (not yet) integrated into the document structure. Such items could, for instance, "float" around the document structure, or be displayed in a "tiled" fashion around the edges of the editor window.

We are developing a shared pointer system, but that was not available at the time of writing. In the system used for writing this chapter the floor holder could highlight sections so the other conferees could see what she was referring to, but without actually transferring the floor there was no way for non-floor holders to do this. Although this was not essential, it would have made some discussions a little more natural.

7.5 Conclusions

The main aim of this case study was to determine if multimedia conferencing can provide the rich channel of communication that collaborative writing requires. We found that the process of collaborative writing is not dissimilar to the process of designing an artefact. Therefore an electronic environment such as CAR, which aims to support design work, could be effectively employed to support collaborative writing of documents.

In addition, we wanted to explore whether the use of computer-based tools would interfere with creative processes between authors. The factors that distinguish rich channels of communication are interactivity and expressiveness (Chalfonte et al. 1991). As far as interactivity is concerned, the speed of feedback provided by synchronous conferencing facilities can hardly be improved. We would also consider the feedback provided through both audio and video channels to be appropriate, since removing either of them seriously constrains the range of feedback provided to authors (see Section 7.4.1.4). The expressiveness of communication in multimedia conferencing does not reach the same level as it does in a face-to-face meeting: there is no eye contact between participants, and the impact of facial expressions, gestures and body language is reduced (Heath and Luff 1990). The participants in this study adapted quickly and changed their style of communication accordingly. The expressiveness of feedback in multimedia conferencing goes beyond that of any other communication medium.

Computer-based tools can offer valuable functionality to a team of authors: shared filestores and version control mechanisms help to keep track of a document's evolution and preserve its integrity. In the course of this case study, however, we realized that, to work effectively with these tools in a collaborative environment, a set of rules governing their use was required. We first realized this when we had to develop a very explicit protocol for the use of SCCS (see Section 7.2.4); later, we did the same for conflict resolution, and to a lesser extent for commenting, structuring and partitioning of the document. While explicit protocols have been developed for the interaction of components in complex systems at different levels of hardware and software, e.g. the ISO basic reference model, there are no such protocols for the interaction between authors, or the use of tools. We feel that to ensure effective and efficient collaboration, a set of protocols needs to be defined. At the moment, each team of authors will have to define its own rules, depending on the task, the project goals, and the channels of communication that are available. More research is required to establish areas of commonality of collaborative writing projects, so that such protocols can be defined.

Acknowledgements   We wish to thank Professor Steve Wilbur of UCL, Dr Mike Sharples of the University of Sussex, and the anonymous reviewer for their constructive comments on the first draft of this chapter. We would also like to thank all our colleagues in the CAR project, who are involved in the development of the tools we used and made it possible for us to write this chapter.

This work was funded by the CAR project of the CEC RACE Programme and the Department of Computer Science, UCL. Any correspondence should be addressed to Angela Sasse, Department of Computer Science, University College London, Gower Street, London WC1E 6BT; email: a.sasse@uk.ac.ucl.cs.

Chapter *8*

Reviewing Designs for a Synchronous–Asynchronous Group Editing Environment

V.C. Miles, J.C. McCarthy, A.J. Dix, M.D. Harrison and A.F. Monk

8.1 Introduction

The roots of computer supported cooperative work (CSCW) are in the observation that a great deal of our daily activity involves some form of collaboration (Olson 1989). Much early research in CSCW considered ways of supporting a general concept, that of cooperative work. More recently CSCW research has begun to focus on specific applications. Computer support for collaborative writing, particularly in the form of a shared editing environment, emphasizes a more task-focused approach to CSCW applications.

Collaborative writing involves two or more people working together to produce a document. It involves phases of writing and phases of communicating (Beck, this volume; Newman and Newman, this volume). It also involves periods of synchronous activity, where the group works together at the same time, and periods of asynchronous activity, where group members work at different times. The diverse range of activities involved and the different modes of interaction (synchronous and asynchronous) make collaborative writing a particularly interesting domain for CSCW support. The CSCW literature discusses a number of shared editor applications that aim to support collaborative writing. It is interesting to note that many of these systems will support either synchronous or asynchronous interaction, but not both.

Work at York on CSCW has echoed the general pattern of CSCW research mentioned earlier. We began by looking at computer-mediated communication, building the Conferencer as a "generic" conferencing environment (McCarthy and Miles 1990; McCarthy et al. 1991a, b). This work was valuable in clarifying our thoughts on CSCW. A natural progression, we felt, would be to attempt to support a more focused task than conferencing. We chose to examine collaborative writing within the shared editor application domain. By focusing on shared editing, we are taking a narrow definition of collaborative writing. We concentrate on that part of the collaborative writing process which is concerned with the actual creation of text: "putting pen to paper". Our proposed shared editing environment does not aim to provide specific support for activities such as brainstorming, idea organizing and decision making, although these are important parts of the overall writing process. However, as this chapter will show, we did not deem it sufficient to design a shared text editor alone, but also considered the design of accompanying conversation spaces.

This chapter, then, marks the first steps in the design of our shared editor environment. We consider literature on collaborative writing, computer-mediated communication and group editor applications to come up with some design ideas for our shared editor environment. We start, in the next section, by touching on some of the issues surrounding collaborative writing. This is done with reference to a conceptual model of cooperative work. This section sets up the broad requirements for our shared editor environment. Sections 8.3 and 8.4 deconstruct the model into its component parts. These sections include discussion of designs for supporting computer-mediated communication and group editing. Sections 8.3 and 8.4 see a move from the conceptual model to ideas for design. Section 8.5 attempts to reconstruct the model in the light of these design ideas. The chapter concludes with a discussion section.

8.2 Cooperative Work

This section looks at collaborative writing, using a conceptual model of cooperative work as a focus. This model is shown in Fig. 8.1.

8.2.1 Direct Communication

Arrow *a* in the model of cooperative work shown in Fig. 8.1 refers to direct communication between participants. Direct communication implies that participants are aware of each other, and will address messages to their co-participant(s). Direct communication takes place in face-to-face interaction, for example, in informal conversation, formal meetings and so on. It can also be mediated, for example by telephone, or electronic messaging.

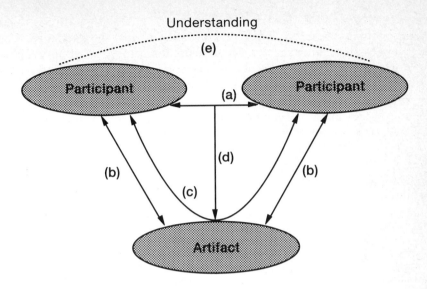

Fig. 8.1. Conceptual model of cooperative work.

Computer support for direct communication is often referred to as computer-mediated communication (CMC). If we take the example of a group of people writing a document together, direct communication may include the communication of ideas about what to include in the document, how to go about the task, relevant expertise, comment and so on.

Successful direct communication implies the achievement of a common understanding between participants. This can be difficult, particularly when group members have a diversity of backgrounds. Different perspectives and different areas of expertise often mean different languages for addressing a problem (McCarthy et al. 1991a). Olson refers to this as a coordination cost (Olson 1989).

The complexity of the coordination problem is elucidated by Begeman et al. (1986) in their analysis of meetings. This analysis itemizes the variety of activities, information items, contexts and goals which constitute a meeting.

Only a subset of these items will be considered by each participant in a meeting. Clearly the nature of this subset will depend on the participant's background, and disparate backgrounds might be expected to result in ineffective meetings, as there may only be a small degree of overlap between subsets. Thus we see the importance of successful direct communication. If each participant can successfully communicate their perspective, a *common understanding* can be achieved, with each participant having some knowledge of how other's perspectives differ from their own.

Clark and Brennan (1991) maintain that it will be easier to reach a common understanding in face-to-face interaction, where a high degree of contextual information is available to participants. They maintain that in direct, face-to-face communication, context is shared through: co-presence; visibility; audibility; co-temporality (where one person receives an utterance at roughly the same time as another produces it), simultaneity (where people can send and receive simultaneously) and sequentiality.

In the model of cooperative work, line e in Fig. 8.1 represents common understanding. Understanding need not only be an emergent property of direct communication, it may also come from interaction through shared artefacts, discussed in the next section.

8.2.2 Shared Artefacts

Cooperative work emphasizes some shared task, or common purpose. Often, this shared task will involve some artefacts that are the subject of the work. These artefacts may be entirely conceptual, for example a joint decision, or be physical, such as a shared document. The artefacts may or may not be part of a computer system. So, a report being prepared by two or more people may be a conceptual plan they share, a paper artefact, or a document that is represented on a computer.

The model of cooperative work in Fig. 8.1 includes a physical artefact. The b arrows represent each participant's interaction with the artefact. Interaction with a common artefact can take place synchronously, where participants work concurrently, or asynchronously, where participants work at different times. One shared artefact central to collaborative writing is the shared document. Posner et al.'s (1991) research into the group writing process has suggested that participants' interaction with a document artefact will be characterized by periods of synchronous and asynchronous activity. They comment on the need groups have to change writing strategies at any time during a collaborative authoring project. Writing strategies identified include: a single person writing the document based on discussion with the group; a scribe in a group meeting; a division of labour, with different members of a group authoring different sections; and a group writing together. The division of labour strategy proved the most widely used.

In addition to each participant's interaction with the artefact, communication can take place through the artefact. One can think of this as indirect communication. In Fig. 8.1 indirect communication, through the artefact, is shown by the curved arrow, c, which links participants and artefact. Imagine two authors sharing paper and pens to write a document. The text of the document, and annotations to it, acts as a means of communication, helping to establish the task in which they are engaged, and perhaps indicating to each participant the expertise, perspective and/or role of the other. The style in which the text is written is informative, as is the type of paper and pen. Cheap paper and sketchy notes written in pencil indicate to participants an informal interaction. A carefully penned letter suggests something more polished. The orientation of the writing material between authors is another form of communication. When one participant pushes the paper across the desk to his partner, the implicit message is, "it's your turn now". Pettersson (1989) has examined the communicative power of the shared artefact in her analysis of document reading within two intensive care units. She analysed the type, use and recognition of documents in the wards. She found that information can be transmitted through: the location of a document; its spatial layout; the appearance of a field, filled or unfilled; and the nature of the handwriting and the pen used to produce it.

In addition to interacting with and though the artefact, participants will use various means to refer to particular artefacts. This is illustrated by arrow *d* in Fig. 8.1. Clark and Brennan (1991) talk about the importance of mutually establishing references to artefacts. They maintain that many conversations focus on objects and their identities, and they discuss several common techniques for establishing "referential identity", that is, the mutual belief that addressees have correctly identified a referent. In face-to-face conversation one such technique is "indicative gesture", which highlights the importance of pointing, looking and touching as a means of grounding references.

Support for artefact sharing is another target for computerization. Group editing applications, shared calendars and shared drawing tools all provide computer support for artefact sharing. Such applications will embody the characteristics of arrows *b* and *c* in Fig. 8.1. Participants will interact with the shared artefact, shown by arrows *b*, and will communicate indirectly through the shared artefact, shown by arrow *c*.

8.2.3 Broad-Based Requirements

This brief look at the cooperative work of collaborative writing has highlighted some important issues that can be translated into some broad-based requirements for our group editing environment. Many of the shared editor applications implemented to date will support either synchronous or asynchronous interaction, but not both. Yet Posner et al.'s analysis of the writing process suggests that a joint writing effort can last from several days to several years, and groups are likely to adopt both synchronous and asynchronous modes at some time during a project. Our choice, then, is to design an editing environment that is capable of supporting synchronous and asynchronous group interaction. In so doing, the aim is to support different modes of writing. For example, support for synchronous interaction would allow group members to write together, at the same time: one of the writing strategies identified by Posner et al. Supporting asynchronous interaction will allow group members to follow the widely used division of labour strategy: each individual writer will be able to produce their part of the text, in their own time, using a single environment. Provision of support for both synchronous and asynchronous interaction is favoured by Posner and her colleagues. She writes:

> Technology needs to be flexible and permissive, allowing groups to change strategies ... . Smooth transitions should be supported between ... synchronous and asynchronous work by group members.

For a more detailed look at synchronous and asynchronous collaborative writing, see Baydere et al. in this volume. When a shared editor is to support synchronous interaction only, then a designer can reply on face-to-face interaction, video and/or audio for direct communication between participants (arrow *b* in Fig. 8.1). When asynchronous interaction is also to be supported, then designers must consider other means of facilitating the group's direct communication. One (inexpensive) option is to use textual communication, that is, textual messages displayed at the workstation interface. Direct communication, therefore, is mediated by means of computer support for textual messaging. Other means of mediating asynchronous communication include asynchronous voice. Unfortunately we do not have the facilities to support this at York, so for practical reasons the choice is textual messaging.

In terms of the conceptual model, we are suggesting that our group editing environment should provide support for both direct communication and work artefact interaction. We require text-based conversation space for direct communication, and shared editing facilities for interaction with and through the document artefact.

8.3 Issues in Computer Support for Direct Communication

In this section we begin the process of deconstructing the conceptual model of cooperative work. This section looks at design issues in computer support for direct communication between participants. The analysis is limited to textual messaging.

CSCW systems vary in the approaches they take to structuring direct communication. There are two broadly differing approaches. On the one hand, there are systems that *enforce* a dialogue structure; and on the other, there are systems that encourage users to structure their own conversation. Gibbs (1989) describes these approaches in terms of a "social versus software protocol". Miles et al. (1991) talk of "local" and "global" structuring. Local structuring is an emergent property of a particular interaction: global structuring is embedded at design time, and is enforced in the same way for every interaction.

Coordinator, an application designed to make clear the commitments of communicating partners, provides an example of a system which *enforces* a dialogue between its users. A central feature of Coordinator is its use of conversational templates, which are based on speech act theory. These templates define a rigid dialogue structure, which the system enforces. Thus, when a user opens a "conversation for action" with another user, he is able to predict a closure of some kind, because this is defined within the template. User testing revealed a negative reaction towards Coordinator (Carasik and Grantham 1988). Carasik and Grantham blame this in part on the rigidity of the conversational structure. For example, they argue that it may be the norm within a task-orientated group that only certain statements need a response, yet Coordinator required an explicit response, violating interaction norms. This suggests a lack of *context sensitivity*. Given a certain relationship between participants, there may be no need for the intermediate steps in a "conversation for action": one utterance might be sufficient to make a number of speech acts. Coordinator's enforced structure limits participants' potential for novel intervention. To that extent, it is an unnecessary constraint on the group process, since it limits the options available for solving the problem under consideration. Carasik and Grantham's evaluation is that "the conversational templates appeared to be more a straight-jacket than a communications medium" (Carasik and Grantham 1988).

Work on the Amsterdam Conversation Environment (ACE) contrasts greatly with the approach taken with Coordinator. Designers of the ACE system (Dykstra and Carasik 1991) adhere to the principle that users rather than the system should structure communication. ACE is designed for synchronous use only, and aims to support conversation and stimulate interaction among group members. The support that is available is for the expression and preservation of people's views, rather than enforcement of a dialogue structure. Hypertext provides the means by which exchanges can be recorded. Designers of ACE are scornful of systems that "institutionalize a conversation space". They maintain that system enforcement of formalized methods of conversation leads to bureaucracy, and rules that stop conversation.

In terms of a conversation space for our proposed group editing environment, allowing user structuring and hypertext support for conversation may present problems for asynchronous users. The nonlinearity inherent in hypertext may make it difficult for asynchronous users to follow a previous conversation. In other words, the relationship between a piece of text and its context may be lost. Our earlier discussion of direct communication indicated that context can play a significant role in situating text. When the context of a text is unclear there is potential for that text to be misunderstood. Indeed, Conklin and Begeman, in their examination of linear versus nonlinear text, found that the nonlinearity of hypertext meant that users found it difficult to follow the thread of a writer's thoughts as it wound through several nodes. They suggest that "traditional linear text provides a continuous, unwinding thread of context as ideas are proposed and discussed" (Conklin and Begeman 1989).

Lying somewhere between the rigid dialogue structuring of Coordinator, and the fluidity of conversation permitted by ACE are systems such as the Information LENS system (Malone et al. 1987a), which support semi-structured messages. LENS presents users with a range of semi-structured message types, which they can use for information sharing. The writer is aided in structuring a complete message without any constraint on express-ivity, while the reader is provided with a recognizable structure that facilitates efficient search and comprehension. Semi-structured messages can be an effective means of establishing the context of a textual message (McCarthy et al. 1991b). This is an important consideration, since LENS is designed for asynchronous use, where the time lag between messages can lead to the relationship between the text and its context being lost. The message templates in LENS and the message frames used in KMS (Yoder et al. 1989) provide information about the subject of the message, the identity of participants in the conversation, and so on. In both cases the template or frame surrounds the text of the message. In effect, the message is embedded within its context border.

Semi-structured messaging systems may not be suitable for synchronous use. Message templates must be explicitly filled before the information is shared. It may take some time to complete a template, slowing the pace of interaction. Designers of some synchronous systems view the grain of text transmission inherent in semi-structured messages as too coarse for their needs. Fine grain updating may present valuable contextual information to users, allowing them to review the text as it is generated.

The importance of the grain of message sending is highlighted by Tatar et al. (1991), in their discussion of the development of Colab's Cognoter tool. Cognoter, a shared whiteboard for idea organization (Stefik et al. 1987) was initially developed to include private edit windows. Users of the Cognoter whiteboard could create an individual item using these private edit windows. When completed, an icon consisting of the first twenty char-acters of the item was created and placed in the Cognoter window. Once there, any user could change or add to any item by opening a private edit window on it. The private editing windows had an "aggregating" (Johnson and Harrison 1990) function, collecting chunks of text before transmission. Studying users' reactions to Cognoter, Tatar et al. found that groups were frustrated by the lack of transparency afforded by the whiteboard. Colab's "What You See Is What I See" (WYSIWIS) principle had been relaxed (Stefik et al. 1987) to such a degree that the group process was being ham-pered. Users wanted a finer grain of message transmission than the private windows would allow. Cognoter was redeveloped as a consequence. The redesign featured a much finer grain transmission, achieved by updating every few characters. This review of CSCW systems which support text-mediated direct communication highlights some of the issues and trade-offs designers must consider. Should the designer support the enforcement of a dialogue structure, or should users be encouraged to structure their own interaction? The rigid system-enforced structure in Coordinator presents users with a ready knowledge of the thread of a conversation, but places unnecessary constraints on expression. Nonlinear representation of participant structured conversation may present difficulties for the asynchronous user, who may be unable to re-establish the context of the text. Semi-structured messages provide an alternative, preserving and presenting the text and its context. However, in synchronous interaction, explicit completion of semi-structured messages may slow the pace of the conversation, and remove the important contextual information inherent in being able to see the emergent text.

8.3.1 Some Ideas for Conversation Space Design

The previous section looked at some CSCW systems that support textual direct communication. These were reviewed in terms of how well they support synchronous and asynchronous interaction. With this review in mind, let us consider possible design ideas for a "conversation space" within our proposed group editor. It should be stressed that these design ideas represent a first step to producing a prototype. Evaluation is required to assess how well these features support synchronous and asynchronous text-based conversation.

8.3.1.1 *Reviewable Text Transcript*

Text-based communication has an advantage over ephemeral speech (Dix 1991) in that it is reviewable. For asynchronous users particularly, it is vital that the text of previous conversations remains to be reviewed. If users were able to delete text irrevocably, then the context history of the interaction, which structures the group process, would be lost. In Conklin and Begeman's (1989) terms, the "existence" of the conversation is important. They use the notion of "existence" to emphasize that information elements and commitments that are forgotten or are not readily accessible have, in a sense, ceased to exist.

It might be of value to asynchronous users if the system indicated new conversational text. That is, text that had been generated since a participant last used the system. For the system to be able to produce such an indicator, users would have to be registered with the system.

Systems like LENS allow "directed messages" between users (Malone et al. 1987a). That is, a user can choose to send messages to a particular person, or to an enumerated group, rather than to "all". Directed messages occur in conventional collaborative writing, and therefore we should seek to support them in the proposed group editing environment. It will be interesting to observe the use of such a facility. Allowing directed messages within a small group (we envisage supporting groups of less than ten people) may present problems, in that the conversation would cease to be common to all.

8.3.1.2 Sequential Linear Text

Presenting the text of a conversation in nonlinear form may confuse asynchronous participants. They may not be able to follow the thread of the conversation. System-enforced, sequential linear text would provide a degree of structure to the conversation. Asynchronous users would be provided with a ready contextual history. Synchronous users would be able to predict that new text is always appended to the transcript. Sequentiality ensures that the presentation and acceptance of text takes place in an orderly way. True sequentiality means appending a message when it is begun, rather than when it is complete.

8.3.1.3 Indicating Participant Activity

Participant activity is a valuable source of contextual information. In face-to-face conversation information about participant activity is maximized. Participants will be aware of the interactions that led to the present utterance, they will know the content of the utterance and from whom it originated. In an environment that supports textual, distributed communication, the contextual clues available are limited. The sorts of contextual information that can be provided at the group interface are likely to vary for synchronous and asynchronous users.

In synchronous conversational interaction context can be established by representing participant status information. Indicating the identity of group members is a necessary part of this. Such information can be provided in a variety of ways. Our Conferencer system maintained a "participant list", giving the name of every user in a session; other systems use face icons. Indicating a participant's conversation space activity is another form of status information. Fine grain updating is one way of indicating synchronous user activity. Our earlier discussion of the grain of text transmission indicates that rapid updating can increase the pace of interaction, and provide an emergent context. An alternative is to allow private message composition, with appropriate activity indicators. Conferencer provided this form of support, by attaching a "compose flag" to a writer's name on the participant list. A participant might prefer to compose in private if his message is complex, requiring careful articulation. We are interested in supporting both fine and coarse grain message sending in our prototype group editing environment. We should like to observe the effects of providing users of a conversation space with a *choice*: either to transmit the message as it is typed, providing others with rapid updates, or to transmit the text when it is complete. By offering this option, users can generate their messages in a manner they consider others will understand. Offering a

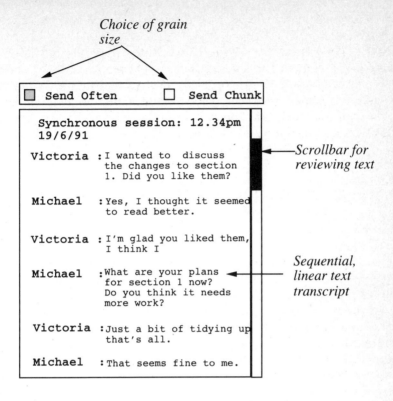

Fig. 8.2. Some conversation space design ideas.

choice of grain size may pose problems for non-expert users, who may find it difficult to understand the distinction between the two choices, and therefore, which choice to make.

We have suggested that users be given a choice of message sending grain. The designers of ACE take a similar approach to empowerment. They consider that systems should be capable of supporting constraints, but that the locus of control should remain with the users. Users should be able to choose and generate their own constraints.

Asynchronous users of our group editing environment would require information about previous activity; a contextual history of interaction. Message templates and frames, in systems like LENS and KMS, surround the text of a message with its context. Asynchronous participants are thereby provided with valuable contextual information about the message. Within a conversation space, contextual clues could be automatically generated to accompany the text. Indicating who wrote a message could be facilitated by having the system prefix a textual message with the writer's name. System-generated messages could be used to indicate when text was generated, and whether it was produced during a synchronous or asynchronous session.

Fig. 8.2 illustrates some of the conversation space design ideas put forward in this section. These design ideas can be seen as striking a balance between system-enforced structure, and user structuring. A conversation space includes some system-enforced structuring, in that a sequential, linear transcript is maintained. However, by giving users a choice of grain size for message sending we are supporting a degree of flexibility in the interaction.

8.4 Issues in Shared Editor Design

This section continues the process of deconstructing the model of cooperative work. Here, we concentrate on the interaction with and through the artefact. The artefact in our shared editing environment is the document. The group's interaction with the document will take place by means of a shared editor. This section examines the literature on shared editor applications. The aim is to consider the design of a shared editor in our proposed group editing environment.

The earlier review of computer support for direct communication discussed the issue of structure. It was suggested that structure can be system-enforced or user-defined. A similar dichotomy can be seen from a review of some existing shared editor applications, and the approaches they take to structuring the collaborative authoring task. There are applications which use a model of a document to enforce a structure. Others apply a system-enforced structure based on roles within the joint authoring task. Others again impose minimal constraint on users, allowing them to structure their own work.

Lubich and Plattner (1990) describe a system-embedded, *document model* approach to structuring a shared editor. Lubich and Plattner are involved in the MultimETH project, working on the design of a multimedia conferencing and collaborative authoring system. The aim is to support the collaborative creation, editing and management of multimedia documents. To this end, use of a formal document model has been proposed, which consists of a number of hierarchically related "structure elements", for example title, headlines, chapters, sections, etc. Each of these "structure elements" has a "content portion", for example, text, graphics, bitmap, etc. The document itself is represented in a shared workspace; the associated document model is shown as a logical tree structure in another window. By clicking on a node in the tree structure and issuing the "lock" command, the user reserves a complete subtree, or a content portion within that subtree, for exclusive write access. The approach taken by Beaudouin-Lafon (1990) is similar to that used in MultimETH, in that the document is given a certain structure. The emphasis of Beaudouin-Lafon's work is on support for collaborative software development, so the shared document might be a program file. A key issue is version control for collaborative software development. A document is defined as a hierarchy of fragments. Fragmentation is usually performed automatically by the system, following a predefined set of fragmentation rules. Each fragment can have an arbitrary number of versions. These versions are embedded in the document, rather than kept externally. When users open a document they can select a version for display according to the context. For example, users can choose to see the original version of the document, or the version held by a particular user, or their own version. Rule-based fragmentation of a document would appear to be particularly well suited to a program file where component procedures are built to follow a regular pattern. Beaudouin-Lafon's work highlights the importance of version control, which, he suggests, is an issue many other shared editing applications ignore.

Having a system-enforced document model means that users are presented with a recognizable and consistent structure. Use in MultimETH of a logical document tree provides a concise representation of the document. This could be particularly useful for asynchronous users, who will be able to establish the current state of a document from its graphical representation. A document tree structure also provides participants with a ready means of establishing a referent within a document. Users can point to a node on the tree rather than to the document itself. A document model approach to structuring a shared editor can be seen as an object-oriented approach. The components of a document model can be viewed as objects, with certain attributes attached to them. One concern with the document model approach is that rigid system enforcement of a model might hinder the group writing process, particularly the initial stages. Conklin and Begeman (1989) discuss the early stages of the individual's writing process. They maintain that "the early phase of consideration of a writing or design problem is critical and fragile, and must be allowed to proceed in a vague, contradictory, and incomplete form for as long as necessary".

Analysis of the writing process by Sharples and Pemberton (1990) maintains that writing is "an open ended design task". They describe a writer as "under-constrained", facing innumerable possible texts that could fit the goal, and a very large number of actions that can be taken at any stage. It is not clear that system level enforcement of a highly structured document model would allow sufficient flexibility.

The document model in MultimETH makes some use of social roles. When a document is created in the shared workspace the corresponding access rights must be declared by a chairman or the owner of the document. Similarly, it is the role of the chairman or document owner to change access rights during a collaboration. Access rights are "write", "read" and "annotate". The Quilt application for asynchronous collaborative document production also makes use of system-enforced social roles (Fish et al. 1988; Leland et al. 1988). Each user of Quilt is assumed to have a specific role in regard to a particular document, for example, "co-author", "commenter", "editor" and "reader". These roles, combined with the chosen document style, define access privileges to the document. Document styles are assigned to sections of text within the document. Setting the document style to "exclusive" means only the author of a section can modify it; "shared" means any co-author can modify any section; "editor" ensures that only a designated editor can modify any section, and other authors must make submissions to the editor. Roles and style must be specifically defined at the beginning of a collaboration.

Role enforcement can be a useful means of structuring and organizing collaborative writing. The allocation of roles helps ensure that activities are neither neglected nor unnecessarily duplicated. Knowledge of the their own and others' roles enables users to predict their responsibilities with the interaction. One contention, however, is that role structure may not always be obvious at the beginning of a collaborative endeavour. It may be an emergent property of the interaction. Neuwirth et al. (1990) make the point that "premature" definition of roles can lead to undesirable consequences. They suggest that if, for example, authorship is denied at the outset, then this may reduce the motivation of someone who has been defined as "non-author", and the person may be disinclined to contribute. Roles formed one element of Posner et al.'s (1991) writing process taxonomy. Their findings support the notion that roles change during a protracted interaction. They cite the example of groups whose members all started out with the intention of contributing. Later the group member with the least time to dedicate to the project fell into a consultant role, and ceased to be an active writer. There may be a conflict between roles and control in a collaborative writing task. Roles in a collaborative writing task may not be accurately reflected when other relationships interfere. A supervisor and a student may both be defined as co-authors, but the relationship between them may make this declared equality hard to sustain.

The applications discussed so far enforce a structure, be it role or document model based, upon users. An alternative is to allow users to structure their own interaction by means of the emergent social protocols. The GROVE group editor (Ellis et al. 1990, 1991) provides an example of an application which imposes minimal system constraint. The default in GROVE is a mode in which every user can see and edit any part of the shared document, and there is absolutely no locking while editing. Mode changes can be achieved by redefining the "view" of some portion of the shared environment. A user can move from the default "public" view to a "private" view, where items can be accessed by that user only, or to a "shared" view, where items are accessible to an enumerated set of users. Studies of the use of GROVE provide evidence of social protocol mediation. Ellis et al. describe how users organized themselves to work in parallel, how they organized "partitioned entry" where the group assigns particular members to refine or reorganize particular parts of the text, and how the individuals avoided colliding with others working on a particular piece of text at a particular time.

ShrEdit, a shared text editor developed at the University of Michigan (Bellotti et al. 1991), also enforces minimal system constraint. ShrEdit is a synchronous shared editing tool designed for use in face-to-face design meetings. Users can work simultaneously in any part of the document, although insertion points are locked, so that no two insertion points can be co-located. No continuous feedback is given to users to indicate the location of other users' editing activity; however users can elect to "find" or "track" other users to gain such information. Bellotti et al. (1991) report users' reactions to ShrEdit. They gave eight groups of three co-located designers three different design problems to solve using ShrEdit. Bellotti et al. were struck by the great diversity of ways in which ShrEdit was used. A number of design themes emerged from their analysis, including users' desires to know what people were doing and where. Users described "bumping into each other" because of the lack of user activity information. One group described constructing a tree representation of the texts they had created, permitting "a fairly quick address for where we were talking". In other words they were providing themselves with the means to make "referential identity" easier.

GROVE and ShrEdit are both designed for synchronous use, they allow parallel editing and are characterized by fine grain (or no) locking, and rapid updating. Frequent updates minimize the divergence between different views on a text (Olson et al. 1990), ensuring that each user sees the most up-to-date version of a shared document. Continuous updating can be thought of as a way of "communicating through the artefact". Participants in a synchronous interaction will be able to watch others' text as it is created. Fine grain text transmission mitigates against what Chafe (1986) cites as one of the advantages of written textual communication. Writers, he claims, can revise and polish their thoughts before communicating them; a facility not available to speakers whose second thoughts and revisions are laid bare before their audience. Providing private workspaces (Olson et al. 1990) gives users the option to carry out this polishing and revision of their contributions before including them in the shared document. Olson et al. (1990) comment that many group editors provide this for free, in that they are embedded in multi-tasking environments where other windows are available for private work. Adopting this solution, however, would mean that important user activity information would be lost to other participants. Ellis et al. (1991) have considered the issue of private work, and suggest a novel means by which private user activity information can be denoted. They suggest that private user text editing activity can be shown in the form of a "cloudburst". Textual modifications are shown immediately to the person who initiates them, but are indicated on other users' screens by the appearance of "clouds" over the original text. The position and size of a cloud indicates the approximate location and extent of the modification.

GROVE and ShrEdit are designed for synchronous use only. They do not attempt to support asynchronous interaction. In ShrEdit, for example, this means that no provision is made for recording the context of a text, for maintaining versions or for reviewing changes. The LENS and KMS asynchronous messaging systems discussed earlier deliberately separate text and context, "framing" the text within a context border. Users can re-establish the context of a message by referring to its border. We require our proposed group editor to support synchronous and asynchronous interaction. It is important, therefore, to consider firstly, the separation and recording of text and context, and then, the means by which asynchronous users are able to re-establish the context of a text. The document model discussed earlier lends itself well to the separation and reinstatement of text and context. Contextual information can be associated with document model "objects". For example, it would be possible to establish who wrote what text object, when it was written, whether it had been changed, by whom and when, whether there were access privileges associated with it and so on.

This review of shared editing applications has once again shown up the various trade-offs that designers must consider. Rigid enforcement of roles or a document model may be too inflexible to encompass the range of techniques groups employ when writing together. Role enforcement, however, can help ensure that activities are not ignored or duplicated. A document model lends itself well to "object" status, and is amenable to graphical representation. Single editor, multiple cursor systems with minimal system intervention allow users to structure their own interaction, but do not support asynchronous interaction.

8.4.1 Some Ideas for Shared Editor Design

The previous section offered a brief review of some existing shared editor applications. In the light of that review, this section considers possible ideas for the design of a shared editor artefact within our proposed group editing environment. Once again it should be made clear that evaluation of the prototype is required to assess how well the system supports the group editing task.

8.4.1.1 Structuring

Group editing systems differ in the support they provide for structuring the editing task. In some systems the shared editor is structured by an embedded model of the document under production. Other applications use system-enforced role assignment to structure the access to a shared document. Others still allow the group to structure their own work, and impose minimal system constraint. We should like to consider combining elements of these approaches in the design of our group editing environment.

An objection to system-enforced document model structuring is that it is too rigid, and does not reflect the way people write together. This would appear to be the case particularly at the initial stages of a collaborative authoring endeavour. An advantage of document model structuring is that it readily supports the graphical representation of a document. Such a logical model could be a useful point of group reference for synchronous users, and a good means of assessing the current state of a document for each asynchronous user.

One might consider allowing users to determine their *own* document structure. Support could be given in the form of a graphical representation of the structure they choose. Users would be able to "chunk" a document into segments which they considered appropriate, as the interaction progressed. Each segment would be graphically illustrated. The graphical representation of the document could be used as a means of gaining edit access to a segment. Thus, clicking on the representation of a segment would allow users access to the editor containing the existing text of that segment. Allowing users to manipulate the graphical representation of their self-structured document could provide a means of refining and altering the ordering of segments.

Each user-defined segment could be given "object" status. Attributes of such an object could include details of when the segment was edited and by whom. Associating such information with the text of the segment would provide asynchronous users with support for re-establishing the context in which a piece of text was written. Users could be provided with a *history* of the current text of a segment. Such information could also be used by the system to indicate automatically new text to each asynchronous user.

There are various ways in which the history of a segment could be presented. One could envisage provision of a "meta-segment". This could take the form of a copy of the text of the segment, suitably annotated with information about who wrote and changed pieces of text and when. Another possibility would be to allow users to query the text of the segment itself. For example, a user selecting a line or paragraph could be presented with the history of that selection.

Included among the ideas for a conversation space design was the suggestion that users be given a *choice* of support for message sending. Continuing this theme of providing optional tool support, one could consider providing users with the option of segment ownership. As owner, a user could be entitled to restrict access to the segment, for example, assign read-only roles to the other members of the group.

8.4.1.2 Version Control

The process by which people write is highly complex. Text will inevitably require revision. Coordinating revisions among a group is a non-trivial task. The work of Beaudouin-Lafon has highlighted the importance of version control in collaborative writing. He has implemented system-supported version control, embedding versions within the parent document or program file.

We are interested to see how groups handle the issue of versioning. To this end we would like to provide optional tools, which users can select to assist in version control if they choose. Participants will be able to use a conversation space discussion to consider different versions. In addition, one might consider the provision of a "dumping bay" where users can off-load segments they do not wish to include in the final document. Such a facility could be operationalized by allowing users to move a graphically represented segment from the logical structure to the "dumping bay".

Another feature which may be useful in version control is a voting tool. Participants may not be able to agree on a particular version using the conversation space. In such a situation an optional voting tool could be used. Design would have to consider notifying asynchronous users that their vote is required.

8.4.1.3 Sharing a Segment

Many existing synchronous CSCW systems provide users with the facility to work privately, as well as publicly. Private workspaces allow participants to polish and revise their contributions before communicating them.

Allowing private work means explicit support must be given to the locking of a segment. When one user cannot see where his colleague is working, then he cannot ensure that he will avoid editing the same text. The potential for contention is obvious. One possibility would be to support segment level locking. Thus when a user selects a graphically represented segment, that segment is locked. A locked segment would allow write access to the lock owner, and read access to the other users. Allowing synchronous users the option to work privately means that the readers of a locked segment will see an out-of-date version of the text. The system must indicate this important contextual information. Informing users of where a colleague is working may be insufficient. The "cloudburst" metaphor suggested by Ellis et al. gives users an idea of the size of text currently under preparation. Information as to the degree of activity in a colleague's private workspace may also be of value.

Our aim is to allow users to alternate freely between private and public work. In this way users are able to choose how they "communicate through the artefact". Segment level locking would avoid the problems of users "bumping into each other" and experiencing unpredictable or chaotic interaction. To facilitate public work, rapid updating is required. Even with public work there may be a need for user activity information to be denoted. Indicating a pause in a colleague's work, for example, may be of value.

Segment level locking ensures that contention is avoided, but at a cost. Users cannot work in parallel on the same segment. However, with a

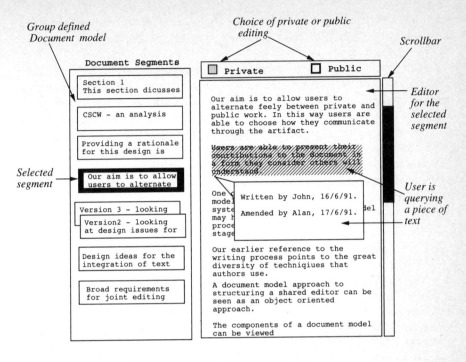

Fig. 8.3. Some shared editor design ideas.

segment-based model, it would be possible for each member of the group to work on a different segment at the same time. Thus there is support for some form of parallel working.

Fig. 8.3 illustrates some of the design ideas proposed. Once again, these ideas can be seen as combining elements of system-enforced structuring and user-defined structure. We are keen that users structure their own document segmentation in a way that is agreeable to the group. We wish to provide a choice of private or public editing. However, a degree of system enforcement is inherent in the segment locking strategy proposed. Many of our design ideas focus on supporting the presentation of contextual information. An important consideration here has been to present not only the current interaction state, but also a context history for asynchronous users.

8.5 Design Ideas for Integrating Conversation Spaces and Shared Editor

The previous two sections deconstructed the model of cooperative work introduced in Section 8.2. First we looked at computer support for direct communication between participants. This involved consideration of designs for a conversation space. Next we looked at interaction with and through the document artefact. This involved reviewing designs for shared editing.

In order to support asynchronous, as well as synchronous interaction, we need both conversation space and shared editing facilities in our shared editing environment. In this section we consider how to support the connectivity between these two communication spaces. We are broaching the subject of how to design an *environment* rather than its individual components. The aim is to consider how the system as a whole would function. In effect, what we want to do here is to *reconstruct* the model of cooperative work, looking at the integration of conversation spaces and shared editor in a single environment.

8.5.1 Establishing Referential Identity

Earlier discussion mentioned the importance of grounding references to artefacts. In face-to-face communication, pointing, looking at and touching the object of a conversation helps the group establish "referential identity". In some CSCW systems, e.g. rIBIS and Boardnoter (Stefik et al. 1987), identifying referents is facilitated by providing telepointers which allow users to "point" to screen objects. Control is usually held by one person at a time, while others see the movement of the pointer on their own screens. Telepointing is suitable for synchronous communication, but not for asynchronous. So what alternatives are there that would be effective for both synchronous and asynchronous interaction? One possibility would be to associate a conversation space with each document segment. Our suggestion is that users should be free to segment a document as they chose, rather than having to follow a rigid document model such as "title", "abstract", "section" and so on. A conversation space could be generated automatically to accompany each segment. The conversation space would be provided for users to talk about the associated segment, while the segment itself would be available for the document text. A criticism of this approach is that it may not be sufficiently *context sensitive*. It would allow a conversation about a segment to be associated with that segment, but would not support the sort of direct deictic reference that telepointing provides.

An alternative option would be to provide a facility more akin to annotation. In traditional paper and pencil authoring, asynchronous communication about the identity of a referent is easily established by annotation, for example, the writing of comments and highlighting of text. There are several CSCW systems which support text annotation. The Collaborative Annotator system (Koszarek et al. 1990) is a multi-user document review system, which allows graphic, voice and video annotations to be associated with a shared document image. The document is scanned, and its image displayed on the group interface. This image can be annotated with soft-ware highlighter pens, multi-font text and yellow "stickies". The Quilt system also supports annotation. It differs from the Collaborative Annotator in that it supports editing of the document as well as review. Indication of an annotation is embedded within the text of a document. This ensures that the referent of the annotation is clear.

We should like to explore the potential for embedding annotations within the shared document of our group editing environment, that is, having annotations that "point" to specific text. In terms of structure, anno-tations could be structured as conversation spaces, allowing sequential, reviewable contributions. Thus, rather than having one conversation space per segment as suggested earlier, users would be able to generate a number of annotation conversation spaces. These they could embed within a seg-ment's text, assisting with accurate referential identity. Annotations that are structured as topic-specific conversation spaces may overcome some of the problems of annotation put forward by Neuwirth et al. (1990). They main-tain that writers are frustrated by the lack of consistency in comments that contradict each other. The more reviews there are, the more pressing this problem becomes. Annotations that are communication spaces may help alleviate such difficulties, since different reviewers would be able to see the comments of others, and add their suggestions to the appropriate topic-specific area.

Fig. 8.4 illustrates these two approaches to establishing referential identity: Fig. 8.4a shows a conversation space accompanying a document segment; and Fig. 8.4b shows annotations embedded within the document segment. These are displayed as "think bubbles" that users can open, read and edit.

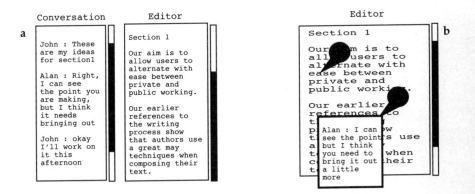

Fig. 8.4. Two alternative ideas for establishing referential identity: **a** segment editor with a conversation space, and **b** annotations.

8.5.2 Providing a "Global" Conversation Space

Design ideas for our proposed group editing environment included support for user-defined document segmentation, with an annotation facility available for each segment. What is lacking is a facility for "global" coordination. A "global", ever-present conversation space may help to provide this function. It would provide a window for procedural group discussion, for example, conversation about how to perform the task, what division of labour is appropriate, what documentation segmentation to choose, and so on.

8.5.3 Playback Facilities

An important requirement of our proposed group editing environment is that both synchronous and asynchronous modes of interaction are supported. For asynchronous users particularly, it is important to make clear the context of previous interactions. One way to support this reconstruction of context is to provide "playback" facilities. These would allow users to see what interaction had taken place since they last used the environment. Playback could be provided for individual components of the group editing environment. For example, users could play back events within a particular document segment. One could also envisage "global playback", where users are invited to step through the changes to all components of the group editing environment in sequence. A degree of context sensitivity is provided with this strategy since users would be able to integrate changes to different components. For example, users would be able to integrate the sequence of changes to the document with new or changed annotations.

8.6 Discussion

This chapter marks the first steps in a design process. The aim has been to consider support for collaborative writing in the form of a shared editing environment.

We began by introducing a model of cooperative work and applying that model to the task of collaborative writing. Group writing involves direct communication between participants, and interaction with and through the document artefact. Group writing can be a protracted exercise and is amenable to both concurrent and asynchronous work. With these observations in mind, we proceeded by deconstructing the model of cooperative work into its component parts. First we considered direct communication and drew from the literature on computer-mediated communication to propose some ideas for conversation space design. Next, we looked at interaction with, and indirect communication through, the shared document. This involved a review of some of the literature on shared editing applications, and some ideas for shared editor design. One fundamental design issue, which affects both computer-mediated communication systems and shared editing applications, concerns the approach to task structuring. One can identify two broadly differing approaches. Some systems are designed to enforce a particular structure, others encourage users to structure their own interaction. The design ideas that have been put forward for possible inclusion in our group editing environment reflect an attempt to strike a balance between these two approaches. An important design consideration has been the presentation of contextual information. One aim has been to present not only the current interaction state, but also a context history for asynchronous users.

By proposing that our group editing environment will have both conversation spaces and shared editing we are suggesting provision of a range of different "channels" for different types of communication. For example, a document segment will provide a task-specific communication channel, while the global conversation space might be used as a channel for general procedural discussion. These "channels" are not physical, in the sense of the visual, auditory and linguistic channels that are available in face-to-face communication. They can be thought of as "virtual channels": these describe the communication media that participants perceive (McCarthy and Miles 1990). Participants' perception of a communication channel will be influenced by its appearance, and the way they interact with it. Giving users a range of differently styled channels can increase the effectiveness of their communication. For example, when a channel is perceived as supporting a particular type of communication, then that channel will help to specify the intended meaning of messages received on it. Receiving related information on more than one channel can have a strengthening effect. For instance, seeing an annotation suggesting a change to a segment, and then seeing the change made to the text, reinforces the intention. Provision of a range of channels also allows for deictic referencing, so users can refer to "this segment" or "that annotation". Deictic references can increase the efficiency of communication (McCarthy and Monk 1991).

Having separated the model of cooperative work into its component parts, we then considered its reconstruction. The focus was on how to integrate conversation spaces and shared editing into a single environment. In conceptual terms the aim is to provide interrelated and complementary channels: interrelated in the sense that the relationship between the channels is made clear, complementary in the sense that different channels can mutually supply each other's lack. For example, document segments and segment annotations will be closely related, both concerned with a particular piece of text. The communication channels they provide will be complementary, with a document segment providing a channel for indirect communication through the document, and the annotations providing a channel of direct communication about the document. The hope is that providing a range of complementary and interrelated channels will help users to achieve the common understanding (*e* in Fig. 8.1) that is central to successful cooperative work.

Acknowledgement   This work was funded by SERC grant GR/F/01895.

Chapter 9

A Case Study in Task Analysis for the Design of a Collaborative Document Production System

I. Denley, A. Whitefield and J. May

9.1 Introduction

Collaborative writing of paper-based documents is a complex activity that is currently poorly supported by interactive computer systems (Sharples et al., this volume). Multimedia documents are complex entities whose storage and presentation in computers has only recently become a tractable research and development problem (Alty 1991). Almost inevitably, therefore, interactive computer systems to support the collaborative production of multimedia documents are complex systems with which we have very little experience at the moment. This chapter describes the design of a prototype multi-author multimedia document production (MAMMDP) system. In particular, the chapter concentrates on how the system's tasks were analysed and represented during the early stages of the design. The aim of the chapter is to relate our ideas and experiences from the analysis and design work, in the hope that some of them may prove useful to others concerned with MAMMDP. We believe that both the processes and the products of our analysis and design work can be informative about the development of MAMMDP systems.

The chapter begins by introducing the context of the design and our reasons for developing the prototype. Section 9.3 presents some basic concepts underlying the task analysis work, while Section 9.4 describes how the analyses were carried out and represented. The chapter concludes by illustrating some features of the final design and discussing the utility of the task analysis approach.

9.2 Context of the Design

The design work reported here was carried out as part of the ongoing RACE 1067 GUIDANCE project. The European Commission's RACE programme is concerned with the development of integrated broadband communication (IBC) systems, which will merge computing, networking and telecommunication technologies to deliver a large number of services to users at a single terminal. The GUIDANCE project addresses the general question of how to ensure that the services provided to the user can be used efficiently and effectively; and more specifically, the question of how might a number of services required by a human end-user be integrated to maximize their ease of use?

9.2.1 IBC and End-User Service Integration

In a typical current office an office worker might use on a daily basis a number of services, including a telephone, a fax machine, a remote database, a word processor and a spreadsheet. With IBC technology, all these services (along with many others) will be delivered to users at the same physical terminal, since the various technologies will be integrated in the same network. However, although the physical problems of moving between and accessing separate items of equipment will largely disappear in IBC systems, the mental problems of learning, conceptualizing and recalling how to use services will not disappear, and may even be compounded by an increasingly large number and variety of services becoming available. Users will almost certainly be faced with service integration problems affecting ease of use, such as: variations in the semantics of input device events; inconsistent screen layout conventions; confusion between operating procedures; incompatibilities between the representations of objects; and differences between representations to support collaborative working. Each of these integration problems will tend to have a negative effect on the ease of use of the set of services. This effect might manifest itself in various ways, for example, increases in learning times, or in data input times, or in command language syntax errors, or in user dissatisfaction, and so on.

9.2.2 Reasons for Undertaking the Design

The GUIDANCE project has explored three related techniques that aim to improve service integration for end-users. First, there is the task analysis technique which is the subject of this chapter. Second, we have developed *service integration principles* aimed at supporting IBC system designers. Third, we have developed a *design method* which incorporates both the task analysis and the principles. An introduction to all three techniques can be found in Whitefield et al. (1992).

Given these activities on the project, there were a number of reasons for designing a prototype system. We wanted to demonstrate that the task analysis and the design method were both usable and effective, and to contribute to their development. We also wanted to demonstrate the efficacy and usability of the principles, and to contribute to their development. In addition, the prototype system would be used in the laboratory evaluation of the principles.

The design of the prototype system, therefore, was undertaken for several reasons. We should like to emphasize, however, the focus of the project in contrast to a project focusing on MAMMDP itself. GUIDANCE is primarily concerned with end-user service integration, and is using MAM-MDP only as an application within which service integration can be explored. This means that we were not specifically aiming to create either a novel document production system or a state-of-the-art system, except with respect to the issues of end-user service integration. The design was undertaken as a scheduled and constrained development activity (within the discipline of a research and development project) to contribute to our understanding of techniques to solve service integration problems; the details and formality of the task observations and analyses described later should be considered with this in mind.

This chapter concentrates on those aspects of the design directly concerned with the task analysis. Further details of the design activity as a whole can be found in May et al. (1992).

9.2.3 The Selection of the Application

IBC systems will support a wide range of applications, in both the domestic and commercial sectors, and it is important, therefore, that our task analysis, principles and design method be generalizable across a range of applications. The choice of application for the prototype design was motivated by a desire to maximize overlap between applications. Eason (1988) regards the main benefits of IBC service integration as likely to occur in the field of computer supported cooperative work (CSCW), where people who may be widely separated geographically can communicate and work together. Additionally, IBC technologies will allow the transmission of many different media (sound, text, static image, moving image, etc.). To satisfy these characteristics of IBC we chose an application dealing with the collaborative production of multimedia documents by distributed authors.

The specific application chosen was the production of multimedia holiday documents (see Section 9.4.2.2). This allowed us to collaborate with another project, RACE 1038 MCPR (Multimedia Communication, Processing and Representation), which was implementing holiday information databases on prototype multimedia terminals. The interface software provided by GUIDANCE runs using the hardware and database software provided by MCPR.

In the context of this book, it is important to recognize that collaborative writing in this instance is not concerned only with text or with paper; rather, it concerns the production of a virtual document which may contain several different media, and which may only be "readable" in its entirety by using a multimedia terminal.

9.3 The Task Analysis Concepts

Before presenting the task analysis that we used in our design, it is necessary to present the basic concepts that underlie it. This section draws heavily on the conception for HCI engineering proposed by Dowell and Long (1989), but incorporates several developments or interpretations of that conception. Although the concepts are presented below with specific reference to IBC systems, we believe they are generally applicable to inter-active systems and are not restricted to IBC. The fundamental distinctions in Dowell and Long's conception are between an interactive work system (IWS), a work domain, and performance. For IBC systems we begin with the concept of an interactive IBC work system (IIWS).

An IIWS consists of a set of *behaviours*, supported by a set of *structures* which enable those behaviours to occur. The scope of the IIWS is those structures and behaviours which a designer may specify as part of a design solution, and therefore includes hardware, software and end-users. The behaviours of an IIWS are the behaviours that are relevant to the perfor-mance of the work for which the IIWS is designed; for example, sending messages, storing and retrieving information, creating documents, and so on. The structures of an IIWS are the components that support those behav-iours; that is, the representations and processes of the communicating entities and of the communication channels between them.

An IIWS is designed to perform work within a *work domain*. A work domain is a set of physical or abstract objects relevant to the work being performed; for example, messages, documents, letters. The objects have attributes, some of which can change state. A *work goal* is a particular desired state of the attributes of work domain objects.

Work is some intended state transformation carried out by an IIWS within its work domain; that is, work changes the states of particular domain object attributes to those specified in a work goal. The IIWS performs work by carrying out *work tasks*, which are sets of IIWS behav-iours directed towards a work goal. Work tasks can be distinguished from *enabling tasks*, which change the state of some IIWS structures, but not the states of domain objects. This distinction between types of task is discussed and developed further in Section 9.4.

The *performance* of an IIWS in carrying out its work can be defined as a function of two factors: the quality of the product (i.e. how well the final state of the domain compares with the state specified in the work goal); and the incurred resource costs (i.e. the resources required by the various IIWS entities in accomplishing the work). A most effective IIWS would minimize the resource costs in performing work with a given product quality. A distinction can be made between actual performance (the level of performance actually achieved by an IIWS) and desired performance (the level of performance an IIWS is intended to achieve).

IBC developers face the problem of designing the behaviour of the IIWS such that it achieves the intended changes in the work domain at the desired level of performance. Designing IIWS behaviours involves specifying and implementing those structures of the communicating entities (including the end-users) and the communicating channels that will support the intended behaviours.

The above conceptual analysis underlies the task analysis described below in that it is explicit in its analysis of the IIWS's work in terms of work tasks, enabling tasks, and work domain objects.

9.4 A Task Analysis of Multi-Author Multimedia Document Production

A task analysis is required as part of the design of any interactive computer system, although it may effectively be performed under another name (e.g. systems analysis) or may only be performed implicitly. Since a task is a set of work system behaviours directed towards some goal, a task analysis is therefore the analysis of the goals the work system is trying to achieve and of the behaviours by which it achieves them; the task analysis may also include the work system structures which support the behaviours, particularly if it represents a description of an extant work system rather than an abstract prescription for a work system to be designed. This section reports a task analysis which is in part intended to ensure end-user service integration in IIWS design, although the analysis is a general one and is not restricted either to IIWSs or to supporting end-user service integration. Section 9.4.1 presents the task observations on which the analysis is based. The detailed product of the analysis is presented in Section 9.4.2, and a specific illustrative instantiation of the tasks in Section 9.4.3.

9.4.1 Task Observations

Since multimedia multi-author production of virtual documents is not possible using existing technology, it was not possible to study this domain directly. Instead, observations were carried out on work domains which share critical features with the target domain. Two cycles of task observations were carried out, all on tasks involving multiple collaborating authors. The first cycle involved three tasks, which were selected to give broad coverage of the data types available with IBC systems. These tasks were:

1. Video editing

2. Desktop publishing

3. Multi-author writing

The results of this first set of task observations were then analysed and represented. The second cycle of task observations was carried out to assess and refine these initial analyses. The tasks studied in this second cycle were:

1. Software product localization

2. Newspaper editing

Each of these five tasks involved several people contributing to the final product, and so were multi-author tasks, although they varied in the simultaneity of contributions and communications between individuals and in the communication methods available. They also varied in terms of the materials being worked upon, but taken together, the tasks provide a spread of functionality over the multimedia area envisaged in the target application. The various interviews mentioned below were all semi-structured, in the sense that although the interviews were formally structured in line with our basic task analysis concepts (work goals, work tasks, enabling tasks, roles, objects and actions) we were also able to explore interesting issues more widely when appropriate. Each of the studies will be described in turn below.

9.4.1.1 *Video Editing Task*

We observed, and discussed with the relevant staff, some video editing tasks carried out within a commercial company specializing in video post-production. The observations were conducted in one period of approximately one and a half hours. The tasks involved editing the final master tapes for television advertisements, and copying the master tapes for distribution to the television companies for transmission. These tasks are therefore the final stages in the preparation of television advertisements.

For the tasks observed, the work system was comprised of: one editor (responsible for specifying the content of the final master tape); one video controller (responsible for performing the actual editing as specified by the editor); one video technician (responsible for loading/unloading the tapes and for maintaining the tape decks in good working order); one control desk; several tape decks; and several video monitors. For other tasks that were discussed the work system might also include: further interested personnel, such as the director, advertising agent and client (any of whom might intervene with additional requirements for the advertisement); one mixing desk; one lettering computer; one digital special video effects computer; and one compact disc player for sound effects.

9.4.1.2 Desktop Publishing Task

We observed, and discussed with the relevant staff, a number of desktop publishing tasks concerned with the production and publication of a widely distributed university newsletter. The tasks involved the editing of submitted articles and graphics, and the overall design and layout of the publication. The observations were conducted in one period of approximately one and a half hours.

The work system for the tasks studied consisted of an editor (responsible for design and layout and content alterations), a high quality office PC as hardware, and desktop publishing software. Other personnel involved at other stages of the work included authors, an editorial panel, an artist and a director.

9.4.1.3 Multi-Author Writing Task

We conducted separate interviews, over approximately two hours, with two academic staff at University College London (UCL) about the writing of:

1. Multi-author academic papers for submission to journals or conferences.

2. Multi-author proposals for research funding.

Since these tasks normally occur over long periods, it was decided that interviews based around case studies would be more productive than direct observations. A total of five case studies were discussed. Three of the case studies related to documents still being written at the times of the interviews. The two authors interviewed were relatively experienced at writing multi-author papers and proposals.

For the paper-writing tasks discussed, the work systems were comprised of: one primary author; one or more co-authors; one or more commentators; and one or more word processors. For the proposal-writing task, additional work system components included one or more coordinators, plus non-paper communications devices i.e. electronic mail (email) facilities and fax.

9.4.1.4 Software Product Localization

We conducted interviews, over a period of approximately three hours, with personnel from a UK computer company that had developed a software package for marketing throughout Europe. The package consisted of a user manual together with a set of diskettes containing the application software. The task was to produce local versions of this package in several European languages including French, German, Spanish, Italian, Dutch, Swedish and Norwegian. The package will be marketed to European companies for use within their data processing departments by staff skilled in the use of personal computers.

For these tasks the work systems were comprised of: a project coordinator responsible for controlling and scheduling the total project from receiving the source material through translating, typesetting, printing and shipping to the countries concerned; a technical writer who checks the source material and legal information appropriate for each target country; a team of translators who produce local language versions of the user manual, the software screen messages, the diskette labels and the binder covers; a typesetter or desktop publishing operator who produces the text in each language from the translators' diskettes; an artist who produces the camera-ready copy by pasting up the translated text and diagrams; and various graphical workstations.

9.4.1.5 *Newspaper Editing*

We interviewed, over approximately six hours, the computer manager for a national Sunday newspaper. We also observed, over approximately six hours, the production of a regional daily newspaper in the south of England, and interviewed various editorial and production personnel. The tasks involved in newspaper production are very varied, but include: materials input (text, artwork, layout, etc.); paste-up; story editing; copy-tasting; and so on.

The complete work systems for the newspapers studied are large and complex, but include at least the following entities: head office reporters and editors (including designers, artists, sub-editors, etc.); branch office reporters and editors; home and field reporters; copytakers; composers; text editing software; layout editing software; graphics editing software; scanners; image setters; raster image processors; printers; phototypesetters; email and remote database access; and so on.

9.4.2 The Task Analysis

9.4.2.1 *Treatment of the Observational Data*

The observations discussed above were analysed to produce the task analysis product described below. It might be felt that the details and extent of the collaborative document production observations are insufficient to support fully the task analysis product. We certainly would not dispute that more detailed and extensive observations would be likely to provide a more valid and reliable product. However, it is important to remember that these observations are part of a short-term development activity within a project focusing on service integration. Our intention was not to produce a definitive model of MAMMDP; the kind of long-term strategy proposed by Sharples et al. (this volume), incorporating observational studies of the process of collaborative authoring, would be much more appropriate for such an intention. Nevertheless, we do believe that the description of MAMMDP presented below is largely consistent with the task framework presented by Sharples et al., and hence with the literature more generally.

The data were analysed to identify the elements most relevant to the design process adopted within GUIDANCE. This meant identifying for each study: the work goal, roles, basic tasks (whether work or enabling), objects, and actions (behaviours). Lists of each of these entities were produced for each task studied by analysis of the data collected (in the form of audio recordings and notes). The strategy for inclusion at this stage was liberal (i.e. go for over-inclusion rather than exclusion).

To complete the analysis, it was necessary to develop a more detailed description of the target application (the collaborative production of multimedia holiday documents). This more detailed description has been termed the *scenario*, and is briefly presented in Section 9.4.2.2. The task analysis product that was developed with respect to this scenario is presented in Section 9.4.2.3.

9.4.2.2 *The Scenario*

There will be two or more users, who may work simultaneously. Users will be adults of either gender, and will share the cultural norms prevalent in the countries of the EC. They will be professionals experienced in at least one of two areas: the holiday industry and/or document production; they will also be experienced in the use of interactive computer work systems. All users will have their own workstations.

In addition to the users, the work system could include all possible IBC services, in any combinations, and will operate in standard office environments.

The organization is a large travel agency or tour operator which is physically distributed (i.e. there can be no face-to-face communications between users – they must all be done via the work system). The organization has a democratic management style (i.e. free communications on any topics between users are encouraged). Management is hierarchic not heterarchic (so ultimately one person has final responsibility for the document). The *work goal* is to have a multimedia document which allows holiday makers to select a suitable holiday from those offered by the organization. The work to be achieved by the work system, therefore, is to agree the content of, and to construct, such a document.

Taking performance as comprising task quality and resource costs, the specification of the desired performance of the work system is that acceptable *task quality* is the construction of a suitable document, and acceptable *resource costs* are minimal cognitive effort by the users in operating the devices.

This scenario does not concern the creation of the data that are used in the document (e.g. calculating hotel prices, filming video clips, writing guidebook information, etc.). All the data to go into the document are assumed to exist in electronic form already – the task is to select, collate, edit, link and organize these data.

9.4.2.3 Details of the Task Analysis

The scenario and the task observations were used to construct the task analysis below. Note that what is presented here is the task analysis product, which was produced iteratively. It should not be inferred from the description below that the details of the work domain were fully specified before the work tasks were specified; rather, the different components of the analysis were produced in an iterative and mutually influential manner. The analysis is presented in three parts, concerning the work domain, the work tasks and the enabling tasks.

The work domain   The work to be achieved by the work system is to plan and to construct a multimedia document that allows holiday makers to select a suitable holiday. Both planning and construction will require communication between the various personnel involved in the complete work system.

Given this description, there are three types of objects in the work domain:

1. A document, which is virtual and comprises linked components in different media.

2. A plan, which indicates the intended structure and content of the document, plus comments about it.

3. A message: a communication between members of the work group.

The highest level transformations in the domain will therefore be transformations of the plan (from incomplete to complete), transformations of the document (from unrelated elements to a related document), and transformations of the messages (between work group members). Note that the concept of a plan is interpreted broadly rather than narrowly: it includes annotations and comments about the document as well as particular requirements and specifications for it. As such the distinction between plan and document corresponds exactly to Sharples et al.'s identification of a need for a clear distinction between the object-level text and the meta-level of written plans, constraints and annotations (this volume).

The plan and document objects can each be decomposed into various sub-objects. The message object, however, has no sub-objects. The plan object has sub-objects of: *requirement* (an indication of desirable qualities of the document); *specification* (an indication of document contents); and *comment* (a statement of an author's views on aspects of the documents or plans). The document object has sub-objects: text, tables, audio, graphics, animation, still image, moving image, and link (which connects the contents of the document). Two examples of sub-objects and their attributes are given below:

OBJECT: plan
SUB-OBJECT: *requirement*

Attributes	*Attribute values*
content:	the details of the requirement
identifier:	unique identifier for the requirement
originator:	name of person who created the requirement
medium:	spoken / textual / other
status:	proposed / rejected / agreed
implementation:	met / unmet
importance:	mandatory / preferred / unimportant
revisor:	person making most recent amendment to the requirement
author:	name (or class) of person responsible for meeting the requirement
reviewer:	name of person who evaluates the requirement
format:	rhetorical organization (e.g. list, table, etc.)

OBJECT: document
SUB-OBJECT: *moving image*

Attributes	*Attribute values*
layout:	the details of the moving image design
format:	frames / clips
style:	picture quality / visual techniques
legibility:	the discriminibility of the moving image
colour:	any value for colour
date:	the date this sub-object was created
history:	any amendments made to this sub-object
size:	the sub-object's spatial / memory requirement
location:	the sub-object's physical / virtual location
version:	the version number
security:	access / locked / unlocked etc.

The work tasks   During the task analysis we tried to identify the various work tasks,[1] i.e. the various work sub-goals and the IIWS behaviours and structures associated with each. After analysing each of the task observations in this way we used the results to develop a behavioural description for the work sub-goals of having planned and constructed a multimedia document that allows readers to select a suitable holiday.

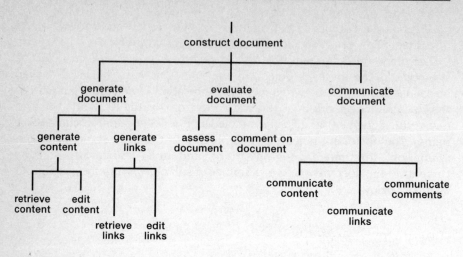

Fig. 9.1. Task hierarchy for high level work task *Construct Document*.

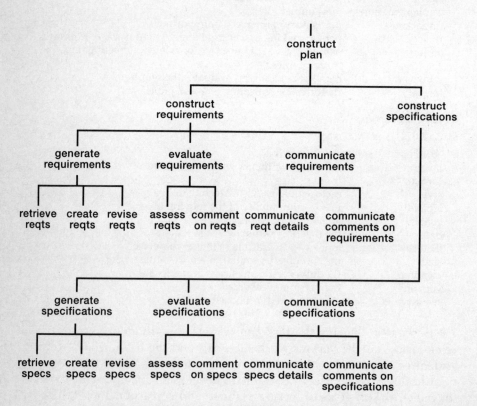

Fig. 9.2. Task hierarchy for high level task *Construct Plan*.

The overall work goal of creating the document is seen as comprising two high level work tasks: *Construct Document* and *Construct Plan*. Figs 9.1 and 9.2, respectively, show how these high level work tasks are decomposed. A work task should be thought of as a behaviour and a work goal; however, because the terms used to describe the behaviour and the goal are usually very similar, in Figs 9.1 and 9.2 only the behaviours are shown and the work goals are omitted. Some comments to assist in interpreting these behavioural decompositions of the work tasks are:

1. No sequencing whatsoever is implied by the diagrams. That is, any work task (on either figure) could follow any other work task; there is no left-to-right (or any other) ordering implied.

2. The figures depict the work tasks of the work system as a whole and not for any role or individual within it. Thus, any one user performing a particular role (such as Editor or Commentator) might carry out only a subset of the work tasks shown.

3. Each work task is expressed, as far as possible, as an action–object pairing. As one moves down a level in the hierarchy, either the action term or the object term changes, but not both. This is simply a heuristic to try to improve the coherence in the figures.

4. The sub-tasks for *Generate Requirement/Specification* are *Create Requirement/Specification*, *Retrieve Requirement/Specification*, and *Revise Requirement/Specification*. The sub-tasks for *Generate Document* are *Retrieve Link/Content* and *Edit Link/Content*, i.e. there is no sub-task *Create Link/Content*. This is because the task in the scenario is described as not being concerned with creating the document data, merely with their collation and editing.

5. Constructing a requirement, specification or document is seen as a process of generation and evaluation. This view is based on the blackboard architecture (Hayes-Roth 1983), in which the basic processes are generation and evaluation; strategic concerns are dealt with by *control* of these processes. This control is opportunistic, incorporating both top-down and bottom-up mechanisms. There is good reason to think that the blackboard architecture is an appropriate one for describing the writing task. Writing has been identified as a design task (Sharples et al., this volume) and the blackboard architecture has been used for modelling other design tasks (e.g. Hayes-Roth et al. 1986; Whitefield 1989). More generally, the architecture has been shown to be capable of modelling a wide variety of creative mental tasks (see Engelmore and Morgan 1988). Finally, as Dillon (this volume) has suggested, most models of writing have a similar set of basic processes, and generation/evaluation can be seen as another instance of this similar basic set.

The IIWS behaviours described in the above decompositions all aim to achieve the IIWS's work sub-goals of planning and creating a multimedia document, in that they will change the states of work domain objects (i.e. of plans and documents) closer to their state as specified in the work goal.

Enabling tasks   The work tasks above are not the *only* behaviours the authors will carry out. In addition, they will need to carry out at least some behaviours which concern the use of communication services, such as a videotelephone. Examples of such behaviours are: setting up a videotelephone link, accessing a video database, invoking and closing down a video editing service, and so on. In the task analysis, these behaviours would *not* be directly associated with the work goal of planning and producing a multimedia document, since none of them changes the states of work domain objects. Rather, they would have the goal of "service established" (whether a communication or editing service); this defines a desired state of the IIWS, but not of the work domain. This IIWS state is therefore a necessary goal to be achieved to enable the authors to achieve their work sub-goal, but it is not itself part of the work sub-goal. This type of goal is therefore termed an *enabling goal*, as distinct from a *work goal*, since it enables the IIWS to perform work tasks by putting it into a state from which it can carry out behaviours to achieve work goals. The term "enabling task" refers to those IIWS behaviours associated with the achievement of enabling goals.

The distinction between work tasks and enabling tasks therefore is that work tasks are those IIWS behaviours which directly achieve some state change of the work domain objects that moves those objects closer to their desired work goal states; in contrast, enabling tasks are those IIWS behaviours which achieve some enabling goal state of the IIWS itself; that is, they alter the state of some part of the IIWS (user, other users, terminals, communication service, etc.), in a way that enables the IIWS to perform its work tasks. Enabling tasks, then, manipulate objects (either in the domain or the IIWS) to put the system into a state from which it can carry out work. For instance, changing a person's role in the IIWS (to give them greater access privileges to the document, say), changes the state of the IIWS and enables work on the document to be carried out. As an example of an object in the IIWS, we identified the need for a work group model object which lists the participants, their roles and their current status. This work group model is discussed in Section 9.5.1.

To give another example, if a work system is given a work goal of some specified changes being made to a text document, then editing a paragraph to improve the punctuation is a work task, because the resulting document will be different (part of the work goal). To perform this work task, however, the work system must be in an enabling goal state which includes having the pointer located at the first editing position within the paragraph; the work system's behaviour in moving the pointer to accomplish this change of location is an enabling task, because the document itself is not changed, but only the state of the work system.

This distinction is indifferent to the agent of the task, in that it does not directly associate either the user or other IIWS entities with work tasks or enabling tasks. The overall work goal is that of the IIWS, not of the user(s), and so the various sub-tasks can in principle be performed by any agent of the IIWS, or any agents in combination. Decisions about which agent or agents perform which task would need to be made in a function allocation stage to the design.

In order to identify the enabling tasks, then, we first need to identify the *enabling goals* which will put the IIWS into a state from which it can carry out the behaviours necessary to achieve the work goals. First, each of the sub-tasks specified in the previous stage is considered, and the state that the work system must be in for the sub-task to be performed is specified. These states are the enabling goals. Once these states have been identified, the enabling tasks which must be performed in order to create and maintain the states are specified.

At the lowest level of the work task decomposition for our prototype, twenty-three sub-tasks have been identified. Since each of these sub-tasks requires the work system to be in a corresponding enabling goal state, there could be as many as twenty-three enabling goal states to be described. It is clear, though, from Figs 9.1 and 9.2 that there is a high degree of similarity between the task hierarchies for Construct Document, Construct Requirement and Construct Specification. While it might appear simpler to create one more abstract task hierarchy that could be applied to all three, the first stage in the method treats them as different to conserve all possible task information. The specification of the objects in the work domain provides the information that allows the decision to be made about which sub-task hierarchies are functionally identical.

In this example, it was now possible to examine the tables representing the two sub-objects of the plan: requirement and specification. Since it was found that they had all but one of their attributes in common, a single set of enabling states could be defined, each of which corresponded to a sub-task to be performed upon *either* a requirement *or* a specification. The attributes of the document object were clearly different, and so despite the similarity in the sub-task hierarchy, the sub-tasks which operated upon it required a separate set of enabling goals.

Because of the limited resources of the project, it was decided not to pursue the specification of the *Construct Document* section of the work at this point in the prototyping study. This was because, for the purposes of the study, it was seen as more important to complete partially all stages of the design method rather than to complete fully only some of the stages. This part of the work also seemed likely to involve mainly the design of tools for the editing and manipulation of the constituent parts of the document, sub-tasks which were anticipated to be not only extensive and complex, and outside the scope of a one-year prototyping study, but also to be supportable by "off-the-shelf" tools that could be incorporated into the prototype at a later stage.

Having reduced the breadth of the specification in this way, seven enabling goals remained to be specified, corresponding to the five sub-tasks of creating, retrieving, revising, communicating and assessing requirements and specifications, and the two sub-tasks of creating and communicating comments about requirements and specifications. These enabling goals were defined as being:

1. Plan creatable.
2. Plan retrievable.
3. Plan revisable.
4. Plan details communicable.
5. Plan assessable.
6. Plan comments creatable.
7. Plan comments communicable.

The next stage is to identify the IIWS behaviours necessary to achieve these enabling goals. In this particular exercise, a first pass identified over sixty possible behaviours, but on further inspection these were clustered together to give just five behaviours that deal with recognizably distinct areas of the work system. The behaviours are:

1. Give user knowledge of task domain.
2. Prepare and maintain channels.
3. Prepare workstation.
4. Prepare and maintain database.
5. Prepare store and forward system.

Fig. 9.3 shows the relationship between the enabling goals and their associated behaviours, and the behaviours associated with the work goals already shown in Figs 9.1 and 9.2. In Figs 9.1 and 9.2 the work goals have not been shown, and therefore, in Fig. 9.3 the enabling goals are shown in reverse highlight to identify them as being distinct from the behaviours which satisfy them. The work goals for all the other behaviours shown have been omitted in order to keep the diagrams simple. Together these enabling goals and their associated behaviours constitute an enabling task.

9.4.3 A Specific Instantiation of the Scenario

As a specific example of the goal task description described above let us consider a holiday firm which has an existing base of multimedia documents (MMDs) which it uses to give tourists information about the places to be visited on its tours and package holidays. A new range of holidays in the Upper Rhine Valley is being assembled, and the marketing department of the firm have suggested that the multimedia system be used to attract

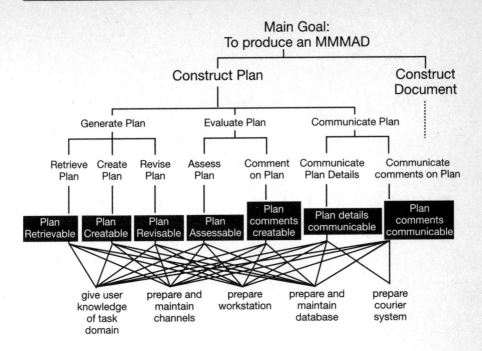

Fig. 9.3. The enabling tasks for the high level work task *Construct Plan*.

prospective customers as well as to assist actual tourists. An editor with responsibility for producing MMDs has been asked by the firm's managers to produce an MMD about the town of Baden-Baden.

The editor has access to a multimedia workstation, which he or she can use to access information on company policy, and to communicate with two authors in different locations, a writer and an artist, both of whom also have workstations. The writer is responsible for producing text, tables and spoken sections of multimedia documents (MMDs), and has access to a database of suitable guidebooks and assorted information for assembling an MMD. The artist, who is responsible for still images, video sequences, soundtracks and graphics, has access to a similar database of all of these forms of information. The editor has responsibilities both to edit and review the document.

There are two other non-human entities, a database which acts as a repository for all created information (e.g. plan and document objects) and a courier system with store and forward functions to allow indirect communication.

Communication channels exist between each user and a workstation, as and when the users work within the system. Each workstation is connected to the database and the courier system, and also directly to each other

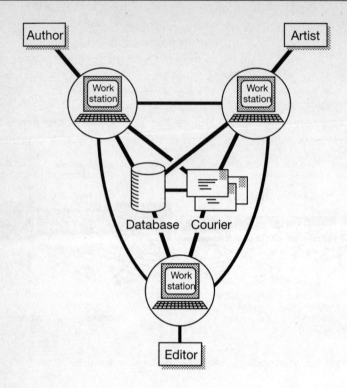

Fig. 9.4. The work system, showing the communicating entities and the communication channels between them.

workstation. The courier system can also access the database. The IIWS described above is shown in Fig. 9.4.

Given this specific scenario and the task analysis above, we can instanti-ate part of the work task decomposition for *Construct Plan*. Fig. 9.5 shows part of the work task decomposition; the lowest level tasks are identified by number, so that they can be easily referenced below. Note that although the tasks are numbered in a left-to-right sequence, this is not the order in which they would occur; for example, the evaluation of the requirement (task 4) would occur before the revision of it (task 3).

Generate requirements:

1. Editor retrieves requirements about need to brief tourists about places in Upper Rhine Brochure (a text memo from management via the courier system).

2. Editor creates requirement (textual, mandatory) for a MMD about Baden-Baden, to be produced by artist and writer (creates text document using word processor).

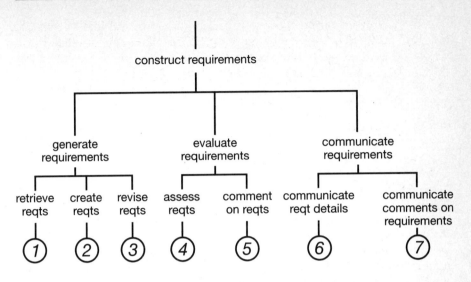

Fig. 9.5. The task hierarchy for sub-goal task *Construct Requirements*.

3. Editor revises requirement about MMD such that it is to be read by prospective tourists as well as actual tourists (edits text document using word processor).

Evaluate requirements:

4. Editor assesses requirement concerning likely users of MMD, and decides that in this case they should include prospective as well as actual tourists (reads text document, communicating with machine to manipulate it).

5. Editor comments that requirement concerning likely users is not appropriate in this case since the purpose is to encourage prospective tourists as well as to inform actual tourists (talks to camera to make an audio/visual memo).

Communicate requirement details:

6. Editor communicates the requirements to the artist and writer about the MMD (videophone session with all three in bidirectional real-time communication, control with editor).

7. Editor communicates comments about the likely users to the writer and artist (forwards prerecorded audio/visual memo via courier system, not real time).

The above, then, serves to illustrate briefly how some of the tasks described in Section 9.4.2.3 might be instantiated in a particular collaborative document production task. In the final section we would like to consider how our prototype design might support the authors in such collaborative tasks, and to discuss the utility of the concepts underlying our task analysis technique.

9.5 Discussion

9.5.1 The Final Design

Further details of later stages of the design process, and how the final design was reached, can be found in May et al. (1992). This section illustrates how the task analysis has influenced the product of the design process by describing some features of the prototype design. It would be almost impossible to present all the influences of the task analysis, since many of them are indirect or are not easily presented diagrammatically. Below are simply some illustrations of different influences.

Fig. 9.6 shows an implemented window of part of a subsystem called the *Browser*. This subsystem coordinates access to a number of services and functions, including:

- editing functions for four classes of media object (text, graphics, audio and audiovisual);

- a real-time audiovisual communication service and a store and forward message service, supporting synchronous and asynchronous communication, respectively;

- overviews of the status and availability of other users of the system and of the workspace (i.e. database retrieval services).

The Browser provides a "shared workspace" in the sense used by Trigg and Suchman (1989) (see also Dillon, this volume), in that it allows users working independently to have access to shared work objects. These work objects can be specified as being public or private by their authors. It also supports both synchronous and asynchronous work by group members (see Beydere et al., this volume, for a discussion of modes of communication in the collaborative writing process), and allows the sending of "directed messages" in any media between particular users, as well as the group as a whole (see Miles et al., this volume). All of the different services that this subsystem makes use of are accessed through a single view called the *Overview*.

The task analysis identified two of the objects in the work domain as being *plans* and *documents*. These two objects are explicitly represented in the final design by different types of interface objects. The icons with "dog-eared" corners along the top of the window represent plan objects (in

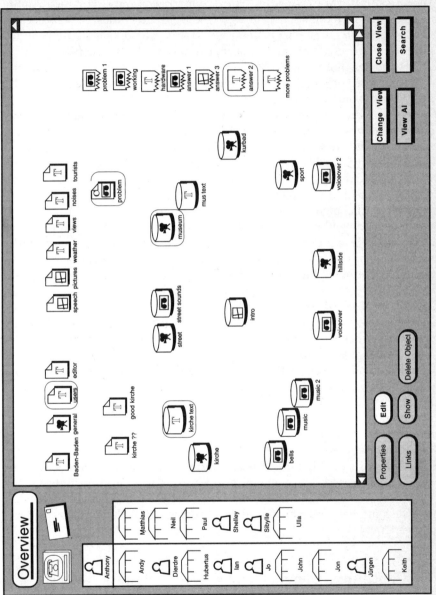

Fig. 9.6. The implemented window corresponding to the overview.

various media). Comments and annotations (a plan sub-object) are shown along the right-hand side of the window and have jagged edges, while the solid, cylindrical icons elsewhere in the window represent document objects (again in various media). Thus, a number of important features of the task analysis have explicit links to the final screen design, i.e. objects that were identified as part of the work domain have contributed to the design. The attributes of these objects can be altered by the user using a property editor (not shown). Again, there is a direct relationship between the objects' attributes identified during the task analysis and the functionality of the implemented property editor.

Another feature of the design which draws upon the task analysis is the *work group overview* shown in the left-hand side of the window. This work group overview shows all the people working in the group, and indicates their availability. A table icon represents that someone is unavailable (either not logged into the system, or logged on but does not want to be disturbed). The properties of users (their role in the work group, for example), can be identified by clicking on their icon. No changes to another person's properties can be made without the correct access privileges (as editor, say).

This work group overview can be seen to be important to both work tasks and enabling tasks described in the task analysis. A work task during the construction of plans is to communicate the plans to other authors. Plans can be communicated either in real time, or using the store and forward facility. To use the store and forward service the user simply selects the object to be communicated and selects the person it is to be sent to from the work group overview while the store and forward service is active. The enabling tasks of setting up and maintaining the appropriate channels and addresses are done automatically. This work group overview, then, explicitly represents three enabling tasks, namely: to give user knowledge about the task domain, prepare store and forward service, or prepare and maintain channels for communication. This leaves the user to concentrate explicitly on the work task of communicating plan information to other authors and editors.

The design of the MAMMDP user interface, then, was influenced by the task analysis carried out on extant multi-author and multimedia tasks. In the next section we would like to consider why the processes and products of the task analysis may be useful to the design of collaborative systems more generally.

9.5.2 Concluding Comments Concerning the Task Analysis

Whitefield et al. (1991) have distinguished between the effectiveness of the task analysis *product* and the effectiveness of the task analysis *method* (where a method consists of a procedure and a notation) in the development of interactive work systems. While the task analysis reported here cannot currently claim to be more than an informal technique, and does not have complete and coherent procedures or notations, we believe there are a number of features of its process and product which warrant the further development of the technique.

First, there are a number of reasons for thinking that distinguishing work tasks and enabling tasks might be useful in the design of interactive work systems. As a minimum, it simply makes explicit an informal and intuitive distinction. We would suggest that most, if not all, users occasionally feel they are doing things for the sake of the computer rather than to achieve their real task goals. This is supported by evidence that users spend a considerable part of their time and effort in operation of the computer in a way that interferes with their ability to perform their real task (Black 1990; Whitefield 1986). The work/enabling task distinction might provide the concepts for an explicit description and interpretation of this evidence. Ongoing research on the GUIDANCE project is addressing this issue.

More than this, however, the distinction might be useful in the design of interactive systems. A weak design use would be in identifying unequivocally those tasks that perform work in the work domain and those that don't; or, put another way, those tasks that any work system would have to perform to achieve the work goal and those tasks the work system has to perform only as a consequence of its own structures and behaviours. This sort of distinction has parallels in the design discipline in identifying functional and structural descriptions (e.g. Pahl and Beitz 1984).

A stronger case for the usefulness of the distinction in design is that it might provide a rationale for structuring a design method that will deliver systems appropriate for their users. This arises from the primary position of the work task and work domain descriptions in a systematic design process, and the way in which they constrain the orientation and language of the design. It is characteristic of systematic design processes that they include at an early stage the formulation of the design problem as an abstract function (or system behaviour) to accomplish some specified state transformation without implying a particular solution (or system structure). See, for example, Pahl and Beitz (1984) for general engineering design, or Fairley (1985) for computer system design. In the terms being used in this chapter, this would be done by specifying the work to be achieved in the work domain, and subsequently decomposing this into the various work tasks. Given careful analysis of how the end-users understand the work domain and the work tasks, these descriptions can be constructed around the users' views of the work. They would contrast with descriptions based on possibly inappropriate views (e.g. those of technologists or even of designers), and also with users' views of other things (e.g. of the computer or network). From the beginning, therefore, the design can be orientated towards how the users perceive the domain and the work. This in itself ought to contribute to systems that have appropriate functionality for their users and that the users understand.

Moreover, the language of the design is strongly constrained by these work descriptions, since the descriptions of the enabling states and enabling tasks are derived *from* those of the work tasks. Consequently, it is difficult for designers to introduce new constructs that are inconsistent with the work task descriptions. The analysis of work tasks and enabling tasks can thus provide a scheme for the design of IIWSs, which can help to ensure that the interactions and device operations are consistently expressed, as far as possible, in terms of the users' conceptions of the work domain and the work tasks.

The final point about design is that the notion of an IIWS as a system including both users and machines as entities, and the fact that the distinction between work tasks and enabling tasks is indifferent to the task agent, mean that design addresses the IIWS as a whole rather than either the users or the machines in isolation. Designers must prescribe the states of the communicating entities and channels, and since users are among those entities, then this can include the states of the users – what knowledge or skills they must have, for example. Right from the start, therefore, system design includes all components of the IIWS. This is an advance over those approaches to design that exclude user concepts until late in the design process, which can leave the user interface designer facing intractable problems, resulting in poor quality user interfaces.

The benefits of the distinction between work and enabling tasks in the task analysis technique described above may be particularly useful in the design of collaborative interactive work systems, since the focus on work goals reduces the likelihood of design simply reproducing existing systems with newer technology, and increases the opportunities for the work allocated to the human end-users of the system to be more effectively supported by other entities including computers, databases, and communications networks.

Acknowledgements This work was carried out as part of the R1067 GUIDANCE project funded by the Commission of the European Communities under the RACE Programme. The project partners are Standard Elektrik Lorenz-AG, Germany; University College London, UK; British Telecom, UK; Roke Manor Research, UK; and Swedish Telecom, Sweden.

---

[1]In previous papers reporting this work (Byerley et al. 1990, 1991) we have used the term "goal task" rather than "work task"; the change here is simply terminological – the underlying concept is the same.

## Chapter 10

MILO: A Computer-Based Tool for (Co-)Authoring Structured Documents

S. Jones

10.1 Introduction

Computer-based tools such as text editors, graphics editors, idea processors, hypertext authoring systems, communication systems and document formatting systems can be useful to both individual and collaborative authors. Unfortunately, these tools are diverse in appearance and behaviour, and are unlikely to be compatible. Jones (1990) has highlighted the fact that although powerful tools are available, no single tool can as yet satisfy the majority of an author's needs.

As a result, authors can be faced with the daunting task of using several different systems during the writing process in order to cater for specific tasks such as idea processing, text entry, diagram production and document formatting. These systems may not even be available on the same hardware platform. Collaborating authors face more difficulties. They need to find a suitable communication system if they are geographically distant, and the tools used by one co-author may not be available to another. Kraut et al. (1988) have observed that collaborators using computer-based tools "had difficulties with the incompatibilities among programs and computing environments".

This paper discusses MILO, a computer-based tool which goes some way towards alleviating these problems. It supports distributed, asynchronous authoring of structured documents that contain both text and graphics, catering for a wide variety of approaches to document production.

The facilities provided by MILO, and how they are related to similar work, will be described, and issues arising from its use will be discussed. Finally, possible future development and investigation of MILO is suggested.

10.2 Designing Systems for Use Now

A common belief in research of computer supported collaborative writing is that computer based systems should not be designed and built until the processes involved in collaborative writing are more clearly understood. There is no guarantee, however, having waited for understanding to be sufficiently advanced, that embedding it in a computer-based system will benefit collaborators. It would be wrong to assume that the technology will be transparent and not affect the process. I would suggest that to provide computer-based support for collaborative writing *now*, systems can and should be designed and implemented, drawing on ideas from sociological/psychological research, but also on concepts, attributes and experiences of existing systems. Evaluation will indicate successful implementation details, those that have failed, and those that need to be added or amended. As Sharples et al., in this volume, point out, the design of highly interactive systems that are intended to support complex tasks cannot be fully specified in advance of implementation.

Such an approach will empirically address issues such as user interface design for collaborative systems, computer support for individual writers, co-authors and communication between collaborators. It is the approach that has been adopted in this work.

10.3 Introducing MILO

Sharples and Pemberton (1990) state that "support for writing should embrace the entire process, from registering the task to producing a finished manuscript". There is a need for a single tool that provides such support, eases communication difficulties and the collaborative process for co-authors, and is hardware-independent. MILO is a step towards such a system.

MILO is intended to be a useful tool for authors of structured documents, into which they may wish to include both text and graphics. It provides facilities both for an individual and for multiple authors.

At the most basic level MILO can be used by an individual author as a text editor to construct a simple linear document. At the other extreme it can meet the needs of geographically distant co-authors who are writing a continually revised document of complex structure containing text and graphics. It also caters for needs anywhere else along this broad spectrum.

MILO can be used as an idea processor, allowing the user to note distinct ideas and create links between them, providing a graphical representation of the resulting structure and allowing its content and form to be edited.

Construction of structured documents is achieved through creation of a hierarchy of logical units called *notes*. The author is provided with alternative representations of the document structure and can take different views of document content. Fast access methods to elements of interest in potentially large document structures are provided.

The use of MILO can ease communication and information exchange between distant colleagues. Although MILO has an advanced graphical user interface, MILO documents are stored in a purely textual manner, allowing geographically distant collaborations to take place via electronic mail (email), and making exchange of MILO-created documents both system and hardware independent.

MILO also allows automatic updating of a document which has multiple authors, drawing together the contributions of all of them into a single version of the document.

10.3.1 Related Systems

Many other computer-based tools exist in the same general application area as MILO. This section indicates how MILO resembles or differs from several other systems.

Firstly, it is not intended to support real-time collaborative creation of documents through a shared screen or shared information on multiple screens. This sets it apart from systems such as AUGMENT (Engelbart 1988) and Cognoter (Stefik et al. 1988), which provide screen images shared between multiple users. It is intended to support single authors and potentially distant co-authors who pass information between them and contribute individually.

Secondly, it does not constrain users to predefined roles within a collaborative task as Quilt (Leland et al. 1988) does, for example. Quilt requires the rights of contributors in a collaboration to be defined at the outset, making change tiresome and difficult when a more apt relationship may become evident during the process. MILO does not constrain users in this way, as a socially-mediated approach between (supposedly trusted) collaborators is far more flexible. Indeed, Ellis et al. (1991) found that users of their unconstrained multi-user editor GROVE implemented social protocols to mediate interaction.

MILO does, however, draw on an approach that several other systems have adopted. Neuwirth et al. (1988) describe benefits of using note cards in the writing process, and suggest further benefits of using computer-based note cards. Tools such as Neuwirth et al.'s Notes, NoteCards (Trigg and Irish 1988), HyperCard (Apple Computer Inc. 1987) and InterNote (Catlin et al. 1989) have each implemented this idea and MILO follows suit. Notes allow flexibility in idea generation, document structuring and revision.

Such systems, however, have variable approaches to the implementation and manipulation of notes. The Notes system, for example, allows the author to view only a limited number of notes at a time and provides no overview as to how the elements within the document are related.

NoteCards is better in this respect, as a graphical element to the system gives the user a view of how the note cards of a document relate to each other, maintaining a user's model of the document as a whole. The Notes system takes advantage of the division of a document into smaller elements to allow the author to take selective views of the content, and can automatically retrieve elements that correspond to user-defined attributes. This is a powerful and desirable function which transcends the possibilities of physical note cards and those that exist within the NoteCards system.

The implementation of MILO also attempts to solve the problem that systems such as NoteCards and InterNote have; namely they are constrained to a single type of hardware platform which is necessary for their use. The pool of potential collaborators and users of these systems is reduced as a result. MILO follows the route of the Virtual Notebook System (Shipman et al. 1989), a distributed hypertext for collaborative research. Its interface is implemented using the X Window System (Scheifler and Gettys 1986), which allows it to be used on a wide variety of hardware platforms.

MILO draws on the approaches of these systems for individual and collaborative writers and offers new ideas to extend and improve support.

Fig. 10.1 shows an example screen layout from a MILO session. It includes the main MILO window containing the menu of functions available for use on the whole document, the hierarchical overview and the linear overview. It also shows several note windows containing both text and graphics.

10.3.2 Notes

A MILO user manipulates a single data element type called a note, to create a document. MILO documents are built from any number of individual notes, and so a valid MILO document could consist of a single note or many interrelated notes existing in a hierarchical structure. Each note occupies its own screen space and there is no limit to the number of notes that can be visible at any one time. The complexity and form of the hierarchical structure is user-defined.

All notes have exactly the same look, feel and behaviour, and consist of three elements. These are:

1. A text field which is intended to hold the header or title for the individual note.

2. An EMACS-like text editor which is intended to hold the main body of text for the note. The text editor behaviour is exactly the same for the two text elements of a note.

3. A simple graphics editor allowing the user to draw lines, rectangles, circles and text in a variety of pen patterns.

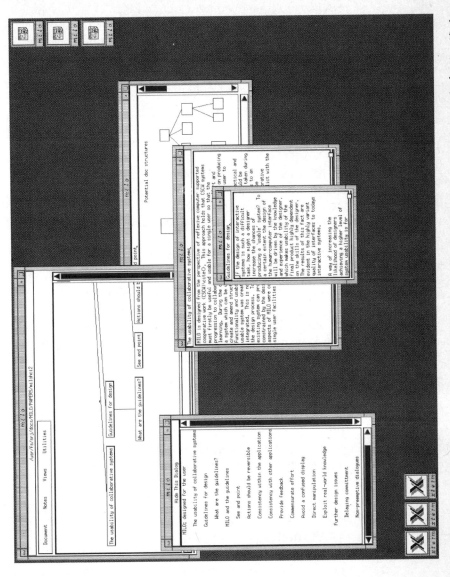

Fig. 10.1. A typical MILO user's screen. It shows the main MILO menu, several note windows and other iconified processes.

A user can also access information about each note, including who created it and when, and who last amended it and when. The information is continually updated, providing users with information about the work patterns of themselves and their co-authors.

Some systems provide multiple document element types, such as annotations, graphics and document text. MILO takes the opposite approach, providing a single, consistent element type. This will maintain conceptual simplicity of document content. Additionally an annotation may well need to contain text and graphics – annotation facilities are then built in to MILO already. An author can therefore use a note in order to annotate existing document contents.

10.3.2.1 Note Relationships

All notes are related to at least one other note (with the exception of one which is the sole note in a document). This relational structure allows each document element to have any number of subordinate elements, providing an author with many possible structures that could underlie a MILO document.

There are three classes of MILO document structure:

1. The simplest MILO document will contain a single note, which may contain text only, graphics only, or both. In theory, this should not restrict the user in the size of the document that she wishes to create, allowing anything from an empty note to a full paper within one note. In this instance the system is being used in a similar manner to a conventional text editor without MILO, but with the added power of the integrated graphics editor.

2. A structure where each note has only one subordinate element will create a document of a simple sequential nature where the text of each note has a sequential relationship with its parent or children.

3. A more complex structure where notes have multiple children, indicating a greater segmentation of the document into smaller, logical, hierarchical units.

10.3.3 Creating Documents

An author creates a MILO document by adding notes to the existing document structure as they are required, specifying the position that the new element will occupy in the structure.

Fig. 10.2 shows a simplified version of Hayes and Flower's (1980) three-phase model of the writing process. This indicates that although planning, translating (text creation) and revision are central to the writing process,

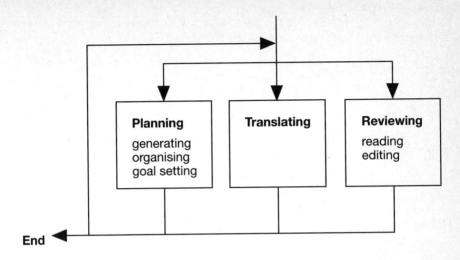

Fig. 10.2. A simplified version of Hayes and Flower's three-phase model of the writing process.

they are repeated and have no constraints on order of execution. This provides a loose description of how people write – that approaches vary greatly. To embed a model of an author's approach to creating a document in a computer-based tool may benefit those writers who adopt that specific approach, but can only alienate those who do not.

MILO tackles this problem by catering for diverse approaches to creating a document. At one extreme the author might create the structure of the document before entering any text or graphics. This indicates the initial hierarchy of the notes, and the relationships between document elements before the author needs to concentrate on text generation. At the other extreme, the author may begin by "writing to discover what she has to say" and generating a large amount of unstructured text, which is then manipulated into a structured document. Of course it is possible for an author to want to use an approach somewhere between these two extremes, and MILO will allow this, catering for the diversity of writing styles that exist along the continuum.

The author can move the focus of her attention from one part of the structure to another, from one note to another at any time, and all notes are always easily accessible. During the creation of a document, text and graphics can be updated, added or deleted at any point.

10.3.3.1 *Storing Documents*

A MILO document can be saved to a file. The file is a standard text file, accessible to other text-based applications available to the user and its contents will reflect the entire structure of the document. The information written to the file can take one of three forms:

1. LaTeX (Lamport 1986) format. When this option is selected, the hierarchical structure of notes in the MILO document is emulated in a LaTeX document. The LaTeX commands to create a structured document are generated automatically and impose a predefined mapping of MILO document structure to LaTeX structure. LaTeX picture environment commands are also generated in order to create figures in the LaTeX document which correspond to the contents of the graphics editors of each note in the MILO document.

2. Plain text. This option will store only the textual contents and the title of each note. It imposes no structure on the document and contains no information about the notes or any of the graphical information contained within the MILO document. A file stored in this format allows an author to mark up the document for formatting in any way she wishes, without MILO.

3. A textual representation of the MILO document and its structure and attributes is stored. This will allow the user to retrieve a document's text, graphics and structure from a text file and it will have exactly the same appearance as it did when saved. An author can also send the exact contents and appearance of a MILO document to someone else using this format. This format allows another author to alter the document from within MILO at another site. New notes, text and graphics can be introduced and the structure itself can be changed.

10.3.4 Amending MILO Documents

The importance of revision in the writing process is stressed by Nold (1981). To be a useful writing tool, MILO must then provide facilities for repeated revision of a MILO document during its lifetime. The author must be able to revise easily not only the textual and graphical content of a document but also its structure. There should also be no time constraint on revisions to a MILO document. It is always possible to revise a document during the current MILO session, but it should also be possible to return to the document at a later date in order to carry out more revisions.

Hence, an author can read a MILO document from a file, restoring both the content and the structure of the document, and not only the textual and graphical content of each note but also the relationship between notes in the structure.

10.3.4.1 Editing Content

The title and textual body of each note can be edited using the text editor provided. It supports commands for movement, text deletion, insertion and selection. Text can also be selected using a pointing device with movement and button clicks. Once text has been selected it can be deleted or copied into another note within the MILO document currently being edited. Additionally, it can be copied to any other application running under the X Window System (see Section 10.6 for details of MILO implementation) which recognizes the X selection mechanism. Similarly, information can be selected in another X application and copied into a document being created or edited using MILO. This eases the problem of incompatibility with other systems.

The graphical content of each note can be edited in a basic manner. Objects can be added to the canvas at any time. The objects available are lines, rectangles, filled rectangles, circles, filled circles and text. A pattern in which drawing and filling takes place can be selected from a palette. Once an object has been drawn on to the canvas it is not possible to manipulate it individually, and in order to remove objects it is necessary to erase all the objects present on the canvas.

10.3.4.2 Editing Structure

Matsuhashi (1987) has found that the continual presence of text (as is the case with conventional word processors or text editors) can encourage low level revision (such as correction of spelling errors) of the text. However, it also reduces the likelihood of more global changes, such as amendments to the structure. MILO therefore encourages the author to consider both structure and content by providing representations of structure, via which content is accessed. This structural representation can then be used for addition, deletion and relocation of document elements, without the need to manipulate large portions of text.

An author can alter the structure of a MILO document by one of three actions:

1. Adding notes to the structure. Notes can be added at any point in time to any position in the note hierarchy.

2. Deleting notes. Individual notes or groups of notes within the structure can be deleted. MILO provides an undo facility for deletion, which allows an author to backtrack through all delete operations that have been carried out during the current session.

3. Altering the position of notes in the structure. A user wishing to move a note to another position in the hierarchical structure can do so by indicating which of the other notes it is to become a sub-element of. Sub-elements of the relocated note remain so, and hence the effect of this action is to alter the position of a subtree of the structure.

10.3.5 Collaboration

Cockburn and Thimbleby (1991) have highlighted the importance of a reflexive perspective of computer supported cooperative work (CSCW), "an emphasis on the importance of catering for the individual's requirements and preferences in cooperative environments". By blurring the distinction between individual and collaborative tools, there is less overhead in transferring from one work mode to another and the group work environment is more predictable. This can encourage collaboration.

MILO is designed from this perspective, ensuring useful and usable facilities for non-collaborative authors so that collaborative use of the system can be eased into.

The facilities described so far indicate that MILO may well be a useful tool for the creation and manipulation of structured documents containing text and graphics that is as independent of hardware as possible and can easily be used in conjunction with other tools for text manipulation. This is a firm base on which to build collaborative aspects.

10.3.6 Communicating via MILO

In order to achieve its aim of being a useful co-authoring tool, MILO supports the author in communicating with colleagues. Communicating authors using MILO will transfer information via purely textual email. Pliskin (1989) describes problems posed by the use of email, and drawbacks of email systems in general. Email is used in MILO, however, for two reasons. Firstly it is an easily accessible, widely used and cheap method of information exchange. Secondly, a user need not directly interact with an email system, as MILO indicates when a MILO document has arrived in the user's mail box, and such documents can be read directly into MILO from the mail box.

The author is supported in selecting a mail target by the system. A reasonable assumption is that authors will generally communicate with the same people most of the time, and when writing a document collaboratively, will in the main be sending the document to their co-authors.

As a result when the author has indicated that she wishes to send a document to a colleague, the names of people who appear in her mail alias file appear as buttons. Clicking on a button produces the email address for the person whose name appears in the button. Additionally, the names of people who have contributed as authors to the current MILO document appear. This goes some way towards alleviating the problems of remembering complex email addresses, and keeping track of who has contributed to the document. This is useful when a document has been distributed to numerous people for review, say, and consequently may have many co-authors at different parts of the document structure. Alternatively the user will enter any email address via the keyboard, as she will do with the name of the file to be sent.

The author is free to select any file rather than just the document currently being worked on, to allow greater flexibility. The current document can then be sent (if it has been saved to a file), or any other document the user desires. It may not necessarily have been created by MILO. MILO will structure the mailing command for the user, alleviating the need to remember its format.

10.3.6.1 *Supporting Collaborative Writing Strategies*

Collaborating groups of writers can adopt varying approaches to creation of documents. Sharples et al., in this volume, outline two approaches that may be used in the kind of distributed, asynchronous task which MILO is intended to support. Sequential partitioning of the task entails dividing it into a sequence of stages, each of which is completed by a different individual or group. MILO supports this approach through its encouraged division of the document into logical elements, the information it provides about the author/amender history of individual notes and the filtering of notes of interest (see Section 10.3.7.2). The context of each group's work can be made clearer through these facilities. In parallel partitioning, different individuals or groups produce different sections of the document. Again the logical subdivision of a MILO document, and the accessible information about co-authors' work support this approach.

If the co-authors were communicating via paper, not only could this be a very slow process if they were a great distance apart, but generating a new document from the multiple versions will be laborious.

Similarly, communication via purely textual email will have its disadvantages although it will be somewhat faster than written communication. A co-author will still be faced with multiple versions of a document that need to be amalgamated into the single entity. This is even more difficult using text held on a computer system because, unlike paper, it will not generally have the comments, scribbles and directions that are usually present on paper, in the form of a standard mark-up language or informal notes.

A useful facility would be semi-automated merging of versions of a document created with MILO to produce a single, up-to-date version. This process is described as semi-automated as the receiving author will have to, in some cases, intervene to make decisions about which changes will prevail.

10.3.6.2 *MILO and Liveware*

Liveware (Witten et al. 1991) is a novel approach to sharing data in social networks. It is designed to take maximum advantage of irregular communication for information exchange. Liveware is a concept rather than a system, and its principles can be applied effectively to a co-authoring environment. Witten et al. describe a Liveware database system, where automatic updates occur in order to maintain consistency and promote information sharing.

There are similarities between a structured document and a database. New elements are introduced into a database, and existing elements are amended, deleted or not acted upon. This same principle can be applied to MILO, with the notes that make up a document corresponding to the data elements of a database. There is therefore a potential advantage in introducing Liveware concepts into the functionality of MILO.

Liveware is used in MILO to automate the process of merging two versions of a single document into a new updated version. This is a useful facility for authors. Firstly it benefits co-authors of a single document as the work of each individual can be drawn together easily into a single cohesive text. There is no limit to the number of co-authors whose work can be amalgamated in such a way. Secondly, the facility can be used by the single author to combine work from multiple incarnations of the same document. Many drafts of a document are usually produced during the authoring process and automation can allow the author to retrieve elements easily from previous versions.

The implementation of Liveware in MILO goes beyond a one-to-one correspondence with the application of Liveware concepts to database manipulation. In addition to handling additions and deletions of notes, and amendments to note contents, the merging process embedded in MILO also takes into account restructuring of the hierarchical document.

The facilities required in a Liveware system will differ from application to application. The current implementation of Liveware concepts in MILO is a basic one, and work on development of this Liveware implementation is ongoing. Currently the merge is destructive, with the most recent amendments to a document prevailing, and several issues are yet to be addressed:

1. How can equally valid changes to a note by different authors at different times be maintained during a merge?

2. Should a contributor to the document be allowed to amend the contents of a note created by another author?

3. Should a contributor's more recent amendments to a note give way to less recent amendments by the note's author?

4. To what extent should the user be prompted to control the merging operation?

A central principle of Liveware is that information exchange is two-way; that is two Liveware versions of a database are identical after an update. MILO relies on authors sending information to each other via email, and so a single author is concerned with merging different versions of the same document. There is no need to update both versions as long as the author is clear about which is the new version to be sent to co-authors.

Witten et al. advise access rights to units of information, with alterations only possible by the owner. This might be suitable for a database implementation, but is not desirable for a co-authoring system where free access to all elements of the document is vital.

10.3.7 Viewing MILO Documents

If an author is to create and manipulate structured documents with MILO successfully then that structure and its content must be accessible and easily understood. When creating a document of structural complexity it is important for the author to be supported by the system in maintaining a correct model of the document at all times. Developing such a document on paper or with an ordinary text editor can be difficult, as, regardless of the model the author has of the structure, the document has no other appearance than linear. Additionally, text editors and word processors generally only show the author a small portion of the whole text, making contextualization of current work difficult. This may well degrade the quality of the final product.

To maximize an author's ability to manipulate document structure and content to best effect, MILO provides different kinds of structure overview, and allows an author to search out sections fulfilling certain criteria, and search for instances of specific text patterns.

10.3.7.1 *Different Views Of Document Structure*

MILO provides two distinct types of graphical structure overview for documents.

1. A tree-like graphic represents the hierarchical relationships between all notes contained within the document. Notes are represented using the text that has been entered in the title bar for each one. The graphical presentation reinforces the hierarchical model of a MILO document, showing elements and their subelements.

2. A graphic resembling an indented table of contents presents a linear representation of the structure. This corresponds to the mapping from hierarchical structure to linear document which is implemented if the author stores the structure in a LaTeX format file.

The first overview aids the author in manipulating the structure for optimal effect, arranging and rearranging ideas and sections of text. The second shows the author a potential linear form for the document. The two overviews should complement each other in helping the author refine the document until the desired result is achieved. The two overviews are shown in Fig. 10.1.

10.3.7.2 Applying Filters to Documents

In addition to wishing to take different views of the structure of a MILO document, an author may also wish to take different views of the content of the document. MILO allows a user to view portions of the document selectively by filtering notes within the document based on rules provided by the user.

Consider an example. A tutor has produced a document within MILO and as part of their assessment her students must comment on the document. She sends each student a version of the original via email, they complete their assignment by adding, removing and amending notes and return the MILO document, again via email. The tutor then merges the work of each student into a single document using MILO's Liveware facility. Now she is faced with a very large document, containing many notes, and has the task of assessing the work of each student.

The tutor might well then wish to view the work of one individual at a time, or to see the work of more than one student at a time if she suspects collusion. She might wish to see when certain students began their project, or when they completed work on it. Using the filtering functions of MILO it is possible to do each of these things. The user can specify individual keys, such as note creation time or note author, to be used for searching for and highlighting notes. Combinations of keys can also be used to find sections of the document satisfying more specific criteria.

The filters can also be used by a single author in order to keep a track of her own work, providing the ability to access parts of a document based on when work was last done on them.

Any notes satisfying criteria specified for the filtering process are brought to the user's attention visually.

10.3.7.3 Time Ordered View

It is sometimes difficult for an author to keep track of work on a document, especially if there are gaps between the work phases. Remembering which elements were being worked on, or the order in which tasks were being dealt with may pose problems which MILO helps to alleviate. It provides a view of the document elements labelled with the time when they were last amended, and ordered from most to least recent amendment. The elements are represented by their title. An author can therefore very quickly see a history of work on the document and, via this view, access elements of interest.

The provision of this view, the ability to filter elements of interest from the document and the information available about each note go some way towards providing the context history of interaction which Miles et al. (this volume) indicate is important in asynchronous collaboration.

10.3.7.4 Searching Documents

There are two reasons why an author using MILO will require a facility to search the contents of a document. She may have forgotten in which note certain subjects were being discussed and need to find it to re-read or amend what has been previously written. It may also be desirable to consider elements of the document that are related in subject matter.

The facility for finding text within a MILO document provides for both reasons. The user can specify not just individual words but a text string that is to be searched for. Any notes that contain the text are brought visually to the user attention, as with the filtering process. Automating the finding of document elements provides accuracy and efficiency benefits for the user.

10.3.7.5 Spell Checking

MILO provides a spell checking facility that can be used within MILO, without the need to save the current document and access such a tool from outside. The spell checker conforms to British spellings, and errors are reported to the user within MILO, indicating in which note they have occurred.

10.4 Observations from Use of MILO

This document was written using MILO, and several points of interest have arisen from this process. Continuing development of the system has gone hand-in-hand with its intensive use to generate reasonably large, structured documents, and several changes have been made:

1. MILO originally provided functions to process and preview LaTeX documents. These were removed simply because they were redundant – they were merely an interface between MILO and the relevant tools. Formatting and previewing can be done outside MILO using the relevant applications, simultaneous with the current MILO session if required, as the user will in general be using a windowing environment. Additionally, it is desirable to keep MILO as independent of any text formatting system as possible. Storing documents in LaTeX format is a convenience function, which could easily make use of an alternative document formatting system; to provide further functions linking MILO and LaTeX would reduce user formatting options.

2. The *filter* and *find text* functions would result in only notes meeting the criteria indicated by the user remaining visible on the screen. If not

visible initially they would be made so, and any notes that were initially visible but did not meet the criteria would be removed from the screen. This was found to be unacceptable, as use of this function does not indicate that the user has no further interest in the current working set of visible notes. These functions are used for reference to notes outside the current working set, and thus were amended so as not to remove any notes from the screen.

3. The provision of a view of document elements ordered on the times that they were last amended and of a spelling checker came out of the needs of this author, which became evident during the use of MILO.

More general observations made during use of MILO are:

1. MILO provides well for various approaches to document creation. The structure of this chapter was originally created and amended, with potential section headings generated for note titles. Text generation began after the initial structure had been refined. However, during the process of writing, necessary structural changes became evident and could be achieved quickly and simply. Parts of the chapter were also added without a predetermined structure in a brainstorming process, and a suitable structure could easily be imposed later.

2. The *find text* facility is very useful for finding and simultaneously viewing document segments concerning or mentioning the same thing. It helps the author to be consistent, and can highlight a need to introduce concepts or terms at different points of the document.

3. The *filter* facility is useful for bringing to attention recent additions to the structure, serving to remind the author of recent or current points of interest in the document.

4. The linear structure overview was of limited use. It served to indicate the linear balance of the document but did not influence how the document was structured.

5. The provision of automatic mapping from the hierarchical structure of a MILO document to a LaTeX format document resulted in this author including LaTeX formatting commands in the text of notes. This then ties the MILO document to LaTeX format – an undesirable situation.

6. In contrast, however, the user is provided with an automatically marked up, structured LaTeX document, saving both time and effort in the formatting stage of the authoring process.

7. The provision of a view of document elements based on time ordering is very useful for orientating the author at the start of a MILO session by giving a possible indication of work to be completed and showing the author their path through amendment and creating of the document.

10.5 Future Work

MILO is a work in progress. To render a tool for collaboration useful, it must first be useful and usable to a single user (Cockburn and Thimbleby 1991). The majority of work to date has been to achieve this aim while providing facilities for collaborative writing.

Evaluation by the author of the current facilities has been ongoing, and changes and developments have been implemented. MILO has been proven to be a useful and usable tool, being used in creation of this chapter and several other documents. The next step, which has just begun, is to gather feedback from use by a wider group of users, some of whom will already be computer literate and some of whom will not. It is expected that this information will address both functionality and interface issues, and it will have to be analysed from both perspectives.

A collaborative writing task using MILO is about to be undertaken. This will highlight whether the facilities provided are effective and will give indications as to how they may be developed. Attention has now been turned to developing the Liveware aspect of the system more fully without increasing the necessary user involvement to an unreasonable level. The current simplicity of the system (single document element types, limited but widely used functions, little user intervention) is seen by the author as a positive aspect. The benefits of overloading the user with functionality are dubious.

Among further facilities being considered for incorporation are folding of levels of the structure to provide less detailed views, integrating annotations while maintaining the simplicity of the single element type, allowing access to facilities for users of text-based non-graphic hardware and indicators of the position which sub-elements occupy within higher level elements.

10.6 Implementation

The interface to MILO is implemented in the X Window system (Scheifler and Gettys 1986) using the Xt Intrinsics and Hewlett-Packard X Widgets (Hewlett-Packard Company 1988). It incorporates many standard graphic user interface objects such as multiple windows, menus, buttons, dialogues and scrollbars to provide a powerful direct manipulation graphic user interface.

X is suitable for the task of developing a complex user interface to MILO for three reasons. Firstly, extensive libraries of high level user interface objects which can be combined into a cohesive interface are provided, using libraries of routines to manipulate those objects. These libraries are abstracted from the most basic programming level in X, simplifying the development task, but still allowing the programmer access to lower level but useful routines. Secondly, the use of X is becoming more widespread and with the support of many major hardware manufacturers it is almost provided by default with powerful graphic workstations. Its use in MILO will increase the potential user base for the system. Thirdly, because of its client-server architecture, any applications developed under X will be device-independent. This again potentially increases the user base by allowing users (even collaborating ones) to utilize it on many different hardware platforms.

10.7 Summary

The motivation and need for a system such as MILO have been described – existing tools to support writers are many and varied and in general incompatible. The functionality provided by MILO and its relationship to other tools to support writers has been discussed, and some issues resulting from its use outlined. It has been seen through use to be a useful and usable tool, although further evaluation is being undertaken. Finally, possible future developments concentrating mainly on collaborative aspects have been suggested.

Acknowledgements   Many thanks to Mike Sharples and James Goodlet for their constructive comments on earlier drafts of this chapter.

References

Achtert WS and Gibaldi J (1985) The MLA Style Manual. MLA, New York

Allen N, Atkinson D, Morgan M, Moore T and Snow C (1987) What experienced collaborators say about collaborative writing. Journal of Business and Technical Communication 1(2): 70–90

Alty JL (1991) Multimedia –what is it and how do we exploit it? In: Diaper D and Hammond N (ed) People and Computers VI. Proceedings of the HCI '91 Conference, 20–23 August 1991. Cambridge University Press, Cambridge

Apple Computer Inc. (1987) Apple Macintosh HyperCard User's Guide. Cupertino, CA

Bachrach P and Baratz M (1962) Two faces of power. American Political Science Review 56: 266–279

Bacsich P (1990) Electronic publishing in distance teaching universities. In: Bates A (ed) Media and Technology in European Distance Education. EADTU, Heerlen, pp 49–56

Bales RF (1950) Interaction Process Analysis: A Method for the Study of Small Groups. Addison-Wesley, Reading, MA

Bass BM (1980) Team productivity and individual member competence. Small Group Behavior 11(4): 431–504

Baxter LA (1982) Conflict management: an episodic approach. Small Group Behavior 13(1): 23–42

Beaudouin-Lafon M (1990) Collaborative development of software. In: Gibbs S and Verrijn-Stuart AA (ed) Multi-User Interfaces and Applications. Elsevier / North-Holland, Amsterdam

Beck EE (1991) A methodology for studying the dynamics of co-authoring for the design of CSCW writing systems. In: Dallaway R, del Soldato T and Moser L (ed) The Fourth White House Papers: Graduate Research at the School of Cognitive and Computing Sciences. CSRP 200. School of Cognitive and Computing Sciences, University of Sussex

Begeman M, Cook P, Ellis C, Graf M, Rein G and Smith T (1986) Project nick: meetings augmentation and analysis. In: Peterson D (ed) Proceedings of the Conference on Computer Supported Cooperative Work (CSCW-86), Austin, TX. ACM, New York

Bellotti V, Dourish P and MacLean A (1991) From user's themes to designers' dreams: developing a design space for shared interactive technologies. AMODEUS RP6/WP7, Rank Xerox EuroPARC, 61 Regent Street, Cambridge CB2 IAB, UK

Benne K and Sheats P (1974) Functional roles of group members. In: Bradford LP (ed) Group Development. University Associates, La Jolla, CA, pp 51–58. (Reprinted from *The Journal of Social Issues* 1948.)

Black A (1990) Visible planning on paper and on screen: the impact of working medium on decision-making by novice graphic designers. Behaviour and Information Technology 9(4): 283–296

Bridwell-Bowles L, Johnson P and Brehe S (1987) Composing and computers: case studies of experienced writers. In: Matsuhashi A (ed) Writing in Real Time: Modelling Production Processes. Ablex, Norwood, NJ, pp 81–107

Brome V (1958) Six Studies in Quarrelling. Cresset Press, London

Brooks F (1982) The Mythical Man-Month: Essays on Software Engineering. Addison-Wesley, Reading, MA

Brown P and Levinson S (1978) Universals in language usage: politeness phenomena. In: Goody E (ed) Questions and Politeness: Strategies in Social Interaction. Cambridge University Press, Cambridge

Bruffee KA (1983) Teaching writing through collaboration. In: Bouton C and Garth RY (ed) Learning in Groups. Jossey-Bass, San Francisco

Bruffee KA (1984) Collaborative learning and the "conversation of mankind". College English 46(7): 635–652

Burkhardt F and Smith S (ed) (1985) The Correspondence of Charles Darwin. Cambridge University Press, Cambridge

Byerley P, May J, Brooks P, Keil K, Whitefield A and Denley I (1990) Enabling states: a new approach to usability. In: Proceedings of the 13th Annual Symposium on Human Factors In Telecommunications, September 1990, Torino, Italy, pp 285–294

Byerley P, May J, Whitefield A and Denley I (1991) The enabling states approach: designing usable telecommunications services. IEEE Journal on Selected Areas in Communications 9(4): 524–530

Carasik RP and Grantham CE (1988) A case study of CSCW in a dispersed organisation. In: Soloway E, Frye D and Sheppard SB (ed) Proceedings of the Human Factors in Computing Systems Conference, CHI-88, Washington. ACM, New York, pp 61–66

Carey L, Flower L, Hayes JR, Schriver KA and Haas C (1989) Differences in writers' initial task representations. Technical Report 35, Center for the Study of Writing, University of California at Berkeley and Carnegie-Mellon University

Cartwright D and Zander A (ed) (1969) Group Dynamics: Research and Theory (3rd edn). Harper and Row, New York

Catlin T, Bush P and Yankelovich N (1989) InterNote: extending a hypermedia framework to support annotative collaboration. In: Proceedings of Hypertext '89, Pittsburgh, PA, November. ACM, New York, pp 365–378

Chafe WL (1986) Writing in the perspective of speaking. In: Cooper CR and Greenbaum S (ed) Studying Writing: Linguistic Approaches. Sage, Beverly Hills, CA

Chalfonte BL, Fish RS and Kraut RE (1991) Expressive richness: a comparison of speech and text as media for revision. In: Robertson S, Olson G and Olson J (ed) Proceedings of the Human Factors in Computing Systems Conference, CHI-91, New Orleans. ACM, New York, pp 21–26

Chandler D (1993) The mediacy of writing. PhD thesis, Department of Education, University College of Wales, Aberystwyth

Cicourel A (1972) Basic and normative rules in the negotiation of status and role. In: Dreitzel H (ed) Recent Sociology, No. 2. Macmillan, London

Cicourel A (1973) Cognitive Sociology: Language and Meaning in Social Interaction. Penguin, Harmondsworth

Clark HH and Brennan SE (1991) Grounding in communication. In: Resnick LB, Levine JM and Teasley SD (ed) Perspectives on Socially Shared Cognition. American Psychological Association, Washington, DC, pp 127–149

Cockburn AJG and Thimbleby H (1991) A reflective perspective of CSCW. SIGCHI Bulletin 23(3): 63–68

Conklin J and Begeman ML (1989) gIBIS: A tool for all reasons. Journal of the American Society for Information Science, March

Couture B and Rymer J (1991) Discourse interaction between writer and supervisor: a primary collaboration in workplace writing. In: Lay MM and Karis WM (ed) Collaborative Writing in Industry: Investigations in Theory and Practice. Beywood, Amityville, NY

Crick M (1980) Course teams: myth and actuality. Distance Education 1(2): 127–141

CSMIL (1989) ShrEdit, a multi-user shared text editor: user's manual. Cognitive Science and Machine Intelligence Laboratory, University of Michigan

CSMIL (1991) ShrEdit 1.2, a shared editor for the Apple Macintosh: user's guide and technical description. Cognitive Science and Machine Intelligence Laboratory, University of Michigan

DeStephen RS and Hirokawa RY (1988) Small group consensus: stability of group support of the decision, task process, and group relationships. Small Group Behaviour 19(2): 227–329

Deutsch M (1973) The Resolution of Conflict. Yale, New Haven and London

Dietz JLG and Widdershoven GAM (1991) Speech acts or communicative action? In: Bannon L, Robinson M and Schmidt K (ed) Proceedings of the Second European Conference on Computer Supported Cooperative Work (EC-CSCW '91), Amsterdam, September. Kluwer, Dordrecht, pp 235–248

Dix AJ (1991) Formal methods for interactive systems. Academic Press, New York, chapter 10.

Dorner J (1992) Authors and information technology: new challenges in publishing. In: Sharples M (ed) Computers and Writing: Issues and Implementations. Kluwer, Dordrecht

Dowell J and Long JB (1989) Towards a conception for an engineering discipline of human factors. Ergonomics 32(11): 1513–1535

Drake M (1979) The curse of the course team. Teaching at a Distance 16: 50–53

Dubrovsky VJ, Kiesler S and Sethna BN (1991) The equalisation phenomenon: status effects in computer-mediated and face-to-face decision-making groups. Human–Computer Interaction 6(2): 119–146

Dykstra EA and Carasik RP (1991) Structure and support in cooperative environments – the Amsterdam conversation environment. International Journal of Man–Machine Studies 34(3): 419–434

Eason K (1988) Information Technology And Organisational Change. Taylor and Francis, London

Eason K (1991) Ergonomic perspectives on advances in human–computer interaction. Ergonomics 34(6): 721–741

Easterbrook SM, Beck EE, Goodlet JS, Plowman L, Sharples M and Wood CC (1992) A survey of empirical studies of conflict. In: Easterbrook SM (ed) CSCW: Cooperation or Conflict? Springer-Verlag, London

Ede L and Lunsford A (1990) Singular Texts/Plural Authors: Perspectives on Collaborative Writing. Southern Illinois University Press, Carbondale

Eklundh K (1992) Problems in achieving a global perspective in computer-based writing. In: Sharples M (ed) Computers and Writing: Issues and Implementations. Kluwer, Dordrecht

Ellis CA, Gibbs SJ and Rein GL (1990) Design and use of a group editor. In: Cockton G (ed) Proceedings of the IFIP Engineering for Human–Computer Interaction Conference. North-Holland, Amsterdam, pp 13–25. Also published as MCC Technical Report STP-263-88

Ellis CA, Gibbs SJ and Rein GL (1991) Groupware: some issues and experiences. Communications of the ACM 34(1): 39–58. Also published as MCC Technical Report STP-414-88

Engelbart DC (1988) Authorship provisions in AUGMENT. In: Greif I (ed) Computer Supported Cooperative Work: A Book of Readings. Morgan Kaufmann, San Mateo, CA, pp 107–126

Engelbart D and Lehtman H (1988) Working together. Byte, December, 245–252

Engelmore R and Morgan T (1988) Blackboard Systems. Addison-Wesley, Reading, MA

Fafchamps D, Reynolds D and Kuchinsky A (1989) The dynamics of small group decision-making over the e-mail channel. In: Proceedings of the First European Conference on Computer Supported Cooperative Work (EC-CSCW '89), Gatwick, 13–15 September. Computer Sciences House, Slough

Fairley RE (1985) Software Engineering Concepts. McGraw-Hill, New York

Fanning T and Raphael B (1986) Computer tele-conferencing experience at Hewlett-Packard. In: Peterson D (ed) Proceedings of the Conference on Computer Supported Cooperative Work (CSCW-86), Austin, TX. ACM, New York, pp 291–306

Fish RS, Kraut RE, Leland MDP and Cohen M (1988) Quilt: A collaborative tool for cooperative writing. In: Proceedings of the Conference on Office Information Systems. ACM, New York, pp 30–37

Finholt T, Sproull L and Kiesler S (1990) Communication and performance in *ad hoc* task groups. In: Galegher J, Kraut RE and Egido C (ed) Intellectual Teamwork: The Social and Technological Foundations of Cooperative Work. Lawrence Erlbaum, Hillsdale, NJ, pp 291–326

Flower LS (1989a) Cognition, context, and theory building. Occasional Paper 11, Center for the Study of Writing, University of California at Berkeley and Carnegie-Mellon University

Flower LS (1989b) Studying cognition in context: introduction to the study. Technical Report 21, Center for the Study of Writing, University of California at Berkeley and Carnegie-Mellon University

Flower LS and Hayes JR (1980) The dynamics of composing: making plans and juggling constraints. In: Gregg LW and Steinberg ER (ed) Cognitive Processes in Writing: An Interdisciplinary Approach. Lawrence Erlbaum, Hillsdale, NJ

Flower LS and Hayes JR (1981) A cognitive process theory of writing. College Composition and Communication 32(4): 365–387

Galegher J and Kraut R (1989) Computer-mediated communication for intellectual teamwork: a field experiment in group writing. Mimeo, University of Arizona

Galegher J and Kraut R (1990a) Technology for intellectual teamwork: perspectives on research and design. In: Galegher J, Kraut RE and Egido C (ed) Intellectual Teamwork: The Social and Technological Foundations of Cooperative Work. Lawrence Erlbaum, Hillsdale, NJ, pp 1–20

Galegher J and Kraut RE (1990b) Computer-mediated communication for intellectual teamwork: a field experiment in group writing. In: Proceedings of the Conference on Computer Supported Cooperative Work (CSCW-90), Los Angeles, CA, 7–10 October. ACM, New York, pp 65–78

Garfinkel H and Sacks H (1969) On formal structures of practical actions. In: McKinney JC and Tiryakian E (ed) Theoretical Sociology: Perspectives and Developments. Appleton-Century-Crofts, New York

Gemmill G and Wynkoop C (1991) The psychodynamics of small group transformation. Small Group Research 22(1): 4–23

Gere AR and Abbott RD (1985) Talking about writing: the language of writing groups. Research in the Teaching of English 19(4): 362–385

Gibbs SJ (1989) LIZA: an extensible groupware toolkit. In: Proceedings of the Human Factors in Computing Systems Conference, CHI-89, Austin, TX. ACM, New York, pp 29–35

Gupta A (1989) Instructional design in distance education: promises and pitfalls. In: Parer M (ed) Development, Design, and Distance Education. Centre for Distance Learning, Gippsland Institute, Victoria, Australia, pp 169–180

Hackman J (1983) The design of work teams. In: Lorsch JW (ed) Handbook of Organisational Behaviour. Prentice-Hall, Englewood Cliffs, NJ, pp 315–342

Hahn U, Jarke M, Kreplin K, Farusi M and Pimpinelli F (1989) CoAUTHOR – a hypermedia group authoring environment. In: Proceedings of the First European Conference on Computer Supported Cooperative Work (EC-CSCW '89), Gatwick, 13–15 September. Computer Sciences House, Slough, pp 226–244

Hahn U, Jarke M, Eherer S and Kreplin K (1991) CoAUTHOR: a hypermedia group authoring environment. In: Bowers J and Benford S (ed) Studies in Computer Supported Collaborative Work: Theory, Practice and Design. North-Holland, Amsterdam

Harasim L (1990) Online Education: Perspectives on a New Environment. Praeger, New York

Hartley J and Branthwaite A (1989) The psychologist as wordsmith: a questionnaire study of the writing strategies of productive British psychologists. Higher Education 18: 423–452

Hawisher GE and Selfe CL (ed) (1991) Evolving Perspectives on Computers and Composition Studies. NCTE, Urbana, IL

Hayes J and Flower L (1980) Identifying the organization of writing processes. In: Gregg LW and Steinberg ER (ed) Cognitive Processes in Writing: An Interdisciplinary Approach. Lawrence Erlbaum, Hillsdale, NJ

Hayes-Roth B (1983) The blackboard architecture: a general framework for problem solving? Report HPP-83-30, Heuristic Programming Project, Computer Science Department, Stanford University, Palo Alto, CA

Hayes-Roth B, Johnson MV, Garvey A and Hewett M (1986) Application of the BB1 blackboard control architecture to arrangement assembly tasks. Artificial Intelligence in Engineering 1(2): 85–94

Heath C and Luff P (1990) Disembodied conduct: communication through video in a multi-media office environment. In: Chew JC and Whiteside J (ed) Proceedings of the Human Factors in Computing Systems Conference, CHI-90. ACM, New York, pp 99–103

Heath C and Luff P (1991) Collaborative activity and technological design: task coordination in London Underground control rooms. In: Bannon L, Robinson M and Schmidt K (ed) Proceedings of the Second European Conference on Computer-Supported Cooperative Work (EC-CSCW '91), Amsterdam, September. Kluwer, Dordrecht

Henri F and Kaye AR (ed) (1985) Le Savoir Domicile: Pedagogie et problematique de la formation a distance. Les Presses de l'Universite du Quebec, Quebec

Hewitt B, Gilbert N, Jirotka M and Wilbur S (1990) Theories of multi party interaction. Report, University of Surrey and Queen Mary and Westfield College

Hewitt B, Wilbur S and Gilbert GN (1991) Truth, lies 'n' negotiation. In: Proceedings of the IEE Colloquium on CSCW: Some Fundamental Issues. IEE Digest 065

Hewlett-Packard Company (1988) Programming with the HP X Widgets and the Xt Intrinsics. Corvallis, OR

Hiltz SR and Turoff M (1978) The Network Nation: Human Communication via Computer. Addison-Wesley, Reading, MA

Hutchins E (1991) Individual and socially distributed cognition. Cognitive Science 234 Course Notes, Cognitive Science Department, University of California at San Diego

ISO/IEC JTC 1 (1991) N1557 US. Contribution to the JTC 1/SWG on procedures regarding teleconferencing and electronic messaging, 19 September

Janda MA (1988) Talk into writing: writers in collaboration. PhD thesis, University of Illinois at Chicago

Janis IL (1972) Victims of Group-Think: A Psychological Study of Foreign-Policy Decisions and Fiascoes. Houghton Mifflin, Boston, MA

Janis IL (1982) Groupthink: Psychological Studies of Policy Decisions and Fiascos (2nd edn). Houghton Mifflin, Boston, MA

Jenkins J (1989) Working with writers. In: Parer M (ed) Development, Design, and Distance Education. Centre for Distance Learning, Gippsland Institute, Victoria, Australia, pp 141–148

Jessup LM, Connolly T and Tansik DA (1990) Toward a theory of automated group work: the deindividuating effects of anonymity. Small Group Research 21(3): 333–348

Johansen R (1988) Groupware: Computer Support for Business Teams. The Free Press, New York

Johnson CW and Harrison MD (1990) Using temporal logic to support the design and implementation of interactive control systems. International Journal Of Man–Machine Studies (in press)

Johnson-Lenz P and Johnson-Lenz T (1991) Post-mechanistic groupware primitives: rhythms, boundaries and containers. In: Greenberg S (ed) Computer-Supported Cooperative Work and Groupware. Academic Press, The Netherlands

Jones S (1990) A discussion of issues and systems relevant to computer supported cooperative work. Technical Report 64, Department of Computing Science and Mathematics, University of Stirling

Kaye AR (1973) The design and evaluation of science courses at the Open University. Instructional Science 2: 119–191

Kaye AR (1992) Computer conferencing and mass distance education. In: Waggoner M (ed) Empowering Networks: Computer Conferencing in Education. Prentice-Hall, Englewood Cliffs, NJ

Kaye A, Mason R and Harasim L (1989) Computer conferencing in the academic environment. CITE paper 91, Institute of Educational Technology, Open University, Milton Keynes

Kiesler S, Siegel J and McGuire TW (1984) Social psychological aspects of computer-mediated communication. American Psychologist 39: 1123–1134

Kille SE (1988) PP – a message transfer agent. In: Stefferud E and Jacobsen O (ed) Proceedings of the IFIP WG 6.5 Conference on Message Handling, Costa Mesa, CA. North-Holland, Amsterdam

Kling R (1991) Cooperation, coordination and control in computer supported work. Communications of the ACM 34(12): 83–88 (Special Issue on Groupware/CSCW)

Koszarek JL, Lindstrom TL, Ensor JR and Ahuja SR (1990) A multi-user document review tool. In: Gibbs S and Verrijn-Stuart AA (ed) Multi-User Interfaces and Applications. Elsevier/North-Holland, Amsterdam, pp 207–214

Kraut R, Galegher J and Egido C (1988) Relationships and tasks in scientific research collaborations. In: Greif I (ed) Computer Supported Cooperative Work: A Book of Readings. Morgan Kaufmann, San Mateo, CA, pp 741–769

Lamport L (1986) LaTeX: A Document Preparation System. Addison-Wesley, Reading, MA

Laurel B, Oren T and Don A (1990) Issues in multimedia interface design: media integration and interface agents. In: Chew JC and Whiteside J (ed) Proceedings of the Human Factors in Computing Systems Conference, CHI-90. ACM, New York

Lawrence G and Young I (1979) Document 2T-271, Tavistock Institute of Human Relations, Open University, mimeo

Lea M and Spears R (1991) Computer-mediated communication, de-individuation and group decision-making. International Journal of Man–Machine Studies 34: 283–301

Leland MDP, Fish RS and Kraut RE (1988) Collaborative document production using Quilt. In: Proceedings of the Conference on Computer Supported Cooperative Work (CSCW-88), Portland, OR, September. ACM, New York, pp 206–215

Lewis BN (1971a) Course production at the Open University II: activities and activity networks. British Journal of Educational Technology 2(2): 111–123

Lewis BN (1971b) Course production at the Open University III: planning and scheduling. British Journal of Educational Technology 3(2): 189–204

Locke M (1980) How to Run Committees and Meetings. Macmillan, London

Lubich H and Plattner B (1990) A proposed model and functionality definition for a collaborative editing and conferencing system. In: Gibbs S and Verrijn-Stuart AA (ed) Multi-User Interfaces and Applications. Elsevier/North-Holland, Amsterdam, pp 215–232

Mackler T (1987) Group produced documents: an exploratory study of collaborative writing processes. PhD thesis, Teachers' College, Columbia University

Malcolm M (1991) GroupWriter: a word processor for collaborative document preparation. Research Report 91/435/19, Department of Computer Science, University of Calgary

Malone TW, Grant KR, Lai K, Rao R and Rosenblatt D (1987a) Semi-structured messages are surprisingly useful for computer supported coordination. ACM Transactions on Office Information Systems 5(2): 115–131

Malone TW, Grant KR, Turbak FA, Brobst SA and Cohen MD (1987b) Intelligent information-sharing systems. Communications of the ACM 30(5): 390–402

Mantei M, Baecker RM, Sellen AJ, Buxton WAS, Milligan T and Wellman B (1991) Experiences in the use of media space. In: Robertson S, Olson G and Olson J (ed) Proceedings of the Human Factors in Computing Systems Conference, CHI-91, New Orleans. ACM, New York, pp 203–208

March JG (1991) How decisions happen in organisations. Human–Computer Interaction 6: 95–117

Martin J (1979) Out of this world –is this the real OU? Open Line 21: 8

Mason J (1976) Life inside the course team. Teaching at a Distance 5: 27–33

Matsuhashi A (1987) Revising the plan and altering the text. In: Matsuhashi A (ed) Writing in Real Time: Modelling Production Processes. Ablex, Norwood, NJ, pp 197–22

May J, Whitefield A, Denley I, Voigt U, Hermann S and Esgate A (1992) Integration of services for human end-users (2): a case study of a cooperative document production system. In: Byerley P and Connell S (ed) Integrated Broadband Communications: Views from RACE –Usage Aspects. Elsevier, Amsterdam (North-Holland Studies in Telecommunication vol 1)

McCarthy JC and Miles VC (1990) Elaborating communication channels in Conferencer. In: Gibbs S and Verrijn-Stuart AA (ed) Multi-User Interfaces and Applications. Elsevier/North-Holland, Amsterdam, pp 181–193

McCarthy JC and Monk AF (1991) Channels, conversation, cooperation and relevance: all you wanted to know about communication but were afraid to ask. Journal of Human–Computer Interaction (in press)

McCarthy JC, Miles VC and Monk AF (1991a) An experimental study of common ground in text-based communication. In: Robertson S, Olson G and Olson J (ed) Proceedings of the Human Factors in Computing Systems Conference, CHI-91, New Orleans. ACM, New York, pp 209–217

McCarthy JC, Miles VC, Monk AF and Harrison MD (1991b) Building expectations from context in on-line conferencing. In: Nurminen MI and Weir GRS (ed) Proceedings of Conference: Human Jobs and Computer Interfaces. North-Holland, Amsterdam

McGrath J (1984) Groups: Interaction and performance. Prentice-Hall, Englewood Cliffs, NJ

McGrath JE (1991) Time, interaction and performance (TIP): a theory of groups. Small Group Research 22(2): 147–174

Miles VC, Johnson CW, McCarthy JC and Harrison MD (1991) Supporting prediction in complex dynamic systems. In: Diaper D and Hammond N (ed) People and Computers VI. Proceedings of the HCI '91 Conference, 20–23 August 1991. Cambridge University Press, Cambridge

Morgan K (1991) The integrated broadband communications requirements in the automotive industry and RACE project CAR. Computer Networks and ISDN Systems 21(4): 321–322

Mudrack PE (1989) Defining group cohesiveness: a legacy of confusion? Small Group Behavior 20(1): 37–49

Neuwirth C and Kaufer DS (1989) The role of external representations in the writing process: implications for the design of hypertext-based writing tools. In: Proceedings of Hypertext '89, Pittsburgh, PA, November. ACM, New York, pp 319–342

Neuwirth C, Kaufer D, Chimera R and Gillespie T (1988) The Notes program: a hypertext application for writing from source texts. In: Proceedings of Hypertext '87, University of North Carolina, North Carolina, 13–15 November. ACM, Baltimore, MD, pp 121–141

Neuwirth CM, Kaufer DS, Chandhok R and Morris JH (1990) Issues in the design of computer support for co-authoring and commenting. In: Proceedings of the Conference on Computer-Supported Cooperative Work (CSCW-90), Los Angeles, CA, 7–10 October. ACM, New York, pp 183–195

Newey C (1975) On being a course team chairman. Teaching at a Distance 5: 27–33

Newman J and Newman R (1992a) Three modes of collaborative authoring. In: Holt P and Williams N (ed) Computers and Writing: State of the Art. Intellect Books, Oxford, pp 17–24

Newman J and Newman R (1992b) Two failures in computer-mediated text communication. In: Sharples M (ed) Computers and Writing: Issues and Implementations. Kluwer, Amsterdam

Newman W (1987) Designing Integrated Systems for the Office Environment. McGraw-Hill, New York

Nicodemus R (1984) Lessons from a course team. Teaching at a Distance 25: 33–39

Nold EW (1981) Revising. In: Frederiksen CH and Dominic JF (ed) Writing: The Nature, Development, and Teaching of Written Communication, vol 2: Writing: Process, Development and Communication. Lawrence Erlbaum, Hillsdale, NJ, pp 67–79

Norman DA (1986) Cognitive engineering. In: Norman DA and Draper SW (ed) User-Centred System Design: New Perspectives on Human–Computer Interaction. Lawrence Erlbaum, Hillsdale, NJ

Nunan T (1990) A case study of research methods course development for Masters awards. In: Evans T (ed) Research in Distance Education. Institute of Distance Education, Deakin University, pp 126–156

Olson GM (1989) The nature of group work. In: Proceedings of the Human Factors Society 33rd Annual Meeting

Olson JS, Olson GM, Mack LA and Wellner P (1990) Concurrent editing: the group's interface. In: Diaper D, Gilmore D, Cockton G and Shackel B (ed) Human–Computer Interaction: Proceedings of INTERACT '90. Elsevier, Amsterdam, pp 835–840

Osborn AF (1957) Applied Imagination. Scribner, New York

Pahl G and Beitz W (1984) Engineering Design. The Design Council, London (English edition, edited by K Wallace)

Palme J (1989) Joint editing as a group communication process. Mimeo, University of Stockholm Computer Centre

Perry W (1976) Open University: A Personal Account by the First Vice-Chancellor. Open University Press, Milton Keynes

Pettersson E (1989) Automatic information processes in document reading: a study of information handling in two intensive care units. In: Proceedings of the First European Conference on Computer Supported Cooperative Work (EC-CSCW '89), Gatwick, 13–15 September. Computer Sciences House, Slough, pp 63–73

Pliskin N (1989) Interacting with electronic mail can be a dream or nightmare: a user's point of view. Interacting With Computers 1(3): 259–272

Plowman L (1992) Talking and writing: a sociocognitive approach to analysing a group writing task. Collaborative Writing Research Group Report 5, School of Cognitive and Computing Sciences, University of Sussex

Posner LR, Baecker RM and Mantei MM (1991) How people write together. Technical Report, Computer Systems Research Institute and Department of Computer Science, University of Toronto, 6 Kings College Road, Toronto, Ontario, Canada M5S 1A1

Rein GL and Ellis CA (1991) rIBIS: a real-time group hypertext system. International Journal of Man–Machine Studies 34(3): 349–368

Reynolds S, Wooley B and Wooley T (1911) Seems So! A Working-class View of Politics. Macmillan, London

Riley J (1979) I wonder what it's like to write a unit? Teaching at a Distance 14: 1–8

Riley J (1983) The preparation of teaching in higher education: a study of the preparation of teaching materials at the Open University. PhD thesis, University of Sussex

Riley J (1984) The problems of writing correspondence lessons. DERG Monograph 11, Open University Distance Education Research Group, Open University, Milton Keynes

Rimmershaw R (1992) Technologies of collaboration. In: Sharples M (ed) Computers and Writing: Issues and Implementations. Kluwer, Dordrecht

Rodden T (1991) A survey of CSCW systems. Interacting with Computers 3(3): 319–353

Root RW (1988) Design of a multi-media vehicle for social browsing. In: Proceedings of the Conference on Computer Supported Cooperative Work (CSCW-88), Portland, OR, September. New York: ACM, pp 25–38

Sacks H, Schegloff E and Jefferson G (1978) A simplest systematics for the organisation of turn-taking in conversation. In: Schenkein J (ed) Studies in the Organisation of Conversational Interaction. Academic Press, New York

Schegloff E (1971) Notes on a conversational practice: formulating place. Reprinted in Gigloioli PP (ed) (1972) Language and Social Context. Penguin, Harmondsworth, pp 95–135

Schegloff EA and Sacks H (1973) Opening up closings. Semiotica 8: 289–327

Scheifler RW and Gettys J (1986) The X window system. ACM Transactions on Graphics 5(2)

Schwartzlose AH and Penter AS (1991) The CAR multi-media conference control experiment: description and implementation. UCL CS Internal Note, IN/91/3

Searle J (1969) Speech Acts. Cambridge University Press, Cambridge

Seel NR, Gilbert GN and Morris ME (1990) A project-oriented view of CSCW. In: Diaper D, Gilmore D, Cockton G and Shackel B (ed) Human–Computer Interaction: Proceedings of INTERACT '90. Elsevier, Amsterdam, pp 903–908

Shackel B (1985) Symposium on computer message and conferencing systems. In: Shackel B (ed) Human–Computer Interaction: Proceedings of INTERACT '84. North-Holland, Amsterdam, pp 671–771

Sharples M (1992) Adding a little structure to collaborative writing. In: Diaper D and Sanger C (ed) CSCW in Practice: An Introduction and Case Studies. Springer-Verlag, London

Sharples M and O'Malley CE (1988) A framework for the design of a Writer's Assistant. In: Self J (ed) Artificial Intelligence and Human Learning: Intelligent Computer-Aided Instruction. Chapman and Hall, London

Sharples M and Pemberton L (1988) Representing writing: an account of the writing process with regard to the writer's external representations. Cognitive Science Research Paper 119, University of Sussex

Sharples M and Pemberton L (1990) Starting from the writer: guidelines for the design of user-centred document processors. Computer Assisted Language Learning 2: 37–57

Sharples M, Goodlet J and Pemberton L (1989) Developing a Writer's Assistant. In: Williams N and Holt P (ed) Computers and Writing. Ablex, Norwood, NJ

Shelley M (1985) Frankenstein. Penguin, Harmondsworth

Shipman FM III, Chaney RJ and Gorry GA (1989) Distributed hypertext for collaborative research: the virtual notebook system. In: Proceedings of Hypertext '89, Pittsburgh, PA, November. ACM, New York

Siegel J, Dubrovsky V, Kiesler S and McGuire TW (1986) Group processes in computer-mediated communication. Organizational Behavior and Human Decision Processes 37: 157–187

Simon HA (1981) The Sciences of the Artificial. MIT Press, Cambridge, MA

Slater PE (1955) Role differentiation in small groups. American Sociological Review 20: 300–310

Smith JB and Lansman M (1989) A cognitive basis for a computer writing environment. In: Britton BK and Glynn SM (ed) Computer Writing Environments: Theory, Research and Design. Lawrence Erlbaum, Hillsdale, NJ

Spitzer M (1990) Local and global networking: implications for the future. In: Holdstein DH and Selfe CL (ed) Computers and Writing: Theory, Research, Practice. MLA, New York

Stefik M, Bobrow DG, Foster G, Lanning S and Tatar D (1987) WYSIWIS revisited: early experiences with multiuser interfaces. ACM Transactions on Office Information Systems 5(2): 147–167

Stefik M, Foster G, Bobrow DG, Kahn K, Lanning S and Suchman L (1988) Beyond the chalkboard: computer-support for collaboration and problem solving in meetings. In: Greif I (ed) Computer Supported Cooperative Work: A Book of Readings. Morgan Kaufmann, San Mateo, CA, pp 335–366

Sun Microsystems Inc (1989) NFS: network file system protocol specification, RFC 1094

Tang JC (1989) Listing, drawing and gesturing in design: a study of the use of shared workspaces by design teams. Xerox PARC Technical Report SSL-89-3 (PhD Dissertation, Stanford University)

Tatar DG, Foster G and Bobrow DG (1991) Design for conversation: lessons from Cognoter. International Journal of Man–Machine Studies 34(2): 185–210

Thompson JD (1967) Organizations in Action. McGraw-Hill, New York

Tight M (1985) Do we really need course teams? Teaching at a Distance 26: 48–50

Timmers S (1986) Microcomputers in course development. Programmed Learning and Educational Technology 23(1): 15–23

Trigg RH (1983) A network-based approach to text handling for the on-line scientific community. PhD thesis, University of Maryland

Trigg RH and Irish PM (1988) Hypertext habitats: experiences of writers in NoteCards. In: Proceedings of Hypertext '87, University of North Carolina, North Carolina, 13–15 November. ACM, Baltimore, MD, pp 89–108

Trigg R and Suchman L (1989) Collaborative writing in NoteCards. In: McAleese R (ed) Hypertext: Theory into Practice. Ablex, Norwood NJ, pp 45–61

Wall VD Jr, Galanes GJ and Love SB (1987) Small, task-oriented groups: conflict, conflict management, satisfaction, and decision quality. Small Group Behavior 18(1): 31–55

Waller R (1977) Notes on transforming. Institute of Educational Technology, Open University, Milton Keynes

Wason P (1980) Specific thoughts on the writing process. In: Gregg LW and Steinberg ER (ed) Cognitive Processes in Writing: An Interdisciplinary Approach. Lawrence Erlbaum, Hillsdale, NJ

Waterhouse K (1992) Through a glass mistily. The Guardian, 30 March

Weber M (1947) The Theory of Social and Economic Organisation. Oxford University Press, Oxford

Whitefield AD (1986) An analysis and comparison of knowledge use in designing with and without CAD. In: Smith A (ed) Knowledge Engineering and Computer Modelling in CAD – Proceedings of CAD '86. Butterworths, London, pp 89–97

Whitefield AD (1989) Constructing appropriate models of computer users: the case of engineering designers. In: Long JB and Whitefield AD (ed) Cognitive Ergonomics and Human–Computer Interaction. Cambridge University Press, Cambridge

Whitefield AD, Wight J, Life A and Colbert M (1991). Assessing the programming language PML as a task analysis method and product. In: Diaper D and Hammond N (ed) People and Computers VI. Proceedings of the HCI '91 Conference, 20–23 August 1991. Cambridge University Press, Cambridge

Whitefield AD, Byerley P, Denley I, Esgate A and May J (1992). Integration of services for human end-users (1): design principles, enabling states analysis and a design method. In: Byerley P and Connell S (ed) Integrated Broadband Communications: Views from RACE – Usage Aspects. Elsevier, Amsterdam (North-Holland Studies in Telecommunication vol 1)

Wicks M (1988) Corporate networks: the new challenges. In: Corporate Telecommunications Networks. IBC Technical Services, London

Winograd T and Flores F (1986) Understanding Computers and Cognition. Ablex, Norwood, NJ

Witten IH, Thimbleby HW, Coulouris G and Greenberg S (1991) Liveware: a new approach to sharing data in social networks. International Journal of Man–Machine Studies 34(3): 337–348

Wright PC and Monk AF (1991) A cost-effective evaluation method for use by designers. International Journal of Man–Machine Studies 35: 891–912

Yoder E, Beavin JH and Jackson DD (1989) Collaboration in KMS, a shared hypermedia system. In: Proceedings of the Human Factors in Computing Systems Conference, CHI-89, Austin, TX. ACM, New York

Zander A (1979) The psychology of group processes. Annual Review of Psychology 30: 417–451

Subject Index

Name Index

Printing: Weihert-Druck GmbH, Darmstadt
Binding: Theo Gansert Buchbinderei GmbH, Weinheim